KING &
SAINT

Peter Rex

King &
Saint

The Life of Edward
The Confessor

For the Staff, Trustees and Friends
of Ely Museum

First published 2008
This paperback edition published 2020

The History Press
97 St George's Place, Cheltenham,
Gloucestershire, GL50 3QB
www.thehistorypress.co.uk

British Library Cataloguing in Publication Data.
A catalogue record for this book is available from the British Library.

ISBN 978 0 7509 9412 5

Typesetting and origination by The History Press
Printed and bound in Great Britain by TJ Books Limited, Padstow, Cornwall.

Contents

Part Three: The Saint

Foreword

I t is now almost forty years since Frank Barlow wrote *Edward the Confessor*. The intervening years have seen the publication annually of the *Proceedings of the Battle Conferences on Anglo-Norman Studies* in the periodical of the same name. Many of the original sources have been re-edited and newly translated and much work has been done on many aspects of the Confessor's reign and the administrative machinery of the Old English State. A number of most interesting works have been published on the pre-Conquest history of England since the year 1000.

This work is an attempt to present an alternative view of the Confessor's life, character and achievements by taking into account much of the work which has been done. It seeks to view events in a manner which discounts much of the over-emphasis on the power and influence of Earl Godwine of Wessex and his sons. Much of what is known of their wealth and land-holding derives from the information provided in Domesday Book which can only have related to the last five or so years of the Confessor's reign and, for that reason alone, should not be so readily applied to the position of the family at the commencement of the reign, wealthy and power-ful though Earl Godwine might have been.

Many scholars who have worked in this field over the last one hundred and fifty years have allowed themselves to be misled by the glib persuasiveness of the Norman accounts of Edward's actions and motives. In an age much more accustomed to the black arts of spin doctors, it is time to view the Norman case more critically, especially where it is unsupported by independent evidence.

More account needs to be taken of the achievements of the Confessor, in foreign policy and statecraft, and of the developments in the administration of the Old English State which were the work of King Edward and his predecessors. Those achievements were to underpin those subsequent ones of William I and his heirs and, indeed, made them possible.

Much more care should be taken in distinguishing the ideologi-cal and theological arguments presented to Rome as part of the case for Edward's canonisation from the known facts of, as opposed to the assumptions about, Edward's marriage.

This work owes a great debt to the labours of the many scholars whose works are listed in the bibliography without which it could not have been written. Where this work differs from the views of others, the responsibility is entirely mine.

Peter Rex

Ely, November 2007.

PART ONE

The *Aetheling*

1002–1042

I

A World in Turmoil

Edward Aethelredsson was born into a society in turmoil. During the first fourteen years of his life his father was dethroned and exiled and his elder brothers and kinsmen were exiled or died. Edward and his brother, Alfred, and sister, Godgifu, were condemned to exile. Edward's exile lasted for twenty-four years. These events, and particularly his own prolonged exile in a strange land, certainly left their mark on Edward's character. He was left with a morbid fear of the return of the Vikings and a determination never to allow England to fall into civil war and so expose itself to the danger of foreign invasion. Like Charles II, he was determined never to go on his travels again.

Aethelred II's reign before the birth of his son, Edward, had seen the comparative peace of the early 990s give way to the renewal of large scale Viking raids. Aethelred turned to the stratagem of buying off the Vikings by paying them *gafol* – tribute – in increasing amounts. The stratagem failed. The King also developed an alternative policy, an attempt, once more, at forging a permanent Norman alliance. He did not want actual military assistance but to persuade the Norman Dukes to close their ports to the Viking raiders who were accustomed to offload their booty in Normandy. Earlier treaties with Normandy had not endured and the problem had loomed large in Aethelred's mind. He even resorted to an abortive naval invasion in a desperate attempt to put pressure on the Duke, Richard I. The first quarrel had occurred in 991 when a short lived treaty was negotiated with Duke Richard, who did nothing to prevent the Vikings from using Norman ports.

Then the quarrel resumed, probably because the Duke had not kept to his side of the bargain. Aethelred was said to have sent a fleet to ravage the Cotentin Peninsula which was repelled by the efforts of Nigel, the Vicomte. Whatever the truth, Richard II needed an English alliance against Viking raiders. The tale may be Norman myth-making for political advantage.[1] The result in 1002 was the arrival of 'The Lady, Richard's daughter', Emma, who married Aethelred.

Emma's mother, Gunnor, was a Danish noblewoman and her daughter had an abiding love of all things Danish.[2] As Edward was the result of Aethelred's marriage to Emma, with her predominantly Scandinavian ancestry, he was in fact Anglo-Danish by blood, a fact of great significance in 1042.[3] Emma was given the English name, almost a title, of *Aelfgifu*. The marriage alliance brought Aethelred valuable contacts among Emma's relatives. It was to be a loveless, diplomatic marriage as is shown by Emma's determination to write it out of the record. Her political testament, the document known as the '*Encomium Emmae*' – 'In Praise of Emma', by an unknown monk of St Bertin, at St Omer, never refers to Aethelred by name, and allows the reader to infer that her children by him, especially Edward, were the offspring of her marriage to Cnut the Great.

Aethelred himself had already fathered ten children by other wives and concubines, and now had three more by Emma. She was also to have a son, Harthacnut, who was King Cnut's son, and a daughter called Gunnhild. The chances that Edward would ever become king himself must have seemed very small to contemporary observers.

The effects of the massacre on St Brice's day, 13 November 1002 when 'all the Danish men who were among the English people' were killed, made themselves felt in the violence of the renewed Viking onslaught and by 1006 a much greater force was ravaging at will over large areas of southern England until persuaded to leave in 1007 by the payment of £36,000, taking with them an abundance of booty.

Aethelred is said to have appealed to Duke Richard for help,[4] but if so none was forthcoming. Richard seems to have continued to cooperate with the Vikings, possibly fearful for the safety of his own duchy or because the trade with them was so profitable. He was bound by treaty to receive sick and wounded Danes and to allow their spoils to be sold in Norman ports.[5] The only aid he ever offered to Aethelred was to give him and his family sanctuary in 1013 and to allow the *Aethelings* to settle in Normandy after 1017.[6]

This was the time when the government of England was plagued by a series of ill-considered decisions, the '*unraedas*' as the chronicler called them, that led to the coining of Aethelred's nickname 'the Unraede' or 'Ill-advised', usually rendered as 'the Unready'. The *Witan* repeatedly had recourse to the payment of tribute, the *gafol* (termed after the Norman Conquest '*Danegeld*'), usually only after immense damage had already been done and the King's campaigns had been undone by the treacheries of Eadric Streona (the Grasper), Ealdorman of Mercia who had married the King's daughter, Edith, and was to be a notorious traitor to both sides from 1007 to 1017.

Edward, the new *Aetheling*,[7] (a title which means that the holder was in the line of succession) was born, at the earliest, sometime in 1003 at Islip in Oxfordshire,[8] according to a writ in which his mother Emma was said to have bestowed Islip on him as a birthday gift.[9] His existence is not recorded until his name appears as 'witness' to two royal charters in 1005.[10] He is listed as the seventh prince, that is '*cild*' (meaning *Aetheling*), and the latest date for these charters is 16 November 1005 (death of Archbishop Aelfric). It was customary to add the names of newly born royal princes to witness lists as a way of acknowledging their existence. Aethelred's new child could have been born at any time between 1003 and 1005. As he was old enough in 1014 to be sent back to England as his father's ambassador, the earlier date of 1003 is more probable. Records from this period are very incomplete. His brother Alfred is not mentioned in a reliable document until 1014. Edward might not have been mentioned until he had safely survived the perilous period of early infancy. His name on one charter is immediately followed by that of his mother as '*Aelfgifu regina*', suggesting that she was now insisting on her son's existence being recognised. Birth early in 1003 would make Edward aged sixty-three when he died in January 1066 and an old man by the standards of the time, as he is shown to be on the Bayeux Tapestry.[11]

Edward's father, Aethelred, it was said, compelled his men to swear that they would recognise Edward as king after Aethelred's own death,[12] although if this did occur it did not prevent the succession of Edmund Ironside. The *Vita Edwardi* says that Edward was 'declared beforehand by the oath of the people to be worthy to be raised at some time to the throne of his ancestral kingdom'. This story could simply be a deduction from the fact, as the charters show, that Edward was recognised as one of the *Aethelings*. Aethelred was perhaps believed to have secured a general oath of fealty in Edward's favour, but as that would have disinherited Edmund Ironside it must be rejected in favour of Edward's recognition as one *Aetheling* among many. He was therefore among those regarded as 'throne-right-worthy'. But though such a claim was perhaps a little stronger than a claim by birth alone, it had to be presented and accepted.[13]

A version of this story was current in Normandy, where it was alleged that Edward had actually been anointed and consecrated king when he was only a boy.[14] This is an enhanced version of the earlier tale. The Norman Duke possibly had hopes that a child born to Emma would ascend the throne of England. Two did so and both were childless and so Norman ambition was to take a very different course.[15] Edward became, in effect, a stalking horse, used in the 1020s and 1030s as an excuse for challenges to Cnut and later on arguments were developed to 'prove' that he was the source of William of Normandy's claim to the English throne. Stories about Edward's recognition as heir to the throne developed simply because Edward did in fact become king whereas when he was born he was the seventh in line. That all six *Aethelings* died, so enabling Edward to become king, must have seemed almost miraculous.

Several of the *Aethelings* disappeared between 1005 and 1016, notably Ecgbert, Eadred and Edgar, probably killed in battle. By 1012 there were still three ahead of Edward; Athelstan, Eadwig and Edmund.[16] Note too that all of these *Aethelings*, including Edward, had 'kingly' names taken from previous kings of Wessex. Some people certainly did see Edward's eventual accession as the work of God.[17] All this is part of the growing legend of 'Edward the Confessor'.[18] The tale is actually denied by Edward himself, according to the *Encomium Emmae*.[19] He tells his mother that in fact the English nobility had never sworn any oath to him. Aethelred himself seems to have done nothing to celebrate Edward's birth and he is given no special significance in the charters, he is merely another *Aetheling* like all the others. On the other hand this may be another of Emma's conceits.

Nothing more is known of his early years other than the claim in the *Liber Eliensis*, that Aethelred and Emma gave Edward as a child to that monastery to be educated as a monk. As presented in the Chronicle this is one more of the improving tales intended to illustrate the nature of Edward's religious life. It is rejected by most authorities as lacking plausibility and has no support elsewhere. Even Osbert of Clare who was careful to collect every possible piece of evidence he could in support of his case for Edward's canonisation, does not have this story.[20] That may be because it would not have suited his purpose to depict Edward as a 'spoiled monk', one who had tried the life and rejected it or had been rejected by his monastery. On the other hand, the story is independent of the Westminster hagiographical tradition and is presented by the compiler of the *Liber Eliensis* as having been handed down by the oldest monks who claimed to have been eyewitnesses of the event.

The monks might well have created the tale, as it is found in the chronicle, to explain their possession of a cloth in which, it was claimed, the child was wrapped when presented to the abbey. It is described as being embroidered 'in the orbiculate style with small roundels of a pale green colour'[21] and to have still been in the possession of the monks. The book comes from the latter part of the twelfth century and would have been completed sometime after 1170, so that Edward was by then a recognised saint. The monks were no doubt hoping to attract pilgrims to view their relic of Saint Edward although the 'pall' itself is unlikely to come from Aethelred's reign. In any case, English kings of this period did not dedicate their sons to the church in this way, only their daughters, and Emma was not the sort of woman to sacrifice her first born. The idea that Edward was ever trained to become a monk at Ely must be rejected as part of the determination to prove that he was indeed a saint.

However, what is certainly true is that the Kings were accustomed to entrust their sons to a bishop or abbot to be educated. King Edgar had received part of his education at the hands of St Aethelwold of Abingdon and his son, Edward the Martyr, was entrusted to Bishop Sideman of Crediton.[22] It is thus just possible that the Ely tale confuses two separate traditions; a dedication story as above and, as the text itself states, another tradition that the prince 'received his upbringing there in the monastery for a long time with the boys and learnt in their company the psalms and hymns of the Lord'. It is that, perhaps, that the older monks recalled. It would presumably have been under Abbot Aelfsige who died in Aethelred's reign, but, as Edward witnesses charters four times between 1007 and 1013, it can only have been for a very short period of time, perhaps a year or eighteen months, possibly to be taught to read and even write. It cannot have been later because of the return of Swein Forkbeard in 1013, whereupon the royal family, Queen Emma first and then the *Aethelings* Edward and Alfred followed by their father, fled for a time to Normandy. This contradicts the *Encomium*'s claim that Emma sent the *Aethelings* to Normandy to be educated.[23] None of the sons of Aethelred by earlier marriages fled abroad, they stayed to fight.

Edward's boyhood otherwise must have been much the same as that of any other *Aetheling*. He would have learnt the protocol and behaviour expected of him at court, he would have been trained in horsemanship and the use of arms and would have learned to enjoy hunting, and would have been instructed in the beliefs and obligations of Catholic Christianity. He would have been taught the Creed and some knowledge of ritual and to recite the psalms. He might also have been more literate than Norman nobles were expected to be. The tradition, from Alfred the Great's time, was that *Aethelings* received some education in the liberal arts, and at least reading if not writing.

As his mother, Emma, spoke both Danish and Old French in the form influenced by the Scandinavian language of the Vikings, Edward as a young man would have heard and learned to understand, even speak, both Old French and the Scandinavian lingua franca as well as Old English. The Normans among whom he was to spend his exile were still not yet divorced from their Scandinavian and Viking heritage, but remained familiar with Scandinavian ways and language. Edward had spent his formative years, from birth to the age of about thirteen, in England and had been brought up as an English *Aetheling*. It is perhaps going too far to imagine that all of this was erased from his mind during his exile. While he showed no friendliness towards the kin of those among whom he had grown up, most of whom were dead, and while he must have remembered much of his youth without pleasure, probably having painful memories, he showed conventional piety towards his father's memory. There is a writ from the period 1061–65 granting land at Wedmore to the clerks of St Andrew's at Wells for prayers to be said for his own soul and that of his father and all his ancestors.[24]

As Barlow remarks, the heroes of Edward's boyhood would have been men like the Ealdorman Bryhtnoth, the hero of Maldon, and the Vikings, Thorkell Havi, Eric son of Hakon, Olaf Haraldsson and Olaf Tryggvason, and his own elder brothers Athelstan and Edmund Ironside.[25] Athelstan seems to have been warlike and possessed a collection of famous swords (one had belonged to King Offa) and fine horses. Edward, according to Scandinavian sources, never forgot the friendship which had existed between his father and Olaf Tryggvason.[26] The saga relates that Orm son of Thorliot lived at Dryness in the Orkneys at the time when Edward was King in England. He used to tell people how he had heard King Edward read the tale of Olaf Tryggvason out of the very same book which Olaf himself had sent to King Aethelred from Jerusalem. It adds that one year the King was reading in the presence of his chief men and the whole court concerning the battle aboard the ship called the Serpent and that he then told his men about the death of King Olaf (who had died in AD 1000).

Norman writers entirely ignore the Anglo-Danish background of the *Aetheling* and the *Vita Edwardi* itself stresses his 'Frenchness', yet England was an Anglo-Danish realm and the traditional culture was Anglo-Scandinavian. Much of the poetry that survives is religious, mainly because those who recorded it were monks, and it is distinctly sad. Men were aware of the insecurity of life, a theme stressed also by the Christian Church, but the old Pagan view emphasising the importance of worldly fame and memorable exploits was still common. There was plenty of court poetry in honour of Scandinavian heroes and some scraps of poetry in honour of Aethelred do survive, but the men of his generation had no sagas written about them. Aethelred's court was a traditional one.

Edward's father Aethelred is shown as a great northern prince, the associate of Viking heroes like Olaf Tryggvason to whom the King is said to have stood as sponsor for his confirmation in 994 and to have been Edward's hero also.[27] Another of Edward's heroes was Olaf Haraldsson (Saint Olaf) whose saga claimed that he came to the aid of Aethelred in the fighting of 1014.[28] Edward as a child might well have met him.

Aethelred, deserted by the English magnates, was driven out by King Swein Forkbeard and his son Cnut in 1013. First Emma took refuge with her brother the Duke, then Bishop Aelfhun took the *Aethelings* Edward and Alfred to join her, and lastly the King took his fleet to Normandy and remained there until Swein's unexpected death on 2 February 1014. Then the leading Englishmen decided to recall Aethelred on condition that he governed them 'more justly' than he had before. He sent ambassadors to England, promising good government if the nobles would support his return to the throne and sent Edward with them as evidence of his good faith. The King must by then have regarded Edward as a possible heir. In consequence Aethelred returned only to find that his son Edmund Ironside was beginning to act independently. Emma for her part seems to have transferred her support to Edmund and from that date seems to have been determined to forget her husband. William of Malmesbury alleges that this was because he had been unfaithful to her but is more likely to have been because of his failure as a king.[29] Edmund, in contrast, is presented in the *Encomium Emmae* as a hero. It was he who was to lead the resistance to the Danes after Aethelred's death on 23 April 1016.

Edward cannot have been more than thirteen years old when his father died but Scandinavian tradition has it that he fought at his brother's side in the battle for London Bridge, distinguishing himself by almost cutting Cnut in two. He and Edmund are regarded almost as joint kings.[30] Edmund might even have felt some alarm at the prominence given to his half-brother by their father, though witness lists do not support any idea of Edward's promotion at Edmund's expense.[31] It might be that Emma had expected Edward to serve Edmund, even if only to unite the people behind Edmund. Edward was too young to take the lead himself so Emma seems to have rested her hopes on Edmund. The Saga says that 'Now in the third spring King Athalrathr (Aethelred) dies and his sons Eathmundr and Eathvathr succeeded to the Kingdom'. They fight jointly against Cnut at the battle for London Bridge.

The young *Aetheling* Edward is said to have struck at Cnut who was saved because Jarl Thorkell the Tall pushed him off his horse and Edward 'smote asunder the saddle and the horse's back ... a blow which men have held in memory in after days'.[32] A remarkable feat for one so young, but perhaps not impossible; men matured early in the eleventh century and Edward is recorded as having been a tall man. Young nobles were expected to engage in warfare at an early age, like the Scandinavians Olaf Tryggvason[33] and Eric Bloodaxe.[34] Edward was descended through his mother Emma from both Danish and Norse ancestors, and would have conformed to the tradition. It is a mistake to separate him from his natural setting, something which both the *Vita Edwardi* and the Norman apologists insist on doing.

Edmund died on 30 November 1016, and Cnut received the submission of the whole of Wessex. By Christmas Edward was in Flanders, as a charter for St Peter's, Ghent from 29 December and dated to 1016 records.[35] It was given by Edward 'unworthy son of Aethelred, King of the English' when 'deprived of his father's kingdom and visiting the abodes of the saints in search of pardon for his sins and of restoration to his ancestral realm by their aid'. He promised to restore to Ghent its English possessions when he became king. The charter was, of course, drawn up by monks eager to secure a grant from an *Aetheling* who might yet one day be a king and might exaggerate the idea that Edward was already claiming to be his father's heir. After Edward became king it was claimed that he confirmed Ghent in possession of lands in England, at Lewisham, Greenwich, Woolwich and other places (in that period part of Kent) granting sundry privileges.

As it stands the charter is rejected by most authorities as spurious but it may be testimony to Ghent's knowledge that Edward had been its benefactor and that he had passed through Ghent on his way to Normandy.[36] He then went into exile with little prospect of ever recovering his father's throne. Edward could have actually visited Ghent at a later point in his exile. The *Vita Edwardi* when first mentioning Edward's exile states that he was 'carried to his kinsmen in Francia so that he could spend his childhood [sic] with them'[37] rather than perish in the devastation wrought by the Danes. The author of the *Vita* was from St Bertin in Flanders, and regarded Normandy as part of Francia. Edmund Ironside's own sons were taken by Cnut who accepted the advice not to kill them and sent them into exile, perhaps hoping that they would be killed there. In fact they ended up as exiles at the court of the kings of Hungary.

Olaf's Saga claims that the sons of Aethelred continued the struggle and allied themselves with Olaf Haroldsson, linking up with him at Rouen and promising him that he should have Northumbria if they recovered England. There is an attempted incursion into England which fails miserably in the face of Cnut's superior forces and the *Aethelings*' return to Rouen. This is presented as occurring in 1016–17. The reality was that Cnut was able to neutralise the *Aethelings* by negotiating his own alliance with Normandy, marrying Emma in 1017, for her political value, and she recovered her position as Queen. Perhaps it was in connection with the marriage that Cnut gave land in Sussex to Fécamp, in recognition that the abbot had undertaken some of the negotiations?[38] It is no wonder that Edward is recorded as maintaining that Emma had 'done less for him than he wished before he was king, and also since'.[39]

Emma paid little attention to Edward. He was out of power with no resources and Cnut was the man in possession. Edward would also have been seen as too young and unable to inspire confidence in others. Emma preferred to try to ensure that England and Denmark would go to any children she had by Cnut.[40] Her brother, Duke Richard II, would not have been prepared to attempt to restore the *Aethelings* by force. In fact the birth of two children to Emma fathered by Cnut, Harthacnut and Gunnhild, would not have improved the *Aethelings'* standing in Normandy. The long separation ensured that relations between Edward and Emma remained cold. Nor had he seen much of his mother during his childhood. The monks of Westminster, in a story which must, like so much of their claims, be treated with caution, were to say that he was brought up by a foster mother called Leofrun identified (improbably) as the 'wife of Earl Tostig', though no such earl of that name can be identified in Aethelred's reign.[41] But there might certainly have been a foster mother.

2

The *Aethelings* in Normandy

Edward was to spend the next twenty-four years of his life as an exile, mainly as a 'guest' of the Norman Dukes, Richard II and Robert ('the Devil' or 'the Magnificent', depending on which source is consulted). It is usually assumed that the *Aethelings* spent the whole of their youth in Normandy but there is nothing much to substantiate this. Indeed, William of Malmesbury insists that Edward was only too willing to revisit his native land at Harthacnut's invitation because he 'was weary of his years of wandering'.[1] Little else is recorded of his actions in Normandy other than the story that he related, when on his deathbed, of having a vision of two monks he had known in his youth in Normandy,[2] and the suggestion that he had worked miracles with the water in which he had washed his hands.[3] Having monks among his acquaintances does not make him a monk! Edward's sister Gode, (Godgifu in English), was soon married off, presumably at the instigation of Duke Richard, to Drogo, Count of Mantes which lay in the Vexin between Normandy and the Île de France around Paris. Her sons were to be Walter, who succeeded his father in

1035, and Ralph, known as 'the Timid', appointed Earl of Hereford by Edward, probably in 1051. Edward and Ralph might well have met in Mantes. Edward would certainly have spent some of his time with his sister as a guest of her husband. Drogo was an intimate friend of Duke Robert and although the Count was actually a vassal of the French King,[4] he wished to become a vassal of the Norman Duke, his neighbour.

Edward, when King, also had Breton courtiers, notably Ralf the Staller and Robert FitzWymarc, the only foreigners at his court, other than his nephew Earl Ralph, who were of the first importance as landowners, neither of them Norman. Ralf the Staller is of interest because he possessed the barony of Gael in Brittany and was one of its greatest lords; the Conqueror was to make him Earl in East Anglia.[5] While Edward could have become acquainted with these men while at the ducal court in Rouen, he might also have visited Brittany and if so have been acquainted with the Bretons who served him later. Several of his bishops were Lotharingians (from the area now known as Alsace-Lorraine) and some of the staff of his household were German. While it may be the case that these men sought his court to obtain patronage, he could also have made contact with them through his acquaintances at St Peter's, Ghent or they might well have met him in Normandy or in Mantes. He could also have visited the French court if the tradition in the *Leges Edwardi Confessoris* (a law book of the twelfth century) is correct. It claims that he banished usurers from England when he became king because he had seen them to be the root of all evil 'when he had stayed in the court of the King of the Franks'.[6]

Other royal and noble English exiles spent their time on the Continent visiting more than one court. Edward was an honoured, and useful, guest of the Norman dukes, not a prisoner, although the dukes held on to the *Aethelings* as useful pawns in their relations with England. It is conceivable that Edward paid visits to other households and became acquainted with other rulers. He was under the protection not only of the Norman dukes but of a number of northern French princes: Drogo of Mantes, Henry, King of France – overlord of the Norman dukes – and perhaps Alan III of Brittany, who was guardian to William of Normandy. The prominent part played by the Norman dukes often sees the possibility of such associations overlooked.[7]

It is accepted that Edward and Alfred completed their upbringing at the ducal court; Edward was about fourteen years of age when he settled in Normandy, old enough for much of his character to have been formed already, and Alfred somewhat younger.[8] There is little evidence to suggest that their upbringing was particularly religious or that they spent any great length of time in the company of monks, other than that of those who frequented the ducal court. Edward certainly knew Abbot John of Fécamp and the man he was to promote as Bishop of London and Archbishop of Canterbury, Robert, Abbot of Jumièges; but this does not mean that he visited their monasteries. It is just as likely that such prominent men visited the ducal court. The *Aethelings* would have lived the normal life of the court and its pursuits; conversation, chess or dice, listening to minstrels or skalds (Scandinavian poets) and being entertained by jesters. If Edward had really taken monastic vows in some monastery, that house would most certainly have boasted of it.

The lives at court of the two *Aethelings* would have been similar to those of other noblemen's sons, especially those of ancient or royal blood. The *Vita Edwardi* records Edward's love of hunting and he most likely engaged in such pursuits in Normandy. Hunting, of stags and wild boar, was part of military training. It was thus that the arts of horsemanship were perfected and men learned to move together, as if on campaign, and to use the bow, the spear and the sword, especially against wild boar. This followed learning the schooling of one's horse and the management of a spear and shield, learning how to strike and not be struck. Serious training began at about the age of twelve and Edward was not much older than that when his exile began. The dukes maintained their own military household, the *familia*, and it was in that household that knightly training was given. It is likely that the *Aethelings* were trained in the company of other would-be knights. Such training ended usually at about the age of twenty-two, and for Edward that would have meant in the late 1020s. Edward would have had the advantage of having had training in England where the battleaxe was the weapon of choice. Such apprenticeship in arms would include breaks for games or sport. The two *Aethelings* remained unmarried because few noblemen married young except for reasons of state and the Norman Dukes made no effort to find a wife for either of them.

There is a curious comment from John of Salisbury,[9] who condemned hunting because hunters were prone to be 'immodest, unchaste and lacking in seriousness' that it would be 'shameful for a huntsman to aspire to rule a kingdom or a bishopric ... whoever heard of a holy hunter?' But he avoids naming names although when he wrote, Edward's cause was being promoted by the monks of Westminster. English nobles were fond of falconry, (as was Edward who delighted in hawks)[10] though the Normans were not. In view of Edward's reputation for chastity (not explicitly celibacy) he probably did not engage in amorous pursuits, as other noblemen often did, including the Dukes, and he is not credited with any bastard children, unlike his contemporaries. There is no record at all of his having actually lived for any length of time in a monastery, other than for a short visit to Fécamp along with the rest of the court. He is unlikely to have taken a vow, either of chastity or of celibacy, since the Church frowned on laymen taking such vows. If a man desired to adopt such a way of life, he was expected to become a monk, as many men did. Such evidence as has survived suggests rather that Edward never forgot his status as an *Aetheling* and that he even thought of himself as the rightful king of England.

He had the opportunity to prepare himself for kingship, not only by learning the art of war, but by observing the manner in which the dukes conducted their government of Normandy, and he and his brother Alfred are found acting as witnesses to charters. He would have been aware of his place in the Anglo-Scandinavian world, stepson in fact if not in practice, of Cnut the Great, half-brother to Harthacnut of Denmark and step-half-brother to Harold I of England. That made him kin to Olaf Tryggvason of Norway and thus of Harald Bluetooth and Swein Forkbeard. He was even, therefore, distant kin to Earl Godwine of Wessex who married Gytha, sister of Earl Ulf who married Cnut's sister Estrith. She in turn was the mother of Swein Ulfsson or Estrithson, King of Denmark during Edward's reign in England.

There is no record of Edward having been knighted but it is not unlikely that he was. It is argued that Harold Godwinson, when in Normandy, accepted knighthood from Duke William, so there is no reason why Duke Robert, who was said to have regarded Edward as a son or brother, should not have done the same for Edward. In 1036 the *Aetheling* led a company of knights in his abortive attempt to visit his mother Emma in Winchester, which would support the suggestion that he was a knight. Edward had a reputation as a soldier in Normandy and in Scandinavia.[11]

No marriage was arranged for Edward, as it was for his sister Godgifu, as provision would have had to be made for the counter-gift, in exchange for the bride, of dower lands. Edward, a landless exile, could not provide it. Despite the assertion of William of Poitiers that Edward received 'great honours and many benefits', there is no evidence of any grant of land.[12] Although he might have had to perform homage to the dukes, it does not appear that he became a vassal in receipt of a fief. Without a prince's estate Edward had little prospect of a noble marriage and even less of launching a comeback. It does not appear that he had so very much to be grateful for. He could even have been emotionally scarred by his experiences in Normandy where he might not, despite Norman assertions to the contrary, have been so well treated. There is no sign, before the rule of Duke Robert, that he was paid any particular marks of respect. He might well have resented any slights visited upon him and to have been very selective in his friendships.[13] He was, as king, to display a degree of stoicism which was later interpreted as resignation worthy of a saint. Edward Augustus Freeman, the historian, once remarked that Edward ought to have been the head of a Norman monastery. It is significant therefore that no attempt was made to make him an abbot.

Military training was a group activity and it is probable that it was from among such men that Edward acquired the following of Frenchmen and Normans who settled in Herefordshire in the early part of his reign, some of whom probably accompanied him on his return to England. These would be landless bachelor knights seeking to make their fortune in the service of a royal lord.[14] Princes' sons were brought up in this way precisely so that they might acquire followers who became their brothers-in-arms and *fideles* or faithful men. The *Vita*'s account of Edward's last days shows that he had French favourites; some of them had been allowed to stay in England after 1052 when most of the Frenchmen and Normans were driven out. Kings were expected to have such an entourage.

Despite the assertions of Norman writers that Edward was grateful to his Norman relatives for the welcome, the treatment and the support he received from them, there is little evidence that anything very much was done for the *Aethelings*. Duke Richard II was quite willing to approve of the marriage of his own sister, Emma, to King Cnut and had no intention of making any hostile move towards the Dane. The two might even have become friends of a sort.[15] The real advantage of Emma's marriage to Cnut, as it had been for her marriage to Aethelred, was that it secured an Anglo-Norman alliance, possibly of benefit to both sides. There is also an unsubstantiated story that at some point Duke Robert contracted a marriage, or perhaps formally betrothed, Cnut's sister, Estrith, but that the alliance did not last or was not completed and Robert repudiated her.[16] She had been married to Earl Ulf, father of Swein 'Esthrithson', King of Denmark, so this would have had to occur after Ulf's death in 1025. Cnut was perhaps trying to strengthen his position, out of fear of Norman support for the *Aethelings*, but this seems unlikely in view of the acceptance of Emma's marriage and as no positive moves were made until 1033.[17] It might have been the Normans who wanted to deter attacks on Normandy.

The only Norman move in favour of the *Aethelings* had been the rather tentative attempt by Duke Robert at a naval expedition to put Edward on the throne of England in 1033, or so William of Jumièges thought.[18] He says that the duke sent an embassy to Cnut demanding the surrender of England to its rightful heir, which was rejected. The whole affair looks quite improbable; the story goes that a fleet was then assembled at Fécamp but that a terrible storm destroyed many of the ships, whereupon the duke decided to campaign against Brittany instead. There is a possibility here that talk of invading England was a diversionary tactic and that Brittany was the intended target all along. The diversion just 'happened' to assist one of the Duke's campaigns there at a time when Mont St Michel was disputed between Normandy and Brittany.[19]

The Duke had summoned a council of his barons at which the summoning of a fleet was ordered. The chronicler concluded that God had decided to restore Edward in His own way and in His own good time and did not intend him to be restored by force. The chronicler's purpose is to give an example of the support Edward received from Normandy which was to lead to feelings of gratitude on his part and a decision to make William of Normandy his heir. One problem with the story is that the Normans were not a seafaring people at this time and had no fleet. Robert certainly did campaign in Brittany. The whole thing reads like an earlier version of Duke William's Council at Lillebonne at which he ordered the construction of the invasion fleet in 1066. It has been carried back and attributed to his father, even down to the damage done by storms in the Channel.

To make matters worse, and even more confusing, William of Jumièges also claimed that Cnut offered a peace treaty and was prepared to cede half his kingdom to Edward, because he was ill and wished to make amends before his death. This is not history but romance, and meant to enhance the reputation of Duke

Robert. The chronicler is embellishing the story to illustrate Edward's indebtedness to the Norman dukes. It echoes Dudo of St Quentin and William of Jumièges who claim that an English King 'Athelstanus' had aided Rollo and they talk of an offer of half the Kingdom.[20] The Duke might have had visions of putting Edward on his throne, in the expectation of earning his gratitude, but real chances of success were slight and nothing substantial in fact was done. It is noteworthy that no hint of any of this is to be found in the Anglo-Saxon Chronicles. Nor, for that matter, do they have much to say about Anglo-Norman relations during Edward's reign. They saw Anglo-Norman diplomacy, if there was any, to be of little interest.[21] The most that can be concluded about Duke Robert is that he was a generous host, up to a point, and possibly personally close to Edward and his family.[22] As Freeman commented, Norman writers never held truth to be of any consequence whenever the relations of Normandy and England were concerned.[23]

Shortly afterwards Robert decided to go on pilgrimage to Jerusalem. He therefore made his vassals do homage to his bastard son William, surrendered the duchy to him, with the support of regents, and caused William to do homage to Henry of France. The Duke then went off to Jerusalem, which he reached safely, but died at Nicaea in 1035 during his return. Interestingly enough Cnut the Great died the same year and Anglo-Norman relations can be said to have entered a new phase.

As there was already a Council of Regency in operation in Normandy, it continued in being and William was recognised as Duke. This did not prevent challenges to his rule and for several years Normandy was plunged into turmoil and outbursts of civil war from which it was eventually rescued by the intervention of Henry of France and the defeat of the rebels at Val-es-Dunes in 1047. The administration of the Duchy never wholly collapsed and the young duke survived his minority, largely due to the policies of King Henry whose support for and recognition of William never wavered. But one thing seems likely: William would have had no interest in or even ability to undertake any action in support of Edward's claim to the throne of England.[24]

It is from the period 1030–1035 that evidence survives of the *Aethelings*' presence in Normandy. They had been kept in the background during the major part of Cnut's rule in England because Duke Richard had cultivated relations with Cnut made possible by his marriage to Emma. But after 1028 they appear to have become more prominent at court in attendance on Duke Robert. A charter for Fécamp from about 1030 is witnessed by the *Aethelings*[25] and a gift to St Wandrille in 1033.[26] Further evidence comes from a somewhat dubious charter for St Michael's Mount. If genuine it might come from about 1042 or earlier and is attested by 'Haduardus rex'. It is partly regarded with suspicion on the grounds that Edward would not have used the title of king at that time. It is a copy not an original. It might have been 'doctored' to include as witnesses Queen Edith and Harold. It might also be that the copyist added the word 'rex' because by the time he made his entry Edward was indeed a king.[27]

The problem that arises is whether Edward could have thought himself able to grant land in England to St Michael's Mount except by anticipation; that is, that it would take effect if he became king. He uses the style 'Edward, by the Grace of God, King of the English' in the body of the charter and the grant is for his own soul and those of his parents. Some even think that the fleet assembled in 1033 might have visited Mont St Michel, which might have moved Edward to make the grant to the English abbey.[28] That would date the charter to 1033. However there is a more reliable charter, of Duke Robert for Fécamp from 1032–35 and both early copies carry the attestation *Edwardi Regis*.[29] The title might have been added by the scribe as a supplement or it could be evidence that Edward was styling himself King. There is no certainty that Edward actually used the royal title while in exile, only probability, but the charters are evidence of his attendance on the duke.[30] It can be suggested that these charters confirm Norman claims that the *Aethelings* kept alive their claims to the English throne during the latter part of their exile. King Henry I of France witnessed a charter for St Wandrille while briefly in exile at Fécamp, so that granting the title 'king' to Edward did Robert's prestige no harm.[31]

Some suggest that Duke Robert did therefore recognise the claims. He seems to have arranged or permitted the marriage of Godgifu to his ally Drogo of Mantes and relations with Cnut certainly worsened after 1030. William of Jumièges gives a rather doubtful explanation for this, alleging that they quarrelled after the repudiation of Cnut's sister Estrith, but such an explanation is not really needed to explain Norman hostility towards Cnut and his power. Robert had every reason to be fearful of the growth of Cnut's influence in the Viking world. That in itself would have predisposed him to at least make gestures of support for the *Aethelings*. But he actually did nothing concrete.

In the year after William's accession came an event that had far more significance for later relations between England and Normandy and, it is argued, for relations between King Edward and his premier Earl, Godwine. In 1036 the younger *Aetheling*, Alfred, came to England. Ostensibly making a visit to his mother Emma at Winchester, Alfred was intercepted by Earl Godwine who was seeking means of ingratiation with the King 'because the popular cry was greatly in favour of Harold.'[32] Godwine seized Alfred and his escort. Many of these men were subsequently put to death, mutilated or sold into slavery, and Alfred himself was handed over to Harold's men. He was taken on board a ship, had his eyes put out and was transported to Ely where he was left to die of his injuries in the care of the monks. The *Liber Eliensis* adds the detail that he was carried to Ely on horseback and naked.[33] He was buried in the abbey church 'at the west end, very near the steeple, in the south side chapel'. His death was commemorated at Ely on 5 February.[34] It was a heinous crime that shocked men of that hard age and left behind it a legacy of hatred and suspicion. Edward seems to have found it impossible to forget and could still charge Godwine with it in 1051.[35]

Queen Emma was to endeavour to create a cult of martyrdom around Alfred. The *Liber Eliensis* testifies to the tradition at Ely, stating that his body 'enjoys due honour in the south aisle in the western part of the church' and that his soul 'enjoys paradisical loveliness'. It says that 'wonderful and beautiful visions of lights and works of power have often occurred'.[36] Emma confessed herself 'dazed beyond consolation' by his murder (or was it at the failure of her scheme?) and fled to Flanders. The encomiast, writing probably after Edward was recalled to England by Harthacnut, claims, for Emma, that Alfred's tomb was the scene of a cult 'it is justly so for he was martyred in his innocence'. She certainly made gifts of costly altar-hangings and palls to cover the shrines of the saints, especially St Aethelthryth (Etheldreda).[37] But the cult eventually petered out and came to nothing. The murder was political and not a religious matter.

Edward is said also to have come over, with a rather more formidable force of Normans as escort, reaching Southampton. William of Poitiers[38] alleges he had forty ships which is certainly a ridiculous exaggeration. That number of ships is the number Cnut retained in England in 1018 after he had been accepted as king.[39] A battle, a skirmish of some sort, took place and Edward withdrew to Normandy. The Norman writer claimed that it was a victory but it is a strange sort of success that causes an immediate retreat. Nonetheless Edward had a certain reputation as a soldier in both Normandy and Scandinavia;[40] most likely he successfully repelled the levies that opposed him and then retreated in the certain knowledge that overwhelming reinforcements were advancing against him.[41] It has been suggested that his retreat was the 'reflex action of a survivor'.[42]

After Queen Emma fled to Bruges she persuaded Edward to pay her a visit there and he came perhaps not yet having given up hope of eventually gaining his throne. She demanded his help for Harthacnut which he rightly refused having no resources of his own with which to provide it. It is further proof, if any be needed, that he did not spend all of his time at the ducal court, certainly not after he had reached manhood. It might have been at Bruges that Emma recruited the encomiast to her service. Harthacnut also came to Bruges, enraged perhaps at the death of Alfred. He had now subdued Norway and, according to the Encomium, had dreamt that the 'unjust usurper' (his half-brother Harold Harefoot) had little longer to live. This may have been wishful thinking or perhaps it was rumoured that Harold was not a well man. It is a typical 'topos' or improving story based on a well known theme, that Harold merited divine retribution for killing Alfred. His death soon afterwards on 17 March 1040 would have appeared to be the fulfilment of the dream. Harthacnut was still in Bruges when the news came. He and Emma returned and he was welcomed as King with his mother as Dowager Queen.

Emma was to claim later, in the *Encomium Emmae*,[43] that the *Aethelings* came to England in 1036 in response to a letter inviting both of them to visit her but that the letter was a forgery put out by King Harold I, Harefoot, to lure the *Aethelings* to their doom. Her protestations do not quite ring true and she might well have been seeking to avoid the charge that she had caused Alfred's death. The *Aethelings* probably did come in response to an invitation from Emma. The context, according to the Encomium, was the situation in which Emma had found herself when Harthacnut delayed his return. She might therefore have turned her thoughts towards her other sons and sent them a letter from 'Emma, Queen in name only' now mourning the death of Cnut. Her sons have been deprived of their inheritance and she asks what they intend to do about it. Their delay has played into the hands of the 'unjust usurper' and English magnates would prefer to be ruled by their *Aethelings*. They are beseeched to visit her privately and she will advise them.[44] They are being dilatory and over-cautious and the writer offers them help.

The encomiast then claims that all this is a forgery, a trap devised by Harold Harefoot using deceitful messengers. Scandinavian sources accuse Emma of using a forged letter to promote Harthacnut's interests in Denmark; if so, it was in character that she should have deceived the *Aethelings*. A forgery by Harold Harefoot is not out of the question, he could easily have had possession of a seal or ring or other token to authenticate a letter, as was the practice. But he had little to gain from deceiving the *Aethelings* into coming to England whereas Emma had much to gain from exonerating herself from responsibility for Alfred's death. The letter only survives because the *Encomium* quotes from it, so, if it was a forgery, how did the Encomiast come by it? There might not have been an actual letter at all, only verbal communications between Emma and the *Aethelings* by way of messengers. Noticeably the *Encomium* blames Harold and is less concerned with Godwine (who rapidly changed sides when Harold died and Harthacnut became king).[45]

Alfred had travelled overland to Flanders and sailed from either Wissant or Boulogne nearby where he could have obtained men and ships. (This could be evidence that the widowed Godgifu had married or was about to marry Eustace of Boulogne and of the close relations between the *Aethelings* and their sister.) Both men found that there was little support for their return.

Earl Godwine's real role in the affair is still something of a mystery because the sources disagree about the extent of his involvement. There are even two charters of King Edward which refer to Alfred's murder. The first blames Harold Harefoot and Harthacnut jointly for Alfred's death and says Edward himself was rescued from them only with difficulty and the second blames the Danes generally. Both may be spurious but they indicate what a forger thought Edward's opinion was.[46] The *Encomium* says that Harold's men took the captives, including Alfred, out of Godwine's hands and were responsible for what followed. One version of the Chronicle ignores the whole thing, another tries to disguise Godwine's part in it. The version in the *Abingdon Chronicle* is possibly nearest to the truth. Godwine and other magnates had concluded that they would have to accept Harold as king, regarded the intervention of the *Aethelings* as an embarrassment, and sought to curry favour with the King by handing Alfred and his entourage over to him.

Godwine himself later, in Harthacnut's reign, swore (in a manner familiar to modern readers from the time of the Second World War) that he was 'only obeying orders' from Harold.[47] He was charged along with Bishop Lyfing of Crediton, who was deprived for a time of his See. What the bishop's part in the affair was is quite unknown. The Earl had to compensate King Harthacnut for his part in the death of the King's half-brother with the gift of a magnificent warship manned by eighty men, fully armed with sword, shield, battle-axe and spear and a triple coat of mail. So the blood-feud was satisfied. According to the *Vita Edwardi* this gesture was repeated in 1042 when Edward became king. Godwine gave him too a great warship with a golden dragon prow 'equipped for six score fearsome warriors'. It may be that on this occasion too the Earl had to purge himself on oath and pay a suitable *wergild*.

In the year after the incursion of the *Aethelings*, Harold Harefoot, son of Cnut by his wife, *more danico*, Aelfgifu of Northampton, was undisputed king and remained so until his unexpected death on 17 March 1040. The *Aethelings* had remained in exile and Emma had to take refuge at Bruges to wait for Harthacnut. He had first to get free of his war with Magnus of Norway as he was too sensible to leave Denmark at the mercy of Magnus while he risked a campaign in England. Somehow or other he made peace with the Norwegian and, possibly leaving Denmark in the hands of cousin Swein Estrithson, returned to claim his kingdom when Harold died. Later writers claimed that he and Magnus had agreed that when either of them died, the other would inherit both northern kingdoms.[48] Magnus and his heir, Harald Hardrada, were to claim that England was included. There is no early confirmation of the story. The *Encomium Emmae* ends with a description of the circumstances under which Harthacnut's half-brother Edward was recalled to England.

3

The *Aetheling* Returns

One result of the elevation to kingship of Harthacnut was the return to England of the *Aetheling* Edward. Nothing is known of the real motives behind Harthacnut's decision to invite his half-brother to return. The Chronicle states simply the fact; Edward returned and was 'sworn in as king'.[1] Thereafter he remained at court until Harthacnut's death. The *Encomium Emmae*[2] presents it as family reunion. Harthacnut is reported to have invited Edward to return out of 'brotherly love' and that 'Emma and her two sons, among whom there is true loyalty, amicably share the Kingdom's revenues'. Harthacnut's benevolence towards his half-brother is confirmed by William of Poitiers in the context of his own specious claim that William of Normandy, then only thirteen years old, had played a part in arranging the return, threatening the use of Norman force.[3] He also explains that Harthacnut was a dying man and wished to be reconciled to Edward before his death. There is, however, no sign that Harthcnut was ill. His death, when it came was sudden and unexpected.

Edward could hardly have expected the invitation, nor could he have returned uninvited as he had no supporters in England as the events of 1036 had shown. There might have been a rapproche-ment between Edward and Emma while she was herself an exile in Bruges. Either of them could have made the first move and Emma might have wanted to bolster Harthacnut's position, aware that he was not over-popular in England. It has even been speculated that Harthacnut, needing to resume his war with Magnus, contemplated making Edward his regent in England.[4] The *Encomium* stresses that Harthacnut's claim to the throne was stronger than that of Edward, though it was not. The Queen does this by implying that Edward was her son by Cnut.

The frontispiece of the *Encomium Emmae*[5] shows Emma enthroned with Harthacnut and Edward in attendance on her so that they are presented as her sons. She had always been ready to make use of the existence of Edward and Alfred for her own purposes, as in 1036. The *Encomium* had claimed that Cnut had promised the throne to Harthacnut, though this cannot be verified. It also implied that Edward had withheld his own claims to allow Harthacnut's accession. Harthacnut had become unpopular by rea-son of heavy taxation, demanding large payments of 'heregeld' for the maintenance of sixty ships' crews which had accompanied him to England and in May 1041 had sent his housecarls out across the country to collect it. Two of them were set upon and murdered by the enraged townsmen of Worcester and the King's response was to have the whole of Worcestershire ravaged in punishment on 12 November 1041.[6] Edward's recall might well have been a bid to appease the English and Florence of Worcester puts the recall shortly after the ravaging.

But it seems to have put Edward in a very favourable position. The Chronicles insist that he was in some way associated in the Kingship and it might be that there was some sort of ceremony in which he was designated as heir to Harthacnut.[7] It was the general practice in most of western Europe for a reigning monarch to secure recognition of his successor by the leading magnates during his own lifetime. A king might indeed be succeeded by a son but also by a brother, or in this case, a half-brother. Even if there was no actual ceremony, it still looks as though Edward was seen as Harthacnut's potential successor.[8] But, although a man might be king-worthy he still had to be made a king.[9] It was probably thought useful to enhance the prestige of the regime by incorporating in it a prince with English royal blood who was also a descendant of Rollo of Normandy. Neither man was married; Harthacnut had no children and showed no sign of intending to marry. He was, it is true, some thirteen years younger than Edward but might well have to fight to retain Denmark. He could easily have feared the possibility of death in battle.

As the two princes were unmarried, Emma became very prominent at court, filling the roles of Queen and close adviser of her son, as the charters bear witness.[10] The *Encomium* presents Emma with Harthacnut and Edward as a trinity of power and she saw herself as a queen mother exercising joint rule with her sons. That can be compared to the position of Queen Eadgifu when Eadwig was King over all England and Edgar was King 'of the Mercians and the Northumbrians' as his charters boasted.[11] In the event Harthacnut died suddenly, probably as a result of a stroke or heart attack. Edward was not, of course, crowned king until after Harthacnut's death. The one charter simply identifies him as the 'King's brother' and none of his men can be identified in the witness list. There are no obviously Norman names.[12] He is not mentioned in other charters and must have really been the junior partner, not exactly a stooge, for Harthacnut could have intended to use him as a regent during absences in Denmark. Emma's preference for Harthacnut explains Edward's complaint that she had done less for him during his exile than he had wanted. If he did give way to his half-brother, then he could dissemble and conceal his aims with the best of them. He might also have resented her elimination of her marriage to his father from her history fostering the idea that he was a son of Cnut. Both the *Encomium Emmae* and Queen Edith's tract, the *Vita Edwardi*, were obsessed with the succession to the throne.[13] Neither supports any claims by William of Normandy.

The Chroniclers believed that Edward, upon his return, was accompanied by a household of Normans and Frenchmen, and William of Poitiers, who maintained that his return had been the result of Norman threats to use force, affected to believe that he was accompanied by a troop of Norman knights. Though that is possible, it is more likely a detail intended to strengthen the claim that Edward was indebted to William for his assistance and support.[14] The *Vita Edwardi* says that he was accompanied by quite a few men from France and that they were by no means base-born. It goes on to add that he made some of these men 'his privy counsellors and administrators of the royal palace'. The composition of this French entourage will be considered later. It is sufficient to point out here that few of these people can be identified as holding major offices or as major landowners and that very few were actually Normans.

There may also already have been some Normans in England since Emma herself must have been accompanied by a retinue when she first arrived, but again they cannot be identified as of major importance. It was Orderic Vitalis who thought that the Normans had won positions of influence as a result of Emma's marriage simply because she must have had an entourage of her own.[15] But she had English servants also including an unnamed goldsmith who looked after her relics, Wulfweard White, a thegn, who later served Queen Edith, and Aelfgar son of Whitgar who served Emma along with a relative called Leofgifu. Aelfgar seems to have been her steward in charge of Thingoe Hundred.

Foreigners, of course, were attracted to Edward's service after he became king. But initially the number of them at court must have been quite small. Twelfth-century tradition looked back to the arrival of Emma as the beginning of a peaceful infiltration of English society which prepared the way for Duke William but that, as has been acutely remarked, is 'a strange historiographical distortion'.[16]

Then on 8 June 1042, Harthacnut, while at the wedding feast of prominent Danish nobleman Tofig the Proud and Gytha, daughter of Osgod Clapa, collapsed and died 'as he stood at his drink'. With his death the male line of the Danish royal house of Cnut came to an end. The succession to both England and Denmark became open to question. In Denmark the choice lay between Harold, son of Thorkell the Tall, and Swein Esthrithson but before the matter could be resolved, Magnus of Norway invaded presumably to enforce his claim derived from his treaty with Harthacnut (if there was one). Harold was murdered in 1043 and Swein was left to lead the Danes in a war of independence against Magnus.

Whether Edward was present at the wedding feast is uncertain. The Chronicles imply that he was in London but do not actually say so. The *Vita Edwardi* has its own account. Seeking, as it does, to enhance the role of Earl Godwine in English affairs, it states that he took the lead in urging the *Witan* to free England from Danish rule and send for Edward, implying that he was not actually in England. Godwine succeeds in his aim and Edward receives a warm welcome. But the *Vita* is not well informed about the affairs of the beginning of the reign and its account telescopes the events of 1041–43 to emphasise Godwine's contribution. It may simply be transferring events which occurred in 1041 to 1042 and exaggerating the Earl's part in the reception of Edward.

The Chronicle account is straightforward enough and of better authority. They say that he was 'received as king, as was his natural right' or that the people 'chose Edward and received him as King'. Florence of Worcester adds that this was 'chiefly by the exertions of Earl Godwin and Lyfing bishop of Worcester'. Only the Peterborough Chronicle (which for this period was based on a text from Kent, probably St Augustine's Canterbury) says 'all the people chose Edward as king in London, may he hold it as long as God grants it to him'.

There is some interesting evidence to substantiate the role of Earl Godwine, information recorded in the twelfth-century lawbook called the Quadripartitus.[17] Chapter nine of that work claims that the recall of Edward to England was the result of the mediation of Aelfwine, Bishop of Winchester,[18] and of Earl Godwine. It says that he came to 'Hurstshevet' where 'all the thegns of England gathered' and 'there it was heard that he would be received as King only if he guaranteed to them upon oath that the Law of Cnut and his sons should continue in his time with unshaken firmness'. He was then 'promoted with such fortunate auspices'.

Maddicott argues that this points to 1041 because the Chronicle states for that year that he was sworn in as king, '*to cinge gesworen*'.[19] So, as the surviving son of Aethelred and Emma, Edward became king because he was indeed the descendant of both Cerdic, the progenitor of the West Saxon Monarchy, and of Rollo of Normandy, the Viking. As such he was acceptable to both English and Danish magnates. It is not known exactly where Edward was when Harthacnut died. William of Malmesbury thought that Edward was in England but that at first he wanted to return to Normandy and was persuaded to stay by Earl Godwine.[20]

The Earl is described as urging the King to put his trust in him as his authority carries great weight in England and no one will dare oppose Edward if Godwine supports him. In return he asks for honours for his son and that Edward marry his daughter. The writer points out that there was nothing Edward would not have promised 'in the need of the moment' and that he accepted Godwine's offer. The Earl then persuades the magnates to accept Edward as king by a combination of his own influence and of bribes. The few who objected were later exiled by Edward.

It is conceivable that he had made a visit to Normandy and that Bishop Aelfwine and Godwine recalled him to England when Harthacnut dropped dead. The situation in the Quadripartitus is that Edward landed in England at a place called 'Hursteshevet', which is usually taken to mean Horsted in Sussex but, as Maddicott has pointed out, 'stede' is not 'shevet'. Nor is Horsted on the coast.

His analysis concludes that as 'heafod' means a head or headland, the location that best fits is Hurst or Hurstbeach off Milford-on-Sea, giving 'heafod-shevet' or Hurst Head off the Solent, the location of Hurst Castle. That would fit a return from Normandy via the Isle of Wight. The location is a sand bank on which Edward could have landed and been welcomed, not by 'all the thegns of England' but by a deputation of magnates and their men. The Quadripartitus is a Hampshire source.

The resulting agreement might then have been circulated by writ, from which the lawbook quotes. If Edward did promise to uphold the Law of Cnut (as he was asked to do on another occasion by the northern rebels in 1065), that would explain why he never issued a law code of his own (that is, none that has survived) and yet has a reputation as a law giver. He would certainly not have returned either in 1041 or 1042 unless he had first been invited to do so. This material also explains why it was claimed that Godwine was responsible for his elevation to the throne. Whichever date is accepted, William of Normandy had nothing to do with it. The most he might have done would have been to give his blessing, some cash and permission for a small escort to accompany the *Aetheling*.

Bishop Aelfwine of Winchester's role in all this is supported by grants of land and money, some fifty hides and £22, made to him as the King's 'familiar bishop' who had 'faithfully shown obedience to me'.[21] Edward also confirmed him by writ in possession of the bishopric of Winchester. There was no accepted procedure for the recognition of a new king and what process there was had been disrupted by disputed successions and the Danish conquest.

The four principal ingredients seem to have been eligibility by birth, designation by the previous king, election or recognition by the magnates of the *Witan* and the Church followed by consecration by the Church, usually the Archbishop of Canterbury. That was when the succession was orderly and on this occasion it was. Edward had clear advantages over all possible rivals and his position rapidly became unchallengeable. No other son of Aethelred was available and all the Danish or Scandinavian candidates were out of the country and in no position to make a claim.

The coronation followed about a year later (a delay which, as the example of other kings, notably in the tenth century, shows, was by no means unusual) and Edward was consecrated as king at Winchester (where Harthacnut had been buried in the Old Minster alongside his father Cnut), probably with the same ritual as that used for Edgar and Aethelred, on the first day of Easter 1043. That would have been 3 April. The Abingdon and Peterborough Chronicles add that he was consecrated by Archbishop Eadsige (Florence adds Aelfric of York) and that the archbishop instructed the new king 'as to his own need and that of all the people'. This looks like a reference to the administration to Edward of the *Promissio Regis* used by Archbishop Dunstan at the coronation of Aethelred. Thus he became fully entitled to the personal allegiance owed to a king by his chief nobles. He was now their Lord King, *cynehlaford*.[22] The England of that time could not function as a state without a single head, the King.

He had been accepted partly because there was no other pretender to the throne in England when Harthacnut died, partly because he was the available *Aetheling* of the English royal house, because he was regarded as the heir and successor to the Danish King Harthacnut, his half-brother, and because as the son of Emma he was a descendant of Rollo. He was thus acceptable to both the English and the Danes. To the English it was his royal blood that mattered.[23] The line of Cnut was a foreign dynasty, descended from Gorm the Old and Harald Bluetooth. This did not prevent the Normans from advancing their own inflated claim that he owed his throne to the support and counsel of the young Duke William[24] who was allegedly threatening to come to England himself with a strong force. The Norman claim is quite absurd. William was scarcely in control of his own duchy. It would appear that when the Norman writers were compiling their accounts many stories about Norman rights were circulating in the duchy, some no doubt propagated by Robert of Jumièges during his exile after 1052.[25]

The new king could draw on a fund of good will, though it was not inexhaustible. He would have had to rally support. The leaders of the King's supporting faction seem to have been Earl Godwine (though his role should not be exaggerated), Bishop Lyfing of Worcester who also held Devon and Cornwall, and Bishop Aelfwine of Winchester (who was to be rewarded with land over the next few years). Godwine might have been expected to press the claim of Swein Estrithson, his nephew, just as he had given support to Harthacnut, and before him Harold Harefoot. But he and Bishop Lyfing had been punished by Harthacnut for their involvement with Harold, and perhaps the death of Alfred. Both had now realised the need to back the right candidate in 1042 and perhaps thought that Edward would be both grateful and malleable. If so, they were to discover their mistake.

Once London and Winchester had decided, Edward would have looked to Mercia and Northumbria. It is there that the promise to uphold the 'Law of Cnut' became vital. It is not known whether Siward and Leofric were at court or took part in the acclamation in 1042 but the fact that they remained singularly loyal until their deaths suggests that they were indeed won over. In the tenth century kings had been recognised and accepted by successive provinces in turn, while conquerors had been acknowledged as they advanced. Edward would have expected Leofric to bring over the Mercian thegns since his father, Leofwine the Ealdorman, had served Edward's father Aethelred and the Earl had favoured the native or English candidate Harold Harefoot, son of Aelfgifu of Northampton, over Emma's son Harthacnut. Leofric's wife Godgifu (Godiva in Latin) was an Englishwoman. He might have delayed his response but, as in 1051, he preferred compromise and the avoidance of civil war.

As for Siward, he tended to follow Leofric's lead. He displayed little interest in the affairs of the court in Wessex as long as he was left to govern his earldom as he pleased and his main interests were focussed on Scotland. So normal procedure was followed. The great men, not only the Earls, but particularly those with an above average stake in the country, holding more than forty hides of taxable land, did homage in the English manner by 'bowing' to the King and taking the prescribed hold-oath. In return their lands were confirmed to them and the King promised them his favour. Such great land holders are termed 'proceres' by the *Liber Eliensis*[26] (a class of thegn regarded as of noble rank, possibly equivalent to King's thegn).

Some confirmations have survived, notably for ecclesiastics who were more likely to preserve the written evidence. So, for example, Ufi, abbot of Bury St Edmunds was confirmed in office and the men of the '*cnihtengild* of London' were to have the good laws they enjoyed under 'Edgar, Aethelred my father, and Cnut'.[27] St Paul's, London received its sake and soke and Aelfwine of Winchester was granted the same judicial and financial rights.[28] Other lay figures received grants of land, notably Ordgar, and Aelfstan[29] and possibly Orc of Abbot's Wootton in Dorset.[30] Archbishop Eadsige was confirmed in possession of Christchurch lands.[31] Aelfwine of Winchester was well rewarded with grants of land in successive years[32] and Earl Godwine was granted land at Millbrook at about the same time.[33]

The gifts were not all one-way. The most prominent gift came from Earl Godwine, who no doubt felt a need to ingratiate himself further with the King since he was probably aware that his involvement in the murder of the *Aetheling* Alfred might give rise to resentment and even hatred on Edward's part. He accordingly made a suitably ostentatious display of his own importance, possibly to underline how necessary his support was for the new government, by giving a fully equipped and manned warship, similar to that which he had given to King Harthacnut.[34] (Godwine was undoubtedly the richest of the Earls, though perhaps not as wealthy as his son Harold was to become, with many estates granted by Cnut. He was an upstart and nouveau riche with no connection to the aristocracy of the tenth century.) The ship is described in the *Vita Edwardi* in the following terms:

Equipped for six score fearsome warriors; A golden lion crowns the
stern.
A winged and golden dragon at the prow affrights the sea and
belches fire
With triple tongue.

It was a richer gift than that given to Harthacnut which had only
eighty splendidly armed men, though they had expensive arms and
armour. Earl Godwine cannot have been quite so sure of his ability
to influence, let alone dominate, the King, for him to have made
such an appeasing move. Gifts from other sources are not recorded
but the *Vita Edwardi* does state that at the coronation gifts came
from the 'Emperor of the Romans' Henry and other ambassadors
made rich gifts as well as doing fealty to the new king. It is only
too probable that other magnates made suitable gifts when offering
their submission.

There is some indication that not everyone welcomed the new
monarch but the identity of his opponents is not recorded. Perhaps
their identity can be sought among those who were punished
shortly after the coronation. Women were prominent among them
as the example of Gunnhildr, daughter of Estrith, Cnut's sister, and
Wyrtgeorn, King of the Wends shows. She was wife to Thorkell
Havi's son Harald and her sons were Hemming and Thorkell. They
were of the highest Scandinavian nobility and might well have been
regarded as a threat to the stability of Edward's position. Certainly
other sources thought the opposition came from disaffected Danes.[35]
The subsequent exiling of the Dane Osgod Clapa (the 'Ruffian')
in 1046 might be a sequel to Gunnhildr's expulsion. But the most
forceful action was that taken against Queen Emma.

She was now an embittered woman, possibly scheming to
hang on to her prominent position at court as Dowager Queen,
widow of Cnut the Great and mother of Kings. She might have
been engaged in some kind of correspondence which could be
interpreted as treasonable, though the Chronicles do not accuse

her of it. She might have been affected by Harthacnut's death, the destruction of her hopes. Rumours emerged some fifty years later that she had been encouraging Magnus of Norway to invade. He had invaded Denmark, causing Harthacnut to delay his return to England and was at war with Swein Estrithsson during the 1040s.[36] Swein was to claim later that Edward had been disturbed by Swein's claim to the English throne and had made a treaty with him in which he made Swein his successor in the event of his failing to have a son. This looks like a rationalisation after the event possibly based on vague promises by Edward later in the reign calculated to keep Swein neutral.[37]

There is no real substance in much of this and the King's action against Emma is explained quite differently in the Chronicles. She cannot really have wanted to aid Magnus and there is no evidence that his ambitions extended to England as early as 1042. The Chroniclers state simply that the King, shortly after his coronation, took into his own hands all of his mother's lands and everything that she owned in gold and silver 'because she had kept it from him too firmly'. Stigand, who was her closest adviser, also lost his lands and bishopric for having, it was supposed, wrongly advised her. The Worcester account is much fuller. It states that the King took action against her in mid-November, after taking counsel at Gloucester (which suggests a meeting of the *Witan*). He descended on the Lady at her residence in Winchester with an escort composed of his own household retainers and those (the *genge* or band) of the three Earls, Leofric, Godwine and Siward (that is the order in the text) and deprived her of lands and treasure.

It is probable that Emma still controlled some of the housecarls who had served both Cnut and Harthacnut, (she had controlled both the treasure and a bodyguard of housecarls in 1035 and had hung on to both early in 1042) and that would explain the need for the King to require the assistance of a small army. The Chronicler says bluntly that he 'robbed' her of all the treasures that she owned, 'which were untold', and all her lands were confiscated 'because earlier she was very hard on the King her son, in that she did less for him than he wanted before he became king, and also afterwards', a possible reference to her having prevented him from having access to the hoard of treasure at Winchester. It is accepted that in all probability Emma had taken control of the royal hoard containing not only money and objects of gold and silver, but the royal collection of relics and important documents, sometimes referred to as the 'haligdom'. Emma's removal from power was neither permanent nor total. That she had power is demonstrated by the fact that it took the King and three earls to remove her. She is found again in possession of some land and wealth and influence and was back acting as a witness to charters almost immediately. Stigand also returned to a place of influence[38] and resumed his career in the Church, as Bishop of Elmham, which culminated in his appointment as Archbishop of Canterbury in 1052. Later legends exaggerated the extent of Emma's disgrace since she continued to witness charters as the King's mother until his marriage. After the marriage she seems to have retired from court until her death on 6 March 1052.

Part Two

The King

1042–1066

4

Coronation and Marriage

Harthacnut had died in June 1042 and the Coronation came at Easter 1043. Such a delay can be accounted for by the King's need to negotiate with all of his magnates, especially those of Mercia and Northumbria, and the Church would have wanted to use the most auspicious date in the calendar for such an important ceremony. Aethelred himself had been crowned on a Sunday, fourteen days after Easter, but Edward was made king on 3 April, Easter Day. He would have wanted the full sacramental endorsement of the Church in an anointing not unlike that of a bishop, making him a quasi-ecclesiastical person, true lord, protector and benefactor of the Church. The *Ordo* or Order of Service provided for the King to be instructed in his duties by the Archbishop of Canterbury, and the Chronicle confirms that this was so, 'Archbishop Eadsige consecrated him and fully instructed him before all the people, and fully admonished him as to his own need and that of the people'.[1]

So he was put in possession of his kingdom, anointed and crowned in a ceremony recognisably similar to that used first by English and now by British monarchs ever since. Florence of Worcester adds that Aelfric Puttoc, Archbishop of York, also took part in the ceremony. The Chronicle is unanimous in all texts that this was done at Winchester and the claim of the *Vita Edwardi* that it was at Christchurch, Canterbury is wrong, as are some manuscripts of William of Malmesbury's *Gesta Regum* which say London. Archbishop Aelfric, as a provost of Winchester, would have known the Winchester liturgical tradition. The *Ordo* used at Edgar's Coronation, at Bath in 973, was used, suitably revised. The text is thought to be that found in the Vita S. Oswaldi.[2] Winchester was also an appropriate location not only because of its association with previous English kings, notably Alfred, but also because it was the burial place of Cnut the Great and Harthacnut, so stressing Edward's links with the Danish dynasty.

The King entered, flanked by the two archbishops and the Choir sang Psalm 88 vv. 14-15. His crown was removed and the King and the bishops prostrated themselves before the altar. The clergy and people were then asked to accept Edward as king and a *Te Deum* was sung. In 1066 there was at this point an Acclamation and it is likely that this was so in 1043. The King swore the terms of the *Promissio Regis*, promising true peace to the Church and all his Christian people, forbidding robbery and all unrighteous deeds and promising enjoining justice and mercy in all cases brought before him. The Unction, or anointing with oil, followed with suitable prayers on the theme of Christian kingship, with the anthem from the Book of Kings,[3] *Zadoc the Priest and Nathan the Prophet*. Investiture with the regalia followed: ring, sword, crown, sceptre and rod. God's blessing was invoked upon him by the Archbishop and the Lord was asked to 'give him increase of children'. The actual coronation ended with the anthem, *Vivat Rex*, Long live the King.[4] If homage was performed it followed the investiture. Mass was celebrated by the archbishops and this was followed by a coronation banquet.

According to the *Vita Edwardi* many foreign princes were present or sent ambassadors. King Henry III (German Emperor after 1047) husband of Edward's half-sister, Gunnhild, sent ambassadors and gifts, as did Henry I, King of the Franks; and Swein Estrithsson, King of Denmark (who is specifically said to have taken Edward as his Lord) attended in person. This king is not named, he is referred to only as 'King of the Danes'. Some have suggested that Magnus, who held Denmark at the time, was meant, which seems unlikely. Swein is more likely to have been seeking support in his war against Magnus. Much diplomatic activity would have resulted as ambassadors carefully assured Edward of the peaceful intentions of their lords and the *Vita* claims that treaties of friendship were offered by both the Germans and the French. Some French counts might have accepted fiefs, probably money fiefs rather than land as no charters exist to confirm such grants. They therefore in effect became Edward's vassals. These diplomatic manoeuvres involved alliances and that helps to explain the peacefulness of Edward's reign and his willingness towards the end of the first decade to ally himself with the German Emperor against Baldwin of Flanders.

The presence of King Swein also explains later claims of a mutual treaty between him and Edward and Swein's assumption that he had been, in some manner, made Edward's heir on much the same terms as the agreement which was alleged to have been forged between Harthacnut and Magnus of Norway. Just as Magnus claimed that Harthacnut and he had agreed that if either died without an heir before the other, the survivor would inherit the dead man's throne, so Swein claimed a similar arrangement with Edward. It looks as though in such agreements there was a perhaps tacit understanding that if either king died before the other, the survivor was entitled to revive any claim he had to the deceased rival's throne. Swein might have temporarily taken refuge in England seeking Harthacnut's aid, only to find that he was dead and Edward had replaced him. Swein would then have been unable to put forward his own claim, derived from Cnut.

It would appear, from the *Vita*'s account, that there were some notable absentees in 1043, despite the known friendship which became apparent later in the reign between Earl Godwine and Baldwin V of Flanders. The *Vita* does not name Baldwin as one of those who sent an ambassador. Significantly, there is no reference to the presence of a Norman embassy either and no Norman source makes any claim that one was sent. Nonetheless the *Vita* does emphasise that 'all Britain, together with the jagged islands of the adjacent kingdoms and monarchies,' settled down to an era of peace under the aegis of a second Solomon, namely Edward.[5] Even allowing for the writer's tendency towards hyperbole, it is true that Edward's reign was a peaceful one with no major external conflicts with Danes and Norsemen such as his father had endured. The only conflicts in which Edward engaged were, for the most part, those that he and his advisors chose to fight, against the Welsh and the Scots, or to repel raiders.

In due course Edward decided on the form of his Seal and according to surviving writs and coins he styled himself 'Edwerd Rex' or 'Eadward Rex Anglorum', King of the English, but on his seal he is *Anglorum basileus*, a style in use by English kings from at least the time of King Edgar. Two charters of somewhat doubtful authenticity give his style in Old English; 'Ic Eadwerd Englalondes cyng'.[6] He was also to use on charters styles similar to those of King Edgar, calling himself 'governor and ruler' or 'defender', either of the English nation or people, or of Albion or Britain or similar rather grandiloquent descriptions. In the *Vita Edwardi* he rules all Britain, surrounded as it is by the British Ocean. But his own style when signing a charter is simply *Rex Anglorum* or occasionally *Rex Anglorum atque Northumhymbrorum*, King of the English and the Northumbrians.

Shortly after the coronation, and as soon as he felt sufficiently established in possession of his kingdom, Edward dealt with the problem of Danish opposition to his rule by carefully calculated expulsions of those he regarded as possible centres of disaffection, and took care to reconcile leading magnates to his rule by continuing the policy of confirming various leading thegns in their sundry offices and lands and most especially took steps to ensure the continued support of the Church by renewing the privileges accorded to bishops and abbots. Most of these magnates, both lay and ecclesiastical, had come to office under Cnut or Harthacnut and it was vital to ensure their continued support. Then he dealt with the problem represented by his mother Emma's hold over the royal treasure at Winchester. It also allowed him to express his anger and displeasure at the way in which she had deserted Edward and his brother and sister in 1018 and the lack of any real attempt to assist him in reclaiming his inheritance. He no doubt regarded her endorsement of Harthacnut's invitation to return as too little, too late.

It also allowed Edward to clear the way for his marriage. Kings were expected to marry in order to provide heirs to the throne. The Chronicles state simply that Edward 'took Edith, the daughter of Earl Godwine, as his wife ten days before Candlemas', that is 23 January 1045[7] and as his queen[8] just under two years after his coronation. As the Chronicles consistently call her queen and twelfth century tradition alleges it as a fact, she was probably anointed and crowned, on the occasion of the wedding.[9] The *Vita Edwardi* is unfortunately lacking the vital pages concerning events after the description of Edward in old age and the poem containing the description of the ship given him by Earl Godwine. Some of what has been lost can be restored from statements made by William of Malmesbury and Osbert of Clare (the Westminster monk who promoted Edward's canonisation) where these two writers are in agreement. Also missing is some material on the members of Earl Godwine's family. It is agreed that the author of the *Vita Edwardi* had described Edward's marriage and possibly Edith's character, abilities and appearance. Osbert's account is rendered less useful by his determination to insist that Edward had remained a virgin all his life, something that Osbert had no way of knowing, in order to add weight to his promotion of Edward's canonisation.

It is Osbert who maintains that there had been a discussion about the need for the King to marry. He says that a search was conducted to find 'a wife worthy of such a husband ... from among the daughters of the princes' and that only one woman was found suitable, 'recommended by the distinction of her family' and by her beauty. This was 'the eldest of the daughters ... of Earl Godwine', Edith by name. She was considered suitable also because of her attainments. She was skilled in spinning and embroidery (essential for an educated noblewoman in the eleventh century) and in both verse and prose. William of Malmesbury adds that she was skilled in the 'liberal arts'.[10] The marriage would have been arranged by the respective parents, presumably in this case Emma and Gytha.

Her father Earl Godwine would have seen the marriage as setting the seal on his career and bringing with it the prospect of a royal grandchild, perhaps a son. It would have signified the healing of any possible breach between the King and the Earl, even as the ending of any feud.[11] Edith 'was delivered to the royal bridal apartments with ceremonial rejoicing, and, anointed by God, was crowned with a diadem'. Such information can be accepted, stripped of Osbert's own additions, as close to the text of the original work. The King could not have been compelled to marry if he was averse to doing so and if merely indifferent, his objections would have easily been dispelled by the clergy. The earls would have wanted an end to political uncertainty. Royal marriages were contracted for political and diplomatic reasons and, even if not always happy, usually produced children.

If matter which emphasises Edward's devotion to a celibate life is discarded, what is left leaves no grounds for assuming that this was anything other than a normal marriage. After the upheavals of the previous forty years, the magnates, both lay and clerical, would have expected Edward to fulfil his duty as king by producing an heir, which would have added to his prospects of continuing the West Saxon dynasty. The prayers used at his coronation included prayer that God would grant Edward children and those at his wedding would have included the sort of blessings that enjoined the couple to produce offspring, and the bride would have been reminded of the relevant texts in Genesis.

The *Vita Edwardi* itself presents the two as united in conjugal love, 'One person dwelling in double form'. Bishop Leofric of Crediton, a friend of Edward from his youth, was to insert in his Pontifical (or Service Book) a prayer for a childless king, praying for heaven's blessings of fertility and fruitfulness and for offspring from his loins.[12] It was only later, when no children appeared, that rumours might have begun to spread about the King, especially after the events of 1051 and the apparent attempt to persuade the King to divorce (or more correctly, to seek an annulment of his marriage to) Edith. There is no contemporary authority for the idea that Edward envisaged a solely companionate marriage or that he remained a virgin. The evidence of the *Vita Edwardi* is ambiguous and will require further careful examination. Edward in fact took a wife at an early point in his reign and his decision was seen as unexceptionable. No writer before the twelfth century saw the decision as in any way unexpected.

Much has also been made of the fact that it was Earl Godwine's daughter that Edward married. Some historians emphasise what they see as the overwhelming influence and power of the Godwines and insist that Edward was to a large degree dominated by Godwine in the 1040s and by his sons, especially Earl Harold, after 1053. They point to the evidence of Domesday Book which records the wealth of the Godwinesons in Edward's reign, and the relatively lesser power and wealth of the Houses of Leofric and Siward. They argue that the King's land holdings were considerably less than the combined holdings of the Godwines and refer that back to the period 1042–52 as though Godwine, and, after 1045, Swein and Harold his sons, were as wealthy and powerful then as the Godwinson family was after about 1060. They see the King as surrounded by the members of this powerful family who are then compared to the 'mayors of the palace' in Carolingian France. It is then alleged that if Edward could do nothing about his situation, he was powerless and that if he accepted it, he was a fool.[13] For the moment it is enough to consider exactly why Edward chose to marry Edith.

Edith was the eldest daughter and, in the view of the author of the *Vita Edwardi*, the eldest child of Godwine and Gytha. She might well have been named Gytha like her mother, (her immediate siblings, Swein, Harold and Tostig all have Danish names) and it would not have been unusual for her to have taken or have been given the English name Eadgyth (in honour of King Edgar's saintly daughter, Edith of Wilton). Queen Edith had been brought up and educated at Wilton and was to expend both time and money rebuilding the nunnery in stone. Her predecessor, Emma, had changed her name to Aelfgifu when she married Aethelred.

Not only was Edith the daughter of the most powerful earl in England, who had been instrumental in the recall of Edward to England and his accession to the throne, but through her mother she was twice related to the Danish royal house. She was daughter to Gytha who was Cnut's sister-in-law, and Gytha herself was a great-granddaughter of Harald Bluetooth, King of Denmark,[14] which made Edith a remote member of the royal house, though not in the line of succession, through Cnut the Great. Edith was therefore a most fitting bride and her lineage, noble enough, helped to cement the King's relationship with his Anglo-Danish subjects.

There is also another aspect to consider and that is whether there was anyone else he could have married. Neither Siward nor Leofric is known to have had a daughter. Some historians have speculated that Gunnhildr, the widow of Thorkell Havi's son Harald, might have been a possibility, but that has little to commend it. She was a foreigner. For Edward to have rejected Edith and chosen, as some of his predecessors had done, to marry the daughter of a prominent king's thegn instead would have been a mortal insult to Godwine and his fellow earls and again fails the test of relevant evidence.

There were several very wealthy king's thegns, though none could match the earls in wealth, but little is known of them and certainly not whether they had suitable daughters. The purpose of a noble marriage was often to cement an alliance of mutual benefit to both families. A bride of the right status maintained the dignity of the family into which she married and brought with her the support, treasure and allegiance of her family members, their kinsmen and commended men. This could often be crucial to the survival of a dynasty.[15] The fortunes of a royal wife and of her family were closely interlinked. By marrying Edith, Edward was signalling an alliance between the throne and its most powerful supporter. The Godwines took the place of the blood relatives that Edward lacked.[16] Marriage, like other Christian rituals such as baptism and confirmation, created strong familial bonds between individuals with no common ancestor, with special words for relationships; *sweor* or father-in-law and *adsum*, sister's husband.[17]

The *Vita Edwardi* makes a great deal out of the support that the King gained from his wife's family, especially the brothers Harold and Tostig (he knows nothing of the renegade eldest son Swein who died in exile). So such a marriage to a nobleman's daughter could be a royal bid to capture the support of that noble family, part of the delicate chess game played between a king and his nobles. It might also lead to the capture of the King himself through the queen, her family's advocate at Court. The *Vita Edwardi* emphasizes Godwine's position as Cnut's most prominent minister, 'earl and office-bearer [*dux et baiulus*] of almost the whole kingdom' who 'flourished in the royal palace, having first place among the highest nobles of the Kingdom', under Cnut and by implication under Edward, and his sons (and daughter) are the 'guarantors of England's peace'.[18]

The queen's position was an integral part of the royal government. As the King was responsible for ruling the Kingdom, the queen had special responsibility for the rule of the palace which was her business and involved direction of the great palace officials in the performance of their duties.[19] Queens ran the day-to-day affairs of the court and maintained the royal dignity. This was because at this time the court was the home of the King and his family as well as the centre and symbol of the entire kingdom. Accordingly a queen gave orders to the stewards and butlers and so on and, as Emma had done, might even control the royal treasure. Edith proved to be virtuous and religious and took great care of the King's worldly dignity and that of his household. The *Vita* suggests that she might well have come into conflict with the imported French members of the household who were 'the privy counsellors and administrators of the royal palace'.[20] He might well have resented Edith's position as being 'in all the royal counsels... strongly preferring the King's interests to power and riches'.[21] As queen she was recognised as such in charters, high in the witness lists as 'conlaterana', she who is at the King's side.

5

In Possession of the
Kingdom

E dward was entitled, as Lord King, to reverence and obedience. Orderic Vitalis was to comment that 'the English are always loyal to their princes'.[1] He now had, as an anointed and crowned monarch, the full support of the Church. There had really been no alternative to him. Edward was much older than most recent kings, other than his father Aethelred, and his very age must have added gravitas to his bearing, making him a figure of power and authority. His wife, Queen Edith, took care to see to it that 'from the beginning of their marriage' he was 'arrayed in many kinds of embroidered robes'[2] which would have added to a dignified and impressive appearance. He would, as Barlow remarks, have been regarded as the cornerstone, uniting the two walls of the English and Danish races,[3] especially as the acceptance of his accession had avoided the possibility of civil war.

As a result of his somewhat peripatetic life in exile, Edward would have acquired knowledge of the workings of a court and the administration of kingdoms and duchies. He was familiar with the work of the ducal court at Rouen and had probably learned something of the working of the courts of Capetian France and Brittany. In England, he would have had clerks to take care of routine administration who could instruct him in the complexities of *geld* collection and the administration of royal estates. From his youth in England he would have been aware of the work of his father's household and the way in which the Kingdom was administered through ealdormanries (converted by Cnut into provincial regions called earldoms), shires and boroughs and courts of shire and hundred, with their lawmen and portreeves and the exactors or tax-collectors. A king had to be competent to make the necessary decisions and act as head of the still developing bureaucracy, and able to present himself as a military leader. So Edward led a small army recruited from his own household and those of the three earls to remove his mother from her powerful position at Winchester and was later to put to sea in command of his own fleet. He was remembered as a soldier in Norman and Scandinavian sources.

Edward would have been wary of making sudden or unnecessary changes. He had not acquired a crown in order to throw it away and he had to take care not to disturb the established powers to which he owed his throne. He had taken good care to promise to maintain the Law of Cnut. As king he had a special responsibility to maintain internal law and order. A charter dated to 1063 illustrates the point. Edward is described as 'appointed king and defender of the English bounds [who] faces everywhere the threat that law and justice will be overthrown, everywhere disputes and discord seethe, everywhere wicked presumption rages, money puts off right and justice'.[4] Thus Edward speaks, through the scribe who wrote the charter, seeing his role as maintaining the effectiveness of existing law rather than making new law. According to the *Vita Edwardi* he appointed skilled churchmen and lay judges (princes and palace lawyers) to determine cases equitably, giving them royal support. It also claimed that he abolished bad laws and enacted good ones and it is clear that he did this not by means of issuing a royal Law Code, like his predecessors, but by means of royal rulings in particular cases, so setting precedents. It might be that he even deserves some small credit for foreshadowing the development of the Common Law. In Henry I's Charter of Liberties (cap.13) the *Laga Edwardi* are the laws of England as they existed before 1066.

As an exile Edward had eaten the bitter bread of other people, having lived under the protection of a number of northern French princes, and he had no intention of doing so again. So he returned to England without evil intent, 'baleless' as the *Vita* puts it, rather than bent on revenge, resolute and cheerful rather than soured or weakened by exile. But the men in power were 'new men', raised to power by Cnut without the established history that had lain behind the power of Aethelred's *ealdormen*. The peace of the Kingdom depended on good relations with the thegns and greater magnates. Ready to meet every challenge to his authority, starting with his mother Emma and the more hostile elements among the Danes, Edward moved with both circumspection and decisiveness, taking from Emma control over the royal treasure at Winchester, exiling the leaders of the Danish opposition and in due course raising his own candidates to power in the Church.

There was no possibility of removing any of the earls but he was prepared to create new ones. His first choices, arguably thrust upon him by Earl Godwine, were the two Godwineson brothers, Swein and Harold, and their cousin Beorn Estrithson. They were, as Godwine no doubt expected, made earls, in 1045–46, but none was given power in the heartland of Wessex. Swein, who might already have had a reputation for wildness, was given an earldom on the Welsh border, holding Herefordshire with the Mercian shires of Gloucestershire and Oxfordshire, acquiring further lands later. It is possible, perhaps, to form a view about the extent of Swein's lands as Earl by looking into the lands held in these shires by Earl Harold after 1053.

Harold was given East Anglia, another contested region at risk from any renewed Viking attack, and his earldom included Norfolk, Suffolk and Essex, and probably Cambridgeshire and

Huntingdonshire.[5] Beorn's earldom centred on Hertfordshire and extended northwards but little more is known of it.[6] The exact limits of these earldoms remain vague. Harold might only have acquired Huntingdonshire after Beorn's murder. Swein's freedom of action could have been restricted by the proximity of Leofric and his control over the rest of Mercia and by the presence in Herefordshire of the King's 'Frenchmen', placed there to see if they could pacify the area through the use of motte and bailey castles. Such castles can hold and dominate an area but cannot resist a siege by a large army. Harold showed himself capable of acting independently of his father, refusing to return to Swein estates acquired after Swein's first exile and then after Beorn's death.[7]

Nothing is really known of the relative wealth and land holdings of the earls in 1043; detailed knowledge only emerges in Domesday Book, referring probably to the period 1060–65. There would have been changes between 1043 and 1066, largely an increase in the holdings of Godwine and his sons, possibly at the expense of the other earls, between 1043 and 1051. A distinction should be drawn between any estimate of the wealth and power of Earl Godwine, along with his two eldest sons, before 1053 and the increase in the power and wealth of the family, and especially of Harold Godwinson after he succeeded his father as Earl of Wessex, in the period 1053–1065.

If this is done it then appears that Edward's position in 1043 was by no means weak. It is likely that no individual earl was as wealthy as the King at that point though his wealth might have been equalled or perhaps slightly outweighed by that of all the earls combined. But they did not act as a group. Godwine possibly did hold more land than the King in some shires, and Leofric also in parts of Mercia, but it cannot be definitely established whether the King's overall superiority compensated for the weakness of his landed position. New kings had to reward those who had supported them and to win over the supporters of the previous king by being generous with gifts of land.

Cnut had owed his throne in no small measure to the support of the Danish Earls, Thorkell Havi and Erik, so early in his reign acted like a man with debts to pay off, making Erik Earl in Northumbria and Thorkell Earl in East Anglia and effectively vice-regent in his absence in 1019; in 1020 Thorkell was exiled (like Godwine in 1051) and allowed back as viceroy in Denmark in 1023.[8] Cnut lost control over much of his empire in Norway and the Baltic and that would have affected his control over England had he lived. Edward had no such losses and had his overlordship extended over Wales and Scotland. It had been Cnut who had made the earldom of Wessex so powerful and it can be argued that he had little choice in the appointments he made as he was a stranger to the thegns of Wessex. By Edward's reign no great matter of state could be decided without the participation of the great earls in the decision and distinctive royal policies could only be put into effect by causing the earls to disagree among themselves.[9] Yet the earls were not the only laymen whose opinion mattered, and other land holders had their part to play, especially when acting collectively as 'all the thegns in Yorkshire' were to do in 1065.

Edward rewarded Bishop Aelfwine of Winchester with a gift of land and was to reward him further. He rewarded in this way men who had served Cnut, such as Ordgar, a Devonshire thegn and Aelfstan, a man of Harthacnut, a Wiltshire land owner, and in 1044 Orc in Dorset. There was in fact a great deal of continuity in the administration and in the composition of the *Witan*. Edward had to accept, naturally, the existing archbishops, bishops and abbots, only appointing new men as vacancies occurred. The same applied to the major earldoms. He made such changes as he could among the thegns and clerks at court, but there is no sign of the wholesale promotion of Frenchmen alleged by the *Vita Edwardi*. It claims that not only was he accompanied on his return from 'Francia' (not specifically Normandy) by 'quite a number of men of that nation', that is Frenchmen, but that he kept them with him and made them 'his privy counsellors and administrators of the royal palace'. Very few of these men can be identified and even fewer, and those mainly clergy, were Norman.[10] Nor can it be shown that those who can be identified arrived with him in 1041 or 1042, though some might have done so.

The three most prominent were his own nephew, Ralph of Mantes, known later as Ralph the Timid, his Breton (or possibly part Norman)[11] 'kinsman' Robert FitzWymarc, possibly accompanied by his son Swein, (a Sheriff in Essex after the Conquest). Robert held the rank of Staller, and was termed 'steward of the royal palace'. Another of Breton extraction was Ralph the Staller (made Earl of East Anglia early in 1067). In addition there were several French or Norman knights who, with their men, were allowed to build castles on lands provided for them on the Welsh border. Osbern Pentecost and his companion named Hugh, were established at Burghill and at Hope under Dinmore in the Wye valley between Hereford and Leominster. Osbern's castle was called 'Pentecost's castle'; the location of Hugh's castle, if he had one of his own, is unknown. There were other castles in the area built before the Conquest but it is by no means certain that they were built before the King's quarrel with the Godwines in 1051 and most were probably permitted afterwards, as a defence against the Welsh. There is really no evidence of the establishment of a 'Norman' colony in Herefordshire as some sort of advance base for a Norman incursion. Any such base would have needed to be on the south coast.[12]

The ecclesiastics when they came proved to be an eclectic mix of Englishmen, Lotharingians (that is, men of Lorraine) and Normans, and the former preceded the latter. So, Herman, a Lotharingian was appointed to Ramsey in 1045 in succession to Beorhtwald. Herman had been in Harthacnut's household. Leofric, English but trained and educated in Lorraine, was appointed to Devon and Cornwall in 1046. He was described as being 'British', which probably means Cornish, and as a *cancellarius*, an official of the King's writing office.[13] Ealdred, an Englishman, abbot of Tavistock, was given Worcester in 1046, and Heca, another Englishman and the King's priest, Sussex in 1047. Robert Champart, former abbot of Jumièges, was appointed to London, possibly as early as 1044 but only certainly from 1046. Stigand, Queen Emma's confidant, received Winchester in 1047 but may not have finally surrendered his East Anglian See of Elmham until 1052 when it passed to his brother Aethelmaer. Finally Ulf, a Norman of poor reputation, received Dorchester as late as 1049. The third Norman, William, Bishop of London, was not appointed until after Robert Champart was promoted to Canterbury in 1051.[14] There were other foreigners who were not promoted until the 1050s, while a few did not win promotion until after the Conquest.

So the path to preferment was, primarily, training abroad, principally in Lorraine but to a much lesser extent in Normandy, followed by service in the royal court and promotion to a bishopric. The King's priests witnessed his charters (and probably wrote them), and modelled his seal on those of the German emperors. The proliferation of Lotharingians rather than Normans suggests the existence of competing interests rooted in the Anglo-Danish past.[15] It is also possible that Edward, while in exile, had encountered and been impressed by the talents of Lotharingian-trained clerics. Edward continued to attract foreign clergy to his court as in the case of Bishop Osmund of Skara from Sweden. He attached himself to the King and it is said that he won great favour.[16]

Apart from this, the *Witan*, as charter witness lists indicate, remained in composition much as it had under the Danish kings. A single surviving charter from 1042[17] lists nine thegns of whom two-thirds were Cnut's men and another two Harthacnut's, and the one new name is never seen again. Another charter, for 1043, lists twenty-three thegns with the same six men from Cnut's time and nine from Harthacnut's court. There are no Frenchmen of any description. Of these men, the first seven appear on Cnut's charters, such as Edward's man, Ordwulf, Osgod Clapa, a Staller, Odda 'of Deerhurst', a kinsman of the King promoted to Earl in 1051, and Orgar and Aelfgar, kinsmen of Edward from the West Country.

Regular witnesses, the '*ministri*' of the charters, that is King's thegns, probably held offices at Court, 'with 'seat and special duty' there, or in their own shires. Some held the title of 'staller', that is place-men, and others would be King's reeves and sheriffs. Some might be the sons of the higher nobility who were being educated at Court, hoping perhaps for preferment to office as stallers or even earls. But it must be disconcerting for those who see Edward as having become French or even Norman in outlook, not to be able to discover the names of the Normans he is supposed to have brought with him. It might well be that the assertion in the *Vita* was, in part at least, propaganda intended to justify Earl Godwine's dispute with the King's Frenchmen led by Robert Champart. The latter does not appear in the record, as Bishop of London, until 1046, though he must have been appointed to succeed Aelfweard who died in 1044. It is possible that he was still at Jumièges and had to be released from there to take up office.

So, for most of the 1040s Edward proceeded cautiously to make himself master in his own kingdom. He certainly assumed the traditional royal control over the Church, appointing bishops and abbots. The bishops he chose are listed above, the abbatial appointments began with that of Siward, abbot of Abingdon, promoted as bishop in Canterbury during Archbishop Eadsige's period of infirmity; he was thus a co-adjutor bishop of St Martins.[18] The sacristan, Athelstan, succeeded to the abbacy of Abingdon. This was all done with 'the leave and counsel of the King and Earl Godwine'. Athelstan was to be replaced when he died in 1048 by a monk from Bury St Edmunds called Spearhavoc (Sparrowhawk) who, on the promotion of Bishop Robert to Canterbury in 1051 was made bishop of London only to be refused consecration by the new Archbishop because 'the pope [Leo] had forbidden it him'. As this man was also the King's goldsmith, it might be that Robert had reason to accuse him of simony. Edward allowed him nonetheless to occupy the episcopal lands and did not replace him until autumn 1051 after Earl Godwine had been expelled.

Florence of Worcester says that Aelfweard of London had retained the abbacy of his former monastery of Evesham and that on his death he was replaced by a monk of Evesham called Wulfmaer (and also known as Manni), at a Council at London held on 10 August 1044. There was no word about any appointment to the Bishopric of London and it was only after 1046 that Robert Champart began to witness charters as a bishop. It is possible that there had been opposition to his appointment or Manni could have been nominated but rejected in favour of Robert. In that case this was the first example of Godwine failing to get his own way. On the other hand, as the parties in dispute cannot be identified, it might have been a case of objections by the canons and by local interests which held up the process. So it could have been an example of a revival of what in the tenth century had been known as 'saeculorum prioratus', the attempt to control preferment in the Church by local magnates. Edward was recovering royal control over appointments. Oswy, abbot of Thorney died in 1049 as also did Wulfnoth of Westminster but no source names their successors. A writ for Westminster from 1049 names the abbot as Edwin.[19] All this suggests a power struggle of some sort eventually won by the King.

The detailed history behind appointments is unknown and unknowable but the *Vita Edwardi* was to claim that the Kingdom had been disturbed and the court divided into two factions and somewhat enigmatically remarks that 'one set of men wanted the vacant sees for their own friends while others were alienating them to strangers'. This situation was to reach a crisis point after the death of Archbishop Eadsige. It is a little facile to suggest that these two parties represented an English and a French party respectively. The situation after the death of Eadsige resulted in conflict between Earl Godwine and his family on the one hand and the King supported at first by the new Archbishop Robert Champart on the other. However, several of the episcopal appointments were of Lotharingians as well as Englishmen and to see conflict arising between a party advocating such appointments and another advocating the appointment of Normans does not fit. It does not explain the appointments actually made. One solution[20] would be to see it as a conflict between local interests (a sort of country party) and a court party. But the conflict might also have been between two different strands of ecclesiastical reform, with reform minded clergy in the royal household supporting the King. The visible evidence is of the King exercising his rights, to his own benefit, choosing his own clerks as bishops and so cutting across local interests.

The Lotharingians and Englishmen might have taken their inspiration (as in the tenth century) from Ghent and Utrecht. Earl Harold Godwinson was to found a house of Canons at Waltham Holy Cross with the assistance of the noted scholar Adelard of Utrecht who introduced there the rules and observances of the Lotharingian church. Throughout Edward's reign bishops from, or familiar with, Lotharingian cathedral organisation introduced canonical life in English cathedrals, notably Exeter, Wells, Hereford and York. Lotharingia was influential throughout the Western Church from 1049 to 1054 during the pontificate of Leo IX, the Lotharingian Pope. Bishop Ealdred of Worcester while on missions to Germany in the 1050s brought to England the Romano-German Pontifical and was a patron of Folcard of St Bertin in Flanders.

Leofric, bishop of Devon and Cornwall had entered Edward's service when he was at Bruges. The bishop was unmistakeably English but educated in Lorraine, probably in a house of canons. He is reputed to have been Edward's *cancellarius* that is scribe (not as in Norman times, chancellor). His canons at Exeter followed the Rule of St Chrodegang of Metz.[21] There was also Regenbald the presbyter, a German, who witnesses the charter uniting the Dioceses of Devon and Cornwall in 1050 and transferring the seat of the bishopric to Exeter.[22] He, like Leofric, was a *cancellarius*, and was the predecessor of King William's actual chancellor Herfast. It is probable that the work of a *cancellarius*[23] was evolving throughout Edward's reign and beginning to undertake the kind of role played by chancellors after the Conquest. After the crisis of 1051 had been resolved, Edward was to recruit further Lotharingians to his service, such as Giso, bishop of Wells, the successor to Dudoc, a survivor from Cnut's reign.

In opposition to that strand of opinion it is possible that if there were, as seems possibly to be the case, a number of Norman clerics in Edward's household, they, pushing perhaps at an open door, persuaded Edward to summon Robert Champart from Normandy, (unless he had come over with Edward in 1041 or 1042) so that there might be a Norman bishop of London who would promote the Norman version of reform through the promotion of monks rather than canons. Who these men might have been is by no means clear, but Bishop Robert must have had other Norman clergy in a position to support him. There was a Hugh or Hugolin, *camerarius*, but no other foreigners are named in the few surviving charters from 1042 to 1050.[24] They cannot be dismissed as non-existent when so little evidence survives. More can be said about this in considering events leading up to the crisis of 1051. Overall, Edward does not seem to have had a specific ecclesiastical policy, other than a readiness to exercise his royal prerogative in all appointments. Those appointments were for the most part sound enough but he does not appear to have been a reformer of the sort Rome would have hoped for. He had his own preferences and these frequently cut across local interests but he was not afraid to do so.

The main effect of his appointments was to increase royal influence in the shires and that meant the appointment of foreign, but never predominantly Norman, clerics. Bishops and abbots, as the reign progressed, increasingly owed their appointment to the King and were therefore a source of royal strength. Stigand's removal in 1043 shows the effect of a loss of royal favour. By 1050 all but two of the eleven bishops witnessing charters were the King's appointees and at least four royal clerks had been promoted. Edward did not habitually 'sell' churches but both King and Queen would expect to receive appropriate 'gifts' in gratitude for promotion. At least two royal clerks, Herman (Sherborne) and Giso (Wells) 'lost' estates to Edith. The *Vita Wulstani*[25] asserted that 'no trader in churches, no money grubber, would ever find in Edward's mind anything which was of profit to his schemes'.

The King's attitude is perhaps best illustrated by the text of a charter from 1050 uniting the Dioceses of Devon and Cornwall and transferring the bishop's seat to Exeter; 'It will be right and proper for us, Edward, who are said to have been appointed by God as ruler over men … especially to take in hand and in kindly measure investigate the affairs of the church, putting right those things which in our eyes do not appear to be just and to establish them correctly.' As a result of his attitude he appoints bishops and abbots and rewards his own clerical friends. He even gave Regenbald the priest, who performed the work of a chancellor, episcopal status in law.[26]

He was expected to accept clerical advice and act on it but he held no great ecclesiastical councils and issued no legislation like Aethelred and Cnut. Church business was dealt with by the King with his *Witan*. Regular church synods were unknown but Edward sent bishops to the reform synods at Rheims and Vercelli in 1049, and to Rome itself in 1050, something which William I never did. Failure to attend legatine councils was liable to result in excommunication, which might in part explain Stigand's isolation. But overall Edward's acceptance of reforms went beyond royal compliance with papal wishes.

6

The King's Wealth

The extent of the royal demesne is a vital aspect of royal power, although the King's wealth also included what he received in terms of taxation and the profits of royal justice. It is necessary to form some idea of the King's wealth in comparison with that of his earls in order to estimate their relative strength. The problem is that the information necessary for this does not exist for the period 1042 to 1052 and probably not for 1052 to 1062 either. The information that does survive comes from Domesday Book, compiled in 1086 on the basis of information collected from all sorts of sources, and especially the testimony of local juries, regarding land holding as it was in England 'when King Edward was alive and dead', that is, taken literally, in 1066 and probably actually based on recollections of the situation as it was in the last five years of the King's reign, together with such written records as had survived from the period before the Conquest.

It is usual to compare the King's land holdings with those of the Godwines and the other major earls, as given in Domesday Book. But that cannot simply be transferred to the period 1042 to 1052. Yet so influential is the wealth of information provided by Domesday that inevitably historians are led to suggest that Earl Godwine must have had the same relative position vis-à-vis the King as his son Earl Harold, simply because both were Earls of Wessex. But there is no real way of knowing just how much land Earl Godwine had at the moment when Edward came to the throne, although it is commonly accepted that he was wealthy indeed. There is, for example, his ability to provide King Harthacnut with a fully equipped and manned warship in 1040 and then to do the same for King Edward in 1042. He had made great strides during the reigns of Cnut and his sons and had indeed become a rich man, but it is by no means certain that he was as wealthy as his son Earl Harold was to be.

Harold, starting from his elevation to the Earldom of East Anglia in about 1046, did accumulate wide lands and great wealth. After the exiling of his elder brother in 1047, Harold and his cousin Beorn were given shares in the lands of the exiled Earl and, on his return in 1048, they refused to give them up so that they could be restored to Swein. Harold also seems to have benefited from the redistribution of Beorn's lands after his murder by Swein. These lands, acquired in this way, seem to have remained in his hands and after he became Earl of Wessex in 1053 he not only retained them but also held on to some of the lands of his earldom which he had been given while Earl of East Anglia. This would have been in addition to any lands he received as heir to his father's earldom and any family lands left to him by his father. It seems very likely therefore, that Harold was much richer than his father had been and that it is not safe to take his wealth in comparison to that of the King as a measure of his father's relative wealth. In any case, Godwine certainly acquired more land from King Edward in the 1040s although records of it are sparse. He did receive an estate at Milbrook, Hampshire in 1045 and another at Sandford-on-Thames in Oxfordshire in 1050, but any others are not recorded in surviving charters. Neither appear as held by Godwine or Harold in Domesday.[1] Both men also received gifts from thegnly families seeking to win their support.

Estimates of the relative wealth of the King and his earls vary quite widely. One estimate puts Earl Harold's lands and those of his commended men at £3,636, as against a holding by the King of £3,840.² Not such a great disparity, especially as it takes no account of royal receipts from other sources. It is, of course, customary to add to Harold's wealth that of the rest of his family, his mother Gytha, and his brothers Gyrth and Leofwine. But it is by no means certain that the family were always in perfect agreement on policy. It takes no account of Edith's resources as Queen. Historians do persist in comparing a total Godwinson holding worth over £5,000, in the 1060s, together with commended men worth over £1400, with the King's holding of almost £4,000. An alternative estimate puts the King's wealth at £5,000 and Queen Edith's at £900. The sons of Godwine are given some £4,000, excluding Earl Tostig, and the Mercian Earls £1,300, with £1,300 also for Northumbria.³

Now it is possible to suggest a way of making a very tentative estimate of Earl Godwine's wealth as Earl of Wessex. If the value of the lands assigned still in Domesday as being held by Earl Godwine, despite the fact that he had been dead for over thirty years, is added to the value of those lands in Wessex held by Earl Harold in his capacity as Earl, Godwine's lands under this heading are valued at about £600. The lands held in Wessex by Earl Harold, together with those assigned to Gyrth, Leofwine and Tostig, come to over £1,800.⁴ That would give Earl Godwine land worth in the region of £2,400. If lands assigned to Earl Gyrth in Norfolk and Suffolk are added to those still held in East Anglia by Earl Harold, the result is a figure of some £850 for the earldom of East Anglia. A calculation to arrive at figures for Swein and Beorn is not possible but there cannot have been much to choose between them and Earl Harold. That allows a figure of about £3,500 to £4,000 for the Godwinson family before 1050. That would tend to confirm the impression that the family, although wealthy, was not as overwhelmingly so as it became after 1053.

Another estimate rates the Godwines in the 1060s at £7,700, as against the King at £5,620, Earl Leofric's descendants at £3,280 and those of Earl Siward at £370. The latter figure is almost certainly an underestimate of Earl Siward's position since Domesday did not extend the survey into the greater part of his earldom.[5] Finally, an attempt to put together land values and revenue puts the King on just over £8,000.[6] These estimates vary because Domesday is by no means consistent in the way in which it records its information and historians can quite legitimately interpret the evidence in different ways. But it is probable that estimates of the King's wealth are grossly underestimated because they take little account of other sources of revenue for which actual figures do not exist. There is no way to estimate the value of tribute paid to King Edward by the Welsh, nor of the irregular tribute occasionally paid by the Scots. Domesday records much about the rights of the King in shires and boroughs but its information is very incomplete. For one example, London was omitted from the survey and Winchester likewise and these boroughs certainly must have paid renders to the King. There is in fact no coherent statement of the extent of the King's regalian rights.

In theory everyone was under the King's power or protection and liable to pay him tribute. He was restrained only by the duties of a good Lord and King, although political reality acted as a check on his actions. He had to act with the consent of his magnates, lay and ecclesiastical. His revenue was undoubtedly considerable and he had the royal demesne, inherited from his predecessors, the profits of boroughs and the Church, the proceeds of justice, many renders and services, and there was the geld, a tax paid on demand from almost the whole cultivated area of the Kingdom and from various boroughs. Rents and services were fixed by custom and were a steady source of income and the King's reeves would not have allowed him to be cheated.

Thus he took every type of profit from his kingdom. No one else could authorise the minting of coins, the silver pennies and when the coinage changed moneyers had to purchase fresh dies sent to them from London. It is thought that there were something of the order of 25 million silver pennies.[7] New issues seem to have been made on a three-yearly cycle, or as short as two years on occasion, (whereas in Edgar's day it was a cycle of six years) so that the King profited each time from the fees for issuing new dies. There were at least eleven issues during the reign, though some issues may have overlapped, and some seventy mints were active. Edward himself added nine new mints and no man in England lived more than fifteen miles from a mint. The King's revenues cannot therefore, as was once held, have been operated from a box under the royal bed. He had a financial officer, Odo of Winchester,[8] who was not called 'chancellor' or 'treasurer' as such individuals were known under the Norman kings, but he was certainly responsible for the safety of the royal treasure. The Court was peripatetic so there had to have been a safe store-house for surplus revenues and for the safe keeping of documents and relics.

In the normal course of events revenue probably never exceeded ordinary expenses by much and as the court travelled from one royal manor to another it would have consumed much of the produce of royal estates as it went. The one great capital expense incurred by Edward was the building of Westminster Abbey, a costly venture but not beyond his means. None of these calculations take any account of the possibility that the King was accustomed to levy a moderate geld, either annually or whenever a particular need arose. He could have raised gelds in the 1040s for the cost of his naval operations against pirates and the Count of Flanders. Gelds could have paid for embassies to the Continent in the 1050s and the cost of operations against the Scots and the Welsh then and in the early 1060s. If they were not unusually heavy they would not have been recorded by the Chroniclers.

The standard coins were stamped from thin sheets of silver, with the King's 'portrait' (a stylised representation of the King as he wished his subjects to visualise him) with his name and title on the obverse and usually the short cross and name of the moneyer on the reverse. A few round halfpennies were issued and, more rarely, gold coins worth thirty silver pennies known as 'mancuses'. The effect of frequent re-issue was to prevent debasement and control the weight of the coins. As milling was unknown coins could be 'clipped' by dishonest moneyers and the clippings melted down to make more coins but when a new issue was made old coins had to be surrendered for new ones of full weight and the old coins could be weighed so that only the equivalent weight of new coins would replace them. Coins might also be tested by 'blanching' which detected whether base metal had been added. In any case the coins did not contain one pennyworth of actual silver and it was unprofitable to melt them down for their silver content.

The King could have been controlling, from issue to issue, the number of coins in circulation. It is suggested that this was so because there had possibly been a sort of deflation after 1053, an indication of rising prosperity with less disease in cattle and better harvests. There was a rise in the weight of coins from 18 to 27 grains following the abolition of the heregeld in 1050, which suggests that fewer coins were needed and a heavier coin could increase the King's prestige. After 1056 the weight was reduced to 21.5 or 20.5 grains then back to 17 grains in 1062 with a return to 21.5 in 1065. It looks like successive inflation and deflation but it is not known whether that effect was known about at the time. The King cannot have been regulating trade or controlling an exchange rate.

There was only a slow general movement of the economy and the King was under constant pressure to be generous and alienate royal land in gifts to 'faithful men'. Such generosity was expected of a king, but Edward is not known to have been easy-going in this respect and there is little evidence to suggest that he dispersed large amounts of land or gave away the profits of jurisdiction. He was no more generous than any of his immediate predecessors. He had no mistresses to provide for and no children and was not over-generous in providing for his great nephew Edgar the *Aetheling*. His foreign favourites were few in number. He did reduce the rate at which some estates were assessed for geld, even remitting it altogether in some instances. That in itself is evidence that the *geld* continued to be collected, though not necessarily annually, as such privileges would have been worthless if there was no tax to be paid.

He did gain land during the reign as well as alienate it. Bookland (held by virtue of possession of a charter) could be forfeited to the King for crimes and outlaws forfeited everything. There were penalties for treason, harbouring outlaws, breach of the peace, desertion from the army, theft, robbery and so on. He must have gained from the 'driving out' of Gunnhild and her family and of Osgod Clapa. Although some of Swein Godwinson's lands ended up in the hands of Harold his brother and Beorn his cousin, some of it doubtless returned to the King. What could happen is illustrated by a charter of 1055.[9] It is spurious as it stands but may nonetheless serve to illustrate what could happen, even forgers used genuine material as a template for their work. The thegns of Gloucestershire had awarded Edward an estate of about three hides of land at Upper Swell as a result of a crime by Eansige son of Hoc. The king granted it to Abbot Manni of Evesham for the provision of victuals for his monks. The Abbot had to pay six marks of gold to the King and one mark to Queen Edith. It was a 'purchased endowment' therefore, as such 'gifts' often were. Legally some 'consideration' had to pass between the parties for the endowment to be lawful. Edward could also break an earl, as the cases of the Godwinsons and Earl Aelfgar show, and when he did he could recover the estates of the earldom, and the service of the thegns who held them, for himself. He could also have kept back some of the lands of an earldom, known conventionally as 'comital' lands, every time an earldom was created or changed hands.

It is argued by many that one handicap suffered by Edward was the existence of the Earldom of Wessex as created by Cnut. It consisted of lands carved out of the old Kingdom of Wessex, and its existence meant that the King now had no province of his own to support him. But, by marrying Edith, daughter of Earl Godwine, Edward had linked the earl's fortunes to his own. It also meant that Mercians, East Anglians, Northumbrians, and those who dwelt in the Danelaw did not regard him as simply a West Saxon king. If the confiscations of 1051 had stood, the King in effect re-possessed Wessex, Edward would have considerably increased the extent of the royal demesne, just as when Harold Godwinson received the throne in 1066, he reunited the lands of the earldom to those of the crown, a policy subsequently followed by William I. However, such comital endowments were only a loss if the services due from the earls and their men were not exacted. There is no real evidence to suggest that such service was not forthcoming and the Chronicle goes out of its way to insist that Earl Harold in particular was a loyal servant of the crown.

If comital land and land assigned to the Church is disregarded, then all other land was administered by the King's reeves who were royal agents, collecting rents and produce. To that can be added the rents and services due from the King's commended men, especially those rich enough to be regarded as members of the nobility, 'proceres' as the *Liber Eliensis* calls them, and his sokemen owing customary dues and services. Some great nobles owed no such services and rendered only the three common burdens, that is service in the Fyrd, repair of bridges and the maintenance of Burhs or fortified towns and strong points.

If Domesday Book is right, then the royal demesne, in effect the King's home farms, was very unequally distributed; nothing in Middlesex, Essex, Hertfordshire, Rutland, Lincolnshire, Cheshire, or Cornwall; very little in East Anglia or Yorkshire. Of Northumbria nothing is known at all. Few of the King's charters relate to land north of a line from Lowestoft to Bristol. Partly this is the effect of the existence of the earldoms which had been provided with large estates and partly the location of monasteries which all lay south of the Wash so that documents regarding northern land have not been preserved. The mere existence of estates in the hands of vassals and servants was not in itself a threat to an energetic king. There were also services which were not written down in charters, of which the most significant was the liability to pay the *geld* which lay on all land assessed to it, some 70 or 80,000 hides or carucates. There were no Counties or Duchies exempt from service or taxation as there were on the Continent. England was about the maximum size of state a king in the eleventh century could successfully govern through his noble and ecclesiastical servants and remain in full command.

The King had control over the design and minting of all coins. The coins changed in weight at various points during the reign. The king's 'portrait' on the coins also changed, probably for propaganda reasons. Edward's early coins were modelled on older designs. On them he is clean-shaven, wears a crown or diadem and faces left. This is the traditional royal image. Then in 1053 (possibly planned during the King's period of rule without Earl Godwine) he is shown facing right, bearded and wearing a pointed helmet, a less classical and more barbaric image, very martial. Then after 1056 a design based on Roman designs was adopted. The King faces forward and is enthroned and there are 'martlets' (probably in fact meant to be eagles) between the arms of the cross on the reverse (taken later in the Middle Ages to have been Edward's coat-of-arms). It changed again in 1059 to a design facing right and crowned, holding sceptre and orb, and finally in 1062 he adopted an image facing to the front. He is again bearded and crowned. It is derived from Byzantine prototypes by way of the issues of the German emperors. His successor, Harold, turned the image to face left. The exact reasons for these changes cannot now be established but possibly represent changes in the way in which Edward wished to be visualised by his people and could indicate the influence of the King's goldsmiths, some of whom were German.[10]

The King's image was also seen on his seal which was of the two-sided type and used to authenticate writs. It was modelled on German imperial prototypes, which says quite a lot about how Edward thought of his position as overlord, *basileus*, of Britain. The King is seen full face, enthroned, crowned, with a beard and moustache (very English), wearing an under-tunic and carrying the royal insignia of orb and sceptre. It is seen as evidence of self-aggrandisement; in having a two-sided seal he was competing with the Pope and the Byzantine and German emperors, and, as enthroned, with the Kings of France. The writs bearing his seal appear to date from 1052. No seals of earlier kings have survived but it is still thought that Edward's seals were revolutionary in design. On the obverse Edward carries a sceptre with a trefoil and on the reverse a long sceptre topped with a bird and has a sword on his left shoulder.

7

The King's *Geld*

E ven in the tenth century King Edgar had been able to
collect general taxes, that is '*geld*'.[1] These were assessed ter-
ritorially and were increased when the Danes returned to
the attack under Aethelred II. He raised tremendous sums with
which to bribe the Danes to cease their depredations for a time.
For example, £36,000 in 1012 and £80,000 in 1017 and in addition about £4,000 a year as '*heregeld*' or army tax which continued
to be levied by the Danish kings and under Edward until 1051.
Over the period from Edgar to Edward the reeves and sheriffs
increased in importance, collecting dues and taxes and general
gelds, assessing liability, assisted by lesser reeves in hundreds and
wapentakes or on manors or in villages. This was to lead to an
increasing reliance on written records.

The abolition of the *heregeld* in 1051 has proved to be a contentious
issue for historians. Commonly it is argued that this meant abolition
of the tax known as *geld* itself, either totally or for a period of uncertain length.[2] More recent arguments centre on the improbability of
any government voluntarily abandoning such a profitable source of

revenue.[3] The very idea is inherently absurd. Attention has therefore focussed on the language used by the Chronicles and it is noted that they use two terms to describe the taxes raised by Aethelred to pay off the Danes and fight his wars. There is *gafol*, literally 'tribute money', even ransom, which came to be called, after the Norman Conquest, *Danegeld*, and there was the aforementioned *heregeld*.[4] It was *gafol* which provided the money, the vast sums, paid in Aethelred's reign, and *heregeld* that was the levy raised by the Danish kings in particular to pay the wages and costs of a force of stipendiary warriors, part soldiers, part sailors.

Under Edward a mercenary fleet was inherited from Harthacnut consisting of fourteen ships' crews which Edward and his *Witan* disbanded in two stages, nine ships in 1050 and another five in 1051. The Chronicle actually says that the King 'ended the contract of the nine ships and they went away with ships and everything'. It adds that the other five were offered only a year's pay and that in 1051 the King 'laid off all his fleet men'.[5] Edward 'abolished that *heregeld* which King Aethelred had earlier established; that was the thirty-ninth year since he had begun it. That tax oppressed the whole English nation ... it always came before other taxes which were variously paid and oppressed men in manifold ways.' The *heregeld* was dispensed with because the fleet for which it paid was no longer employed. One must suspect that the King had doubts about the continued reliability of these Danish sailors.

Historians have tended to use the general term *geld* for both *gafol* and *heregeld*, and after the Conquest it was used for the land-tax levied by the Norman kings at two shillings on the hide, or a multiple thereof. But *gafol* was the tribute paid to raiding armies and cannot still have been being levied in 1050. It was *gafol* which was later referred to as Danegeld. Heregeld was specifically the army tax levied from 1012 to 1051. Neither of these was the 'common geld' used for other purposes. The confusion needs to be dispelled. Fighting men had perhaps had to be retained early in the reign but the removal of *heregeld*, an extra impost, did little to break the continuity of the established land tax. It is arguable that the land tax called *geld* was such a commonplace feature of the English scene that it could be used in a negative way to benefit individuals and religious houses. In about 1051 a writ for Bury St Edmunds declared that its home farm was to be exempt from every render, including heregeld. It was possibly issued before the decision to abolish heregeld altogether. The *geld* was so commonplace that the Chronicles made no comment about it until the exactions of King William became unbearably heavy.

There is a writ of William I referring to a *geld* taken in King Edward's time for the building of ships, which can be neither *gafol* nor *heregeld*. There seems to be no direct pre-conquest evidence, other than the sworn testimony of the jurors in Domesday, but there are many references in it to the collection of the 'common geld' or the 'King's *geld*' when they are describing customs which obtained in King Edward's day. There was the common *geld* 'from which no one can escape when it is laid on the vill' at Guildford.[6] Exeter is recorded to have paid *geld* only when London, York and Winchester did so.[7] At Stamford *geld* was paid 'In the time of King Edward for twelve and a half hundreds, for military service by land and sea and for Danegeld'.[8] The Northamptonshire *geld* Roll, which survives from King William's reign, repeatedly states the Hidage of estates paying *geld* 'as was the case in King Edward's time'. Such rolls had to have been in use before 1066. References found in Anglo-Norman sources show that there were financial records compiled during the Confessor's reign by his reeves and exactors of tax (called collectors or gatherers) and some of these could well have provided some of the information presented to the Domesday Inquests.[9]

Hides (and carucates) were not measured areas of land. When systematically re-assembled they frequently add up to units of five hides or multiples thereof (or of six carucates), which suggests an artificial arrangement independent of any actual area or value. By the eleventh century a hide was worth approximately one pound or, to put it another way, one pound's worth of land tended to be regarded as one hide for the purposes of *geld* assessment.

There were many exceptions, as with all Old English systems, as some shires were more heavily assessed than others and in some areas the original assessment had been reduced. There would have been no point in these adjustments unless the *geld* was actually collected, otherwise no one would benefit from or suffer from decrease or increase in the assessment. The Confessor and his advisers certainly offered great men lighter burdens of taxation in return for co-operation in running the country. For most of the reign, Northumbria and Yorkshire were more lightly assessed than southern England, partly perhaps because the north was less wealthy in agricultural terms and partly because of the greater difficulty in collecting the money. Earl Tostig could have attempted to increase the assessments for the North and if he did that would have contributed to the causes of the rebellion against him.

The vital point is to estimate how much the King could actually have raised whenever he did levy the *geld*. It is variously estimated that there were 70 or 80,000 hides (or their equivalent). If the lower figure is accepted, that allows for the effect of those areas which were not assessed at all (mainly royal estates) or where no *geld* could be collected as the land was 'waste' (devastated by war or raiding).

Under the Conqueror the answer is straightforward. He levied *geld* at a minimum of two shillings on the hide, which was regarded as excessive and severe. That would have raised sums comparable with the *gafols* of Aethelred's reign. At two shillings the *geld* could raise potentially some £7,000 and at six shillings, £21,000. The *geld* Rolls embedded in the Exon Domesday relate to the six shilling *geld* of 1084, paid in two instalments, at Easter and 'after the feast of St Mary' (either 15 August or 8 September). The Peterborough Chronicle for 1084 simply states that the King levied the *geld* 'after Christmas'. It is no wonder that the Conqueror had a reputation for avarice. In practice many men were unable to pay such levies and forfeited their land which was then sold to the highest bidder.

It is unlikely that levies that high were levied by 'good King Edward' (especially after the abolition of the *heregeld*). The clue as to the real burden is in the Berkshire entry in Domesday Book. It states that 'When *geld* was paid commonly in the Time of King Edward throughout the whole of Berkshire, one hide gave three and one half pence before the Feast of the Nativity of the Lord and as much again at Pentecost' (that is at Christmas and Whitsun). It represents a *geld* of seven pence on the hide which, if paid in full, would have raised over £2,000 if applied throughout the Kingdom, as is probable. Similarly at Bury St Edmunds the monks claimed that 'When the Hundred pays one pound in *geld*, then sixty pence goes from the *geld* for the supplies of the monks.' So the monks received most of the levy and the King got forty pence, and five hides were paying one shilling between them. In East Anglia *geld* was raised on a different system, estates paid so many pence when the Hundred paid so many shillings. Yarmouth for example paid twelve pence and Newton near Castle Acre paid nine pence.[10]

8

The Royal Administration

Just as each earldom had its earls, so the shire, by Edward's time, was coming to be administered on a day-to-day basis by a shire-*gerefa* or shire-reeve, that is, a sheriff. There were now too many shires to allow for the earl attending all sessions of the shire court for every shire in his earldom. Accordingly, the sheriff presided over normal sessions. Shire courts might also expect the local bishop to attend but it is unlikely that the bishops attended every meeting of the courts within their dioceses. Possibly they deputed representatives to attend on their behalf, a position regularised in the Norman period by the creation of archdeaconries.

The three earldoms were the work of Cnut the Great. After having conquered the country he found it advisable first of all to reward the jarls who had led the divisions of his armies by creating earldoms for them out of the 'ealdormanries' of Aethelred's time. There had already been a tendency under the Old English kings for *ealdormen*, who had previously been responsible for administering single shires, to become responsible for groups of shires. In Edgar's time East Anglia had been ruled by Aethelstan

'Half-King' (so called for his almost independent control of the eastern counties); Ealdorman Aelfhere had ruled most of Mercia and, under Aethelred, Eadric Streona, Ealdorman of Mercia, had a pre-eminent position, as a result of royal favour, comparable to that attributed under the Danish Kings and King Edward to Earl Godwine.

Cnut soon discovered that his Danish earls were not to be relied on and their services were rapidly dispensed with. The last one, Thorkell Havi, who had ruled East Anglia, was expelled and no earl for that area was appointed to replace him. Instead Cnut promoted two Englishmen and a Dane. First he groomed Godwine for office by making him an Earl responsible only for the western part of Wessex and then finding him reliable, gave him control of all Wessex, as well as the hand of his sister-in-law Gytha. Leofric, son of the ealdorman Leofwine (Eadric Streona's successor in Mercia), was found acceptable as Earl in Mercia, and the Dane Siward, a trustworthy warrior, was put over Northumbria. Leofric married a Mercian noblewoman, Godgifu (Lady Godiva), probably daughter of some well-connected Mercian family, and Siward cannily married into the House of Bamburgh so allying himself to the strongest family in Bernicia. So by the end of Cnut's reign these three earls had become his most trusted advisers and they continued in office throughout the next three reigns until their respective deaths under King Edward.

The 'burhs' or boroughs established by former kings had become islands of royal power. Through these, the King and his agents, *ealdormen*/earls, bishops and reeves dominated the countryside as seats of royal justice, as mints and as market towns. The processes of their development were still ongoing under the Confessor – some shires might not even have been completely developed until his reign – and his rule seems to have been responsible for bringing the system to the level of efficiency which made King William's takeover of the state in 1066 a relatively straightforward matter. The proliferation of the administrative document known as a Writ under King Edward demonstrates how he was able to establish the royal presence throughout his realm.[1]

Writs had first taken the form now in use early in the eleventh century. The earliest use was to licence the holder of an estate to have 'sake and soke'[2] that is judicial and financial rights over his men. Edward, by issue no doubt of a writ, was able to transfer the allegiance of the thegns from Earls Godwine and Harold to himself in 1051. Eadric of Laxfield was outlawed by writ and deprived of the allegiance of his thegns.[3] They were permitted to return by another writ.[4]

It seems likely that the collection of the *geld* was developed under Edward as one of the common renders and that, levied principally to provide finance for his military and naval expeditions, it enabled the monarchy to carry out an adventurous foreign policy which established the security of the realm, and to deal with the ever present threat of disorder arising from the incursions of the Welsh and the Scots.

Building on the precedents set by tenth-century kings, Edward was able to insist that all men had to swear to take Edward 'as lord'. That is, they had to attend shire or hundred court, on reaching the age of twelve years, take an oath of fealty, the Old English 'hold-oath', and 'bow' to the King, promising to 'favour what he favours and discountenance what he discountenances', accepting him as their lord and protector (to *hlaforde* and to *mundbora*).[5] Kingship was a heightened form of lordship but the oath did not mean that every man who swore became a personal retainer of the King. Instead it was a form of commendation requiring men to be faithful to the King as a man was to his lord and most men would have hesitated before foreswearing themselves by defying him. At the level of the nobility, any magnate who deserted his lord forfeited any office he held. Otherwise, those affected by this legislation were those who were obliged to attend the assemblies of shire, burh and hundred.[6] In addition it was held that 'every reeve should exact a pledge from his own shire that they would all observe the decrees for public security'. That, by Cnut's time, meant 'all the thegns of the shire'. There was therefore a specific offence of 'cynges oferhynes' or insubordination to the King, possibly the offence committed by Earl Godwine in 1051 and by Earl Aelfgar in 1055.

Kings were now guaranteeing men's rights and determining what those rights ought to be. From Aethelstan's time onwards lordship had become an instrument of royal government and of social control. Every man was expected to have a lord on pain of outlawry.[7] Lords, like the associations of tithing and hundred to which men were also expected to belong, were expected to be responsible for the lawful behaviour of their dependants.

The judicial functions of shire, borough and hundred paralleled their military functions and were subsumed under the general heading of maintaining the King's peace. Men had to be both *fyrdworthy*, equipped and ready to fight, and *mootworthy*, ready and able to attend court, opposing sides of the same coin. At Hundred Court level 'cases between vills and neighbours and many things of this kind which frequently arise' were dealt with.[8] But no treatise from Edward's reign describes such things as the working of royal government or how mints were managed or courts run; not even the conduct of ordeals which were a vital part of the proceedings in criminal cases. It is known only from the moralising sentiments expressed in some charters that the King was expected to correct the peoples' sins, and offer leadership and protection as well as justice.

The law courts were still in a sense popular assemblies and the law they enforced largely a matter of immemorial custom. There were pleadings and judgements and proofs had to be offered in fixed forms as descriptions of cases in such sources as the *Liber Eliensis* suggest. But kings had created most of the courts, devised the procedures and could both declare and modify the law, either by issuing Codes as Edgar, Aethelred and Cnut had done, or by intervening themselves and making an oral judgement (which was rarely subsequently written down), as seems to have been the case with Edward. In one sense local courts were sections of the King's Court divided up to hear local cases and it is clear that the *Witan* could review cases and make its own judgement. A writ granted to Christchurch, Canterbury rules as follows: 'for my will is that the judgement of my thegns shall be upheld' and Sigweard and his wife's grant to the Church was to stand.[9]

That Edward issued no code of laws did not detract from his authority. It would seem that his determination to remain king and to continue to enforce 'the Law of Cnut' (much of which was in fact the law of Edgar and of Aethelred) made him an acceptable ruler to his people and left him with a reputation for law-making. The laws which operated under Edward were, in the twelfth century, embodied in compilations of the laws of the past such as the *Leges Edwardi Regis*, not the King's own work but that of later scribes. Any written law made by Edward had long since perished by 1140 and his reputation as a law maker rested on tradition and on the survival of memories of his oral judgements. Even his pledge to uphold the law of Cnut was embedded in the lawbook called *Quadripartitus*. That it remained an important element in the King's authority is demonstrated by the insistence of the Northumbria and Yorkshire rebels in 1065 on a re-issue of the pledge as a means of reducing the intensity of Earl Tostig's enforcement of southern standards of government. The *Vita Edwardi* implies that Tostig had cut across northern traditions, possibly the concessions made as long ago as the reign of Edgar.

The King in action with his *Witan* heard cases, gave judgements, even hearing individual petitioners, ratified land deals, pronounced on law and so gave good example to all his agents, the earls and sheriffs and king's thegns. The king could dispatch his agents, like legates, to Northumbria to carry out judicial functions and the earls he appointed regularly attended the royal court. The great families were not provincial. Their lands were not held in blocs (like the baronies of the Anglo-Norman era) but widely scattered. That was one reason why civil war was avoided.[10] The Old English magnates could not in fact function without a single head as king because England was already a nation state with an effective central authority. It had uniformly organised institutions, its own language, its own church and well-defined frontiers. Above all it had a strong sense of national identity and, as Orderic Vitalis observed, 'the English are always loyal to their princes'.[11] England was small enough for the King never to seem too remote even if he rarely left the south. His physical presence in York was rare but the earls and archbishops he chose made his presence felt and his name feared. The sources all imply that all major initiatives were made at the King's instigation and do not refer such decisions to the *Witan* or an individual earl, though the *Witan* might be consulted.

Edward the Confessor had inherited a powerful governmental machine built up by his predecessors and left virtually intact for him by the Anglo-Danish dynasty.[12] The government maintained an extensive set of written records, almost all traces of which have disappeared. The Normans did not take pains to preserve material written in Old English which even their priests were unable to read. The silver coinage was the product of a complex system which has also left little trace, described as the most sophisticated and complex system in the early Middle Ages.

The power of any individual earl had to admit the effect of the collective weight of other nobles, the earls and the King's thegns, as well as that of his bishops and abbots. About thirty-six thegns owned estates worth more than £100 a year (24,000 silver pennies) and another eighty-eight held lands worth more than £40 (9,600 silver pennies). They range from Beorhtric, Aelfgar's son (not the Earl), with £560 worth (almost 135,000 silver pennies) to Osfrith the thegn with only the bare £40, which according to the *Liber Eliensis* made him a *procer* or nobleman. These were the men who bore most of the weight of the *geld* and the opinion of such thegns could not be ignored. Kings or earls who prompted such men to act collectively risked ruin.

Some have argued that Edward gave away financial and judicial rights rather too freely. This theory is based on the study not so much of the land books or charters as on that of Edward's writs which announce that some magnate, lay or ecclesiastical, has been given land not only 'with *sake* and *soke*' but with other rights, such as jurisdiction over various kinds of offences over which other kings had claimed jurisdiction for themselves yet which Cnut had given to the Archbishop of Canterbury.[13] Some rights applied only within the estate to which they were granted and others applied to whole hundreds over which the recipient had jurisdiction, as in the case of the Bishop of Worcester's jurisdiction over Oswaldslow. It is likely that these were a grant of the profits of justice from these areas.

So St Benet of Ramsey had *soke*, – jurisdiction and financial rights – over all the men in a hundred and a half.[14] The abbot had such rights in every shire in which the abbey had land. Other grants of rights depend on evidence from spurious documents which is too unreliable to be accepted. That it probably was only the profits of justice is suggested by a charter for Bury St Edmunds supported by an entry in Domesday Book (although the charter as it stands is of doubtful authenticity), allowing the monks to keep part of the proceeds when the *geld* was levied on the borough.[15] It still seems to have been the case that such rights were claimed only on the basis of royal grants and that they did not arise merely out of the relationship between lord and man or lord and tenant.

It is possible to distinguish the rights a lord had over a man from commendation from rights deriving from the possession of soke, over men or over land. According to a Domesday entry[16] the men of Southwark testified that in Edward's day no one could have the toll from the Strand or in Water Street except the King; if anyone in the act of committing an offence was charged then he paid a fine to the King, but if he escaped and came under the jurisdiction of a lord with *sake* and *soke*, then he paid the fine to that lord. This is not 'seignorial justice' as it existed on the Continent and lords had no right to declare law. This interpretation is verifed by the entry in Domesday for St Mary's, Lincoln: 'With respect to all the thegns who have land in Well Wapentake, St Mary's has two parts of [any] forfeiture, and the earl the third... likewise if they had forfeited their land, two parts [went] to St Mary's and the third to the earl.'[17] The Conqueror took back the two-thirds from St Mary's, showing that these rights had originally been royal and had been granted by the King. It might be that Edward had been making grants of this sort to churches and to some lords in order to buy their support or reward them for support they had given.

Some historians tend to concentrate their attention on what they see as the King's weakness. They talk of his monarchy as leading to the extinction of the West Saxon line, though it became extinct only in the sense of the lack of a direct heir of the body. But kingship was a prize worth having nonetheless, especially with its income derived from royal demesne, profits from boroughs and churches, and from courts of justice, the services of men under the King's direct lordship and from the *geld*. Under Edward, England regained control of Cumbria, established client kingdoms in Wales, and afterwards won the decisive victory over the Norsemen at Stamford Bridge. None of these look like the achievements of a kingdom in terminal decline. Some have claimed that Edward surrendered the substance of power in order to retain its appearance but it is more probable that Edward retained the substance while allowing Harold Godwinson the appearance of power. Earl Godwine won his way back to power in 1052 but only received back what he had lost, his office of earl, a royal official. He did not recover the lands of south west Wessex which remained in the earldom of Odda of Deerhurst.

The King was at the apex, as it were, of the social pyramid, with power to break an earl or a king's thegn and take his lands and thegns; he had sole command over armies and the navy and all others held their land provisionally, owing service and renders and *geld*. The tensions recorded between the King and his earls must not be allowed to distract attention from the cooperative side of the relationship. There were relatively few disputes and their resolution did not disturb the position of the King. The earls continued to support the throne, impose justice, collect taxes and defend and even extend the bounds of the Kingdom. Disputes did not mean that the ruler was weak or that his subjects were over-mighty.

9

All the King's Men

The ecclesiastical appointments of King Edward in his early years have already been considered. In view of the emphasis some have placed on the presence of 'Frenchmen', and more particularly Normans, at Edward's Court, it is worth looking in a little more detail at the make up of English, or to be more exact Anglo-Danish, society in its upper reaches. Those were the men who made up the King's Court and in many cases constituted, (along with major ecclesiastics, the bishops and abbots, and the clerics who staffed what is best termed his writing office), his *Witan*, the assembly, as it were, of the wise or as would be more usual today 'the great and the good'.

All major ecclesiastics, especially the Archbishops of Canterbury and York, and the three great Earls considered that they had a natural right to be consulted by and no doubt to advise and warn the King. Kings also naturally consulted their greater King's thegns, some of whom, possibly as a result of the Anglo-Danish nature of society, became in Edward's reign in particular, known as 'stallers'. As the Court moved around the country, meetings of the *Witan* were held as occasion required in various shires, often in a convenient borough, such as London, Oxford or Gloucester, or a royal manor. Rulers naturally had to take counsel in this manner because it was on these men that kings relied for their commands to be carried out. If the nobles did not agree to go to war and were unwilling to levy warriors from their followers, a king would have a very small army with which to prosecute it. All the processes of government required collective action for their efficient operation. Even a ruler with the most loyal servants could not have afforded enough of them to do all that he wanted to do. The better law and order were maintained and the more taxes that were raised, then the more panels of unpaid subjects would be needed.

Crimes had to be reported, judgements delivered, courts held, taxes assessed and collected. In the absence of any means of coercion (other than the extreme measure occasionally resorted to of ravaging a shire or borough), even free men could be most effectively exploited if they could be induced to organise each other and take collective responsibility for dues and services.[1] The more collective activity there was, the better law and order were maintained.

The *Witan* itself was a group of active governors, which together with the household, was responsible for general administration. To control his *Witan* a king had to be both vigorous and active and Edward in his first ten years showed every sign of being both. His rule was respected all over England. There would have been, at the heart of the *Witan*, a core number of bishops constantly together around the King and it is perhaps the presence of Robert Champart of Jumièges and his fellow Norman, Ulf of Dorchester, at the centre of Edward's *Witan* that has caused so many historians to be misled about the extent of 'Norman' influence on the King. Such clerics had always been close to the Kings, active in administration and legislation. Kings also had been accustomed to have at least one person who was privy to their most closely guarded thoughts, described in the sources as being *a secretis*, knowing the King's secrets or as being his *pedisequus*, one who walks in his footsteps and sits at the foot of the throne. Edgar had the thegn Wulfstan of Dalham, Cnut seems to have confided in Godwine, described in the *Vita* as his *bajulus* or office-bearer 'of almost the whole kingdom, and his constant companion'.[2] The *Vita* complains that Archbishop Robert had become *a secretis* with the King, so displacing Earl Godwine.

An examination of the sources reveals that there might have been, on Edward's part, a policy of gradually reducing the importance of individual earls by multiplying their number, something that he appears to have been able to do without arousing suspicion as to his motives. Because he chose to multiply earldoms, from about 1045 onwards, by promoting the sons of Godwine, the policy has been seen as proof of Earl Godwine's overweening influence over the King. Closer examination reveals flaws in this thinking. The choice of Godwine's eldest son Swein, which could not perhaps have been avoided without openly insulting the earl, actually proved an embarrassment for Godwine. There is in fact a story relating to Swein which does him little credit. He is reputed to have been wont to boast, to the intense disgust of his mother, that Cnut the Great and not Earl Godwine was his real father, evidence perhaps of a highly Danish element in his make up. His subsequent behaviour, the abduction and seduction (if not rape) of the Abbess of Leominster, the kidnapping and murder of his cousin Beorn and his general misbehaviour in Denmark, weakened his father's influence at a critical moment and strengthened the King's hand.[3]

The second son, Harold was also given an earldom in East Anglia and he too proved that he was not just his father's stooge. He refused to return to Swein the lands of his earldom, transferred to Harold and his cousin Beorn (who had also been given an earldom) after Swein's first exile, and took prominent action to provide an honourable burial for Beorn. This suggests disapproval of his father's support for Swein. It might be that the promotion of two Godwinsons was Edward's acknowledgement that, after his marriage to their sister Edith, they were adopted members of the royal kin.

But the policy did not end there. Sometime in the 1050s, possibly as early as the year 1050 itself, Edward created earldoms for two of his kinsmen. His sister's son Ralph of Mantes, who might have come to England with the King in 1041 but, more likely, joined him at the time of his coronation, was made Earl in Herefordshire, endowed with at least some of the estates originally assigned to Swein. At that time, or a little later, another earldom was created in the western shires of Wessex, for Odda of Deerhurst, a thegn found high in the witness lists from the beginning of the reign and a frequent attender at the *Witan*. He held land that could originally have been part of an ealdormanry; Odda himself might have been a descendant of an ealdormanic family and thereby a collateral descendant of the West Saxon kings. The effect of these appointments was felt in 1051 after the expulsion of Earl Godwine. The King retained in his own hands the eastern shires of Wessex from Kent to Wiltshire (no one else is recorded as holding them) and so with Ralph and Odda he controlled the whole of Wessex.

With Earl Godwine's death in 1053, his son Harold became Earl after him, and the earldom he then held, in East Anglia, was transferred to Aelfgar, son of Earl Leofric, who had held it during Harold's brief outlawry 1051–52. So by 1054 there were now six earls. The number remained constant for ten years, probably largely because of the absence of suitable candidates. Tostig Godwinson replaced Earl Siward in Northumbria, in 1055, largely because Siward's own natural successor, his son Osbeorn had died in battle against Macbeth and the surviving son, Waltheof was only a child. The other possible choice, Gospatric, the youngest son of Earl Uhtred, was, as a member of the House of Bamburgh, not acceptable to the King and an unknown quantity.

More earldoms followed in the 1060s as the next generation came to manhood. Aelfgar, who had succeeded his father in 1057, and was dead by 1062 or early 1063, was replaced by his eldest surviving son, Edwin, by 1065, probably as soon as he was old enough, and the remaining Godwines, Gyrth and Leofwine were given earldoms in turn; Gyrth taking over Norfolk and Suffolk when vacated by Aelfgar in 1057 with the addition of Oxfordshire (possibly to compensate him for not getting Essex, Cambridgeshire and Huntingdonshire), while Leofwine had an earldom created for him around London, covering Essex, Hertfordshire, Middlesex and Buckinghamshire on the north bank of the Thames, with Kent and Surrey on the south.[4]

Lastly, almost at the end of the reign, Waltheof, Siward's son, now old enough, was given a small, compact earldom made up of the shires of Cambridgeshire, Huntingdonshire, Northamptonshire and Bedfordshire, probably when lands were redistributed following the fall of Tostig when Edwin's brother Morcar became Earl of Northumbria. The pattern is clear. Earldoms were given to Edward's favourites (none of whom were Normans; even Ralph was French not Norman) chosen from his wife's family or from the King's own kin and sons of other earls were given earldoms as they reached maturity. After about 1057, the emphasis was on Harold's brothers largely because they became old enough to qualify for an earldom earlier than other candidates. Apart from Odda, no attempt was made to promote a thegn rather than the sons of existing earls. It is possible that if Osbeorn, son of Siward, had not died, he and not Tostig might have become Earl in Northumbria. All the other earls' sons became earls in due course and only Ralph had a son, Harold, who did not become an earl because he was still too young in 1066.

There were men with almost as much status as the earls created by the Confessor in the far north; the High Reeves of Bamburgh. Down to 1041 they seem to have been earls and then there was a gap under the Confessor until Oswald son of Eadulf ruled Northumberland under Morcar. The style of 'earl' returned under the Conqueror but with much diminished authority. The cause was the loss of control over Bernicia in exactly the same year as Edward became king in England. Edward entrusted Earl Siward with the task of seeing to it that no more territory was lost, bolstering his authority with money and men and financing his attacks on Scotland.[5] One achievement of Siward was to seize control of Cumberland, as is proved by the grant made in that area, regarding Wigton.[6]

The principal purpose for creating more earldoms was a matter of defence policy. Harold was made Earl of East Anglia to fill the gap left ever since Thorkell Havi had been expelled. The area needed someone to supervise defence in that region, as events after the Conquest demonstrate with the arrival of raiding armies led by Swein of Denmark. Many of the estates belonging to that earldom, some of which were retained by Earl Harold after he became Earl of Wessex, were located at strategic points such as the Blackwater River in Essex. His appointment as Earl might not have been unconnected with the outlawing of the last of the Danish stallers Osgod Clapa[7] who attacked Eadulf's Ness (the Naze) in Essex in 1049.

Similarly Swein Godwinson had been given charge of an earldom on the Welsh border, part of which later formed the Herefordshire earldom of Ralph of Mantes, and his immediate response on becoming Earl had been to engage in preventive action on the frontier allying himself with Gruffydd ap Llewelyn of north Wales against Gruffydd ap Rhydderch of south Wales.[8] In Swein's absence in 1049 Irish pirates entered the Severn and joined up with ap Rhydderch to plunder the area.[9] That explains why Edward made Ralph of Mantes an earl in that area as soon as Swein was out of the way. Herefordshire could not be left without an earl throughout the 1050s. Beorn's earldom in the East Midlands, occupying the place of Thored, Earl of the Middle Angles in Cnut's time, provided support for Earl Harold in East Anglia and after his death was held in part by Ralph who retained the southern shires of the earldom along with his new earldom in Herefordshire. The northern portion of Beorn's earldom seems to have been returned to Northumbria.[10] The southern portion helped to provide lands for Gyrth and Leofwine in the 1060s. Odda's earldom in the south west of Wessex gave support to Ralph.

In what might best be regarded as an intermediate level of authority below that of an earl but superior to reeves and king's thegns, Edward seems to have made good use of the rank of Staller. Cnut seems to have introduced the use of this term, although scholars are divided about whether it was a Scandinavian or Old English term. It could come either from Old Norse *stallari* or Old English *stallere* and was applied to any official in the King's household. Some who held the title under Edward appear to have had specific duties, seen by the scribe who wrote the Waltham Charter[11] as those of the officials of the household known in the Anglo-Norman period, such as stewards or 'dapifers'. It appears simply to mean 'place-holder' and one is reminded of the definition of a king's thegn as one who had 'seat and special duty in the King's hall'.

Tofig the Proud, reputed to have been Cnut's standard bearer, was termed staller as were the Dane Thored and Osgod Clapa.[12] Edward was to have a number of officials bearing this title. They could well have been the sort of men known in the tenth century as *pedisequi*, and so were a higher grade of king's thegn, those closer to the king. Tofig's grandson Esgar was a staller. He might well have had special responsibilities in London possibly as portreeve like his Norman successor Geoffrey de Mandeville. A Breton thegn called Ralph, father of Earl Ralph de Gael, was a staller; another was a thegn named Bondi, possibly sheriff of Bedfordshire. To this list can be added Robert FitzWimarc, whose son Swein was a sheriff in Essex after 1066, Eadnoth who was sheriff in Somerset, a thegn called Leofing *regis pincerna* or butler, and the wealthy thegn Aelfstan of Boscombe.[13]

When at court these men had responsibilities covering duties in the King's (and Queen's) apartments, in the hall and in the surrounding courtyard. Titles of specific offices are rarely found in the charters and other documents but are known from vocabularies used by scribes. They equate quite well to the officials of the Anglo-Norman court. Thus there was the disc-thegn for steward or butler, bur-thegn for chamberlain, and so on. Some of these men, such as Ralph the Staller and Robert FitzWymarc, although they were not earls, received the third penny of the profits of justice from their estates. They attended to the King's interests outside Wessex and each may have had his own sphere of operation. What is noticeable is the complete absence of Normans. That goes far to weaken the idea that Edward's court was packed with them. In fact at the beginning of his reign there were a reasonable number of Danes (or at least men with Scandinavian names) but these faded out during the 1040s and the court became predominantly English, although some, like the Godwines, are better termed Anglo-Scandinavian.

Edward therefore had a highly developed and structured court with officials of the palace and the household not unlike those of the Carolingians. Although he is found to have had a fairly large number of people who could claim some sort of connection, by blood or marriage or through the relationships such as godparents and sponsors at confirmation, there is no sign that he packed his court with them, not even the Norman relatives of his mother. Instead, he had an inner circle of domestic servants. Some can be identified, particularly the stallers listed above, and men like Hugh or Hugolin his chamberlain.

There were some who were relatives. Wigod the thegn of Wallingford was a kinsman, as was Robert FitzWymarc, though the nature of the relationship is not known. Such Frenchmen as there were seem to have been the household priests, some of whom might have been Norman. The rest of the Frenchmen in England were men of very modest means and uncertain origins. The Normans in his entourage are noticed only because there was a Norman Conquest. Their numbers and influence should not be exaggerated. The court was rather cosmopolitan, with Bretons and Frenchmen, Lotharingians and Danes, Germans and a few Normans. It is the author of Edith's political tract, the *Vita Edwardi Regis*, who emphasises for dramatic effect, and so possibly exaggerates, the presence of men from 'Francia' who were

enriched and honoured by Edward and became his 'privy counsellors and administrators of the royal palace'.[14]

Those who worked in the household included clerks, who
looked after the King's relics, discharged secretarial and administrative functions and managed the royal itinerary. They were recruited
very widely from all over western Europe. The various duties
of other members of the household are reflected in the witness
list to the Waltham Charter. Although the charter itself is forged,
probably on the basis of a lost original, the witness list is thought to
be reasonably authentic. It applies to the 1060s. Various stallers are
assigned specific roles: Esgar is overseer of the royal hall, Ralph and
Bondi are officials of the hall and the palace, Baldwin and Peter are
the King's chaplains, Regenbald is his chancellor, Wigod his butler
and Azor and Yfing are his stewards. Also included are his relatives
Robert FitzWimarc and Osbern, and Queen Edith has her butler,
Harding, possibly Eadnoth's son, and Godwine her steward. Other
sources mention ushers, cooks, and goldsmiths, and a lady of the
bedchamber. A woman called Leofgeat was employed to produce
orphrey work, the gold fringing for garments and tapestries. Edward
also had huntsmen, such as Judicael; William, a falconer, and a 'steers-
man', Eadric, of Blakeney in Norfolk, who commanded the King's
ship. It is thought that this reflects a reorganisation of the Court
undertaken in the 1060s by Edith. It is likely that a proto-chancery
was developing out of the earlier king's writing office. There was also
some sort of treasury, developed out of the 'haligdom' or repository
for relics and documents as well as treasure, in use from at least the
tenth century.

The principal reeves were the sheriffs, the *scir gerefas*, who
appear addressed by writ after the local earl and bishop, men
like Blacwine of Cambridgeshire or Toli in Norfolk and Suffolk.
These men profited from administering royal estates, especially
those forfeited for outlawry or crime, they enforced the King's
peace as Domesday testifies, 'the royal peace which the sheriff
gave', and received some fines, though others went directly to the

King.[15] They led expeditions in defence of their shires and some died in doing so, such as Aelfnoth of Hereford.[16] In doing so they led the shire levies as the *ealdormen* used to do.

Also attached to the royal household was the royal *genge* or warband composed of King's thegns and, since Cnut's time and in Edward's reign, housecarls. They were not, as was once fashionable to argue, a standing army[17] but more in the nature of a bodyguard and warband, like the royal companions known in earlier times as *gesiths*. That is, they were household troops and would surround the King during battle. Earls also had such troops and Leofric and Siward were accompanied by their *genge* in 1051 when Edward summoned them to his assistance against Earl Godwine.[18] Hereward in his struggle against the Normans in the 1070s was accompanied by a *genge*, indicative of his status as son of a king's thegn. Probably those thegns under the banners of Godwine and Harold who were required to transfer their allegiance to Edward in 1051 were part of their household contingents.

Men called housecarls in one context, as Domesday shows, might elsewhere be termed freemen or thegns and so might not have been exclusively Danish though most of those who can be identified had Danish names; the castle holder Richard FitzScrob is termed 'Richard, my housecarl'. It is not clear that they performed garrison duty. References to estates 'where the housecarls used to dwell', look more like lands earmarked for those no longer on active service. Other lands are shown providing money '*ad opus huscarlium*', for the work of the housecarls.[19]

Beyond the limits of the Household and outside the ranks of earls, stallers and housecarls, were the rest of the King's thegns. These have been divided into three main categories; those with lands worth more than £100, those with lands worth more than £40, and below them the quite large number of thegns of ordinary rank holding the title either by virtue of having at least five hides of land or by inheritance from a predecessor who did. Of course the five greatest estates were all held by earls and of the twenty greatest, half were held by earls or their wives.

But Beorhtric, Aelfgar's son, held estates worth £560, equal to the three lowest ranking earls in terms of land values. Stallers (five are listed in Domesday) were among these richer thegns. If earls and stallers are omitted, there were about thirty-two men worth more than £100 a year, quite comparable to many Norman barons. The lands of all those worth more than £100 a year total over £6,000. The men with over £40 worth of land, and by implication with more than forty hides, were termed *procer*, implying that they were regarded as chief or leading thegns and therefore noble and not expected to marry below their rank.[20] There are about eighty-eight men of that category. All were in one sense the King's men, some holding land directly of or under King Edward, some specifically termed 'thegn of King Edward'. Many of them were also commended to various earls (some to more than one) or held land from or under them as well as the King.

This reflects the interconnectedness of Old English society. Powerful lords in any area could build up a large number of commended men. Some were commended to bishops and abbots as well as to lay magnates and even quite wealthy or powerful men could be the 'men' of some lord other than the King. It was obviously important in that society to be well connected. Some of the lesser lords, the *procers*, held land under or from nobles wealthier than themselves (who were not earls or stallers), or were commended to such nobles. Lordship was very much a personal rather than a merely tenurial relationship. Those who owned their own land and yet were also commended to a lord were seen as 'median' (*medemra*) or middle-ranking thegns.[21] Lords expected military support from those tied to them personally and from those directly dependent upon them or in their household. But the King, as Edward demonstrated in 1051, could summon the *fyrd* and require the thegns of other lords to join the royal army or forfeit their estates.

The more well-to-do men attended court regularly (they are found in the witness lists) and this gave them the opportunity to give their advice and to be consulted on matters of state. Such men were clearly active during the crisis of 1051–52 and again in 1065. They would have been included in the discussions leading to the return of the *Aetheling* in 1057, the exilings of Aelfgar and the decision to prosecute the war in Wales.

King's thegns had *sake* and *soke* over their own estates and even the *procers* might have had such rights. Those nearest to the King had lands and privileges, led armies, played a part in government and the administration of justice and had power and honour throughout the Kingdom. The very fact that many of them held their land by book right, bestowed on them or their predecessors by charter, made them the King's men. None of this reduced but rather strengthened the royal authority. Those who had supported Aethelred had largely been destroyed or replaced as his reign went on or under Cnut and so Edward would have had to start again and build up a power base of his own. But it was not a case of bringing in Normans but of cultivating support among the thegns. Edward promoted his own supporters as stallers as well as creating smaller earldoms. He was able to make greater progress in this respect after the death of Earl Godwine. The Anglo-Danish nobility had used up much of its resources in dealing with the problems of the succession after the death of Cnut and in the 1040s and 1050s rallied behind Edward. He avoided alienating support during his first six years which may explain why only a small number of Normans ever became influential, and they were ecclesiastics rather than lay magnates.

10

Foreign Wars
and Malice Domestic

Edward, having dealt with the problems posed by the presence of certain Danish elements in the state, by the expulsions of Gunnhild and her family and of Osgod Clapa, embarked on what can only be seen as a forward foreign policy, calculated to demonstrate to other powers that a strong king now ruled in England and so deter any major Scandinavian incursion. The English, throughout the reign of Edward, feared a restoration of a Scandinavian dynasty. At first the threat seemed to be posed by Magnus of Norway, who made various bellicose threats which in fact never materialised. Thus in 1044 Edward spent the summer at Sandwich with the fleet in fear of the arrival of a Norwegian force.[1] He mobilised again in 1045 and 'so great a raiding army was gathered as no one had ever seen in this land'.[2] Magnus was preoccupied with his war in Denmark and did not come. The threat from that quarter disappeared after Magnus' unexpected but, in England, welcome death. There was still the possibility that Swein of Denmark might assert his rights deriving from his descent from Cnut's sister Estrith or that the successor of Magnus in Norway, the dreaded Harald Hardrada, might press the same claims as his predecessor. In practice these two monarchs kept one another busy for the next fifteen years. So traumatised were the English nobility by the wars against Swein Forkbeard and Cnut, that they remained convinced, not without reason, that the principal threat still lay in the North. So in 1051 the two sides in the quarrel between the King and Earl Godwine refused to fight as if they did they 'would be leaving the land open to our enemies'.[3]

Swein of Denmark had held out against King Magnus until 1047 and he then asked for aid from his distant kinsman King Edward. Earl Godwine advised that fifty ships should be sent but Earl Leofric, supported 'by all the people' (that is the influential thegns) advised against it. The King sided with them and refused.[4] The fear was that Magnus, who had his own large fleet, would prove too strong, and that it would be unwise to provoke him.[5] Magnus overwhelmed Swein's defences and took Denmark. Only his death in the autumn saved England from a probable invasion, though that would have been resisted at sea. Edward had not only the fourteen ships of hired fighting men but a fleet of considerable size, with contingents from both Wessex and Mercia.

King Swein again appealed for fifty ships in 1048 after Harald Hardrada succeeded to the throne of Norway and was refused in the same manner, due to Leofric's opposition.[6] Significantly, on both occasions Earl Godwine had advocated action and was defeated; not much evidence there of any overwhelming influence. Hardrada in fact sent ambassadors seeking peace between England and Norway, an offer which was accepted. In practice, continued conflict in Scandinavia caused Hardrada to keep his word. These dangers continued as the pirates (called Lothen and Yrling)[7] attacked Sandwich with twenty-five ships, seizing much booty. But when they turned their attention to Thanet they were repulsed by the local levies and pursued by the King and the earls. A raid on Essex was more successful but they then took refuge with Baldwin of Flanders against reprisals. They made one final effort in 1048, raiding Sandwich and the Isle of Wight but were driven off by the fleet.

Count Baldwin V of Flanders was supporting the Lotharingians in their revolt against the Emperor Henry III and when called upon to blockade Flanders Edward was only too ready to do so. In effect two leagues had formed, that of the Emperor, supported by the Pope, the Count of Anjou and Swein of Denmark, against the Lotharingian rebels, versus the Count of Flanders supported by his brother-in-law the King of France and his vassal, William of Normandy, supporting the Lotharingians. Edward now joined the Emperor's side because it was in English interests to do so since Flanders harboured exiles like Osgod Clapa and gave refuge to Scandinavian pirates. A large fleet was assembled off Sandwich and blockaded Flanders until the Emperor reduced Baldwin to submission.

At this point, Swein Godwinson, who had gone into exile after his abduction of the Abbess of Leominster, had slipped through the blockade to his family's estate at Bosham. He went overland to Sandwich in search of the King's pardon, hoping, it seems, that his cousin Earl Beorn would intercede for him. But both Beorn and Earl Harold were implacably opposed to Swein's restoration and refused to surrender his former lands which had been granted to them by Edward. The King gave Swein four days to return to his ships and leave. News had arrived of the assistance given to Gruffydd ap Rhydderch of south Wales by an Irish Viking fleet, so Edward sent the Wessex Squadron to intervene, commanded by Earls Godwine and Beorn. The Mercian Squadron was dismissed as no longer needed, leaving the King with a few ships of his own, probably the fourteen ships crewed by Danes and paid for out of the *heregeld*.[8]

The exiled Osgod Clapa, with thirty-nine ships, was reported to have anchored near Sluys, so threatening the English coast. Edward hastily recalled the Mercian Squadron; Osgod set his wife ashore at Bruges and sent the bulk of his ships to raid Essex. His men were caught in a storm on their return and few survived it. Osgod fled, possibly to Denmark, and gave no more trouble. Meanwhile the Wessex Squadron had been held by the weather at Pevensey and Swein Godwinson once more appealed to Earl Beorn for help with the King. Foolishly, the Earl agreed to meet Swein, accompanied by only three men, relying for his safety on their kinship. Instead of heading for Sandwich, Swein took Beorn with him to Bosham and, once there, kidnapped him and sailed with his captive to Dartmouth where he murdered his cousin and buried him on the shore.

This was a heinous crime and Swein was declared '*nithing*', a scoundrel, utterly and completely disgraced in the eyes of the King and the whole of his army. Nor could Swein take refuge in Denmark where he would face the wrath of the King, his cousin. Six of his ships' crews deserted him. Two were captured by the men of Hastings and slain and their ships taken to the King. Swein fled to Bruges with his last two ships and was given refuge by Count Baldwin. Earl Godwine's reputation suffered immense damage and his son Harold distanced himself from both Swein and his father, disinterring Beorn's body from its grave in a small local church and giving it honourable burial at Winchester beside his uncle Cnut the Great in the Old Minster.

King Edward, who perhaps had found them unreliable, seized the opportunity in 1050 to reduce the number of hired ships, dismissing nine and retaining only five for another year and then abolishing the *heregeld* raised to pay them. He still had both the West Saxon and Mercian squadrons, and twenty or more smaller ships, perhaps used for patrol duties, from the ports of Dover, Sandwich, Romney, and Fordwich, where the burgesses were granted the profits of justice from the borough courts in return for supplying ships. Hythe and Hastings were probably included.[9] Edward seems to have revived the custom of Kings Edgar and Aethelred of reviewing the fleet once a year at Sandwich. In that way he demonstrated a capacity for leadership in war as he is found with the fleet on most occasions from 1045 until 1052.

Earl Godwine was exerting all the influence he had to secure the reinstatement of his son Swein and in agreeing to the disbandment of the hired fleet, was making necessary concessions. Bishops Hereman and Ealdred returned from the synod at Rome to which Edward had sent them, possibly to secure papal consent for the moving of the See of Crediton to Exeter.[10] They brought with them Earl Swein who was apparently reinstated, though he did not receive all of his former lands, only Herefordshire and perhaps some of Beorn's territory. Possibly Bishop Ealdred felt that the Earl was sufficiently repentant to be allowed back. Edward might have felt that allowing Swein to return would tarnish Earl Godwine's reputation still further. To rub salt into the wound the magnanimous Edward granted his 'faithful earl' Godwine an estate at Sandford-on-Thames.

During 1051 a political storm blew up for which quite different causes have been assigned by the available sources. The Chronicles simply attribute the whole dispute to the actions of Count Eustace of Boulogne and Earl Godwine's refusal to obey the King's orders in consequence of them. The *Vita Edwardi* alleges that friction had been developing between the King and the Earl due to the machinations of Robert of Jumièges, and that the King took steps to divorce Queen Edith. William of Malmesbury[11] while contrasting the views of the English in his own day with those of the Normans says that the two sides blamed the crisis on Archbishop Robert as a 'sower of discord' or on the arrogance and disloyalty of Earl Godwine. He describes the part played by Count Eustace but in the end cannot decide where the truth lies.[12] The approach here is to accept the diverse accounts as two halves of a single escalating crisis.

The Earl had already lost face as a result of the atrocious behaviour of his eldest son and on several occasions the policy he advocated had been rejected out of hand. The king had recently taken the opportunity to rid himself of the encumbrance represented by the hired fleet and won himself increased popularity by ending the collection of the burdensome *heregeld*, an impost which had been greatly resented. The fleet was a survival from the time of the Danish dynasty and had served to prop up the regime. There is no evidence to support it, but it is possible that some of these ships had already left the King's service. Some might have accompanied Osgod Clapa into exile. The Abingdon Chronicle also comments that the King paid off 'all his household troops', which may be a reference to the dismissal of all hired warriors. This does suggest that the King felt secure in his kingdom and had no expectation of trouble.

Early in 1051 Archbishop Aelfric of York died (on 22 January) and a royal clerk, Cynsige, was appointed without difficulty. But the death of the Archbishop of Canterbury, Eadsige, on 29 October 1050, gave rise to a problem. The *Vita Edwardi* explains the matter. When Eadsige died the clergy and monks of Christ Church, Canterbury, followed the process laid down in Canon Law, and 'elected' a local candidate, trained at Christ Church, by the name of Aelric (that is Aethelric), who happened to be distantly related to Earl Godwine. They 'elected him to the office both by general consent and by petition according to the Rule.'[13] There is no reference to this in the Chronicles, but it cannot be dismissed for that reason. As Godwine was the relevant official, as earl, the clergy approached him so that he might obtain the King's approval of their choice, 'elected according to Canon law'.

Godwine did as they asked, and was refused. The king 'lent his ear to the rival party' at Court and appointed his friend of long-standing, Robert Champart, Bishop of London. Bishops were not permitted to move from one see to another without papal approval and Robert needed a pallium, so he went to Rome. While he was absent, the King promoted his goldsmith, a cleric named Spearhavoc (who was engaged on making a new crown) to the bishopric of London. On his return Archbishop Robert announced that he could not consecrate Spearhavoc because 'the Pope had forbiddden it him'. It can be assumed that Robert had accused Spearhavoc of simony. At first the King obstinately refused to accept the ruling and allowed Spearhavoc to occupy the estates of the see and receive its revenues.

The *Vita* alleges that already, as bishop of London, Robert had begun 'to intrude himself more than was necessary in directing the course of the royal councils', causing Edward to ignore 'more useful advice' – from Earl Godwine, presumably. The bishop is accused of disturbing the affairs of the Kingdom by persuading the King to appoint men he recommended when vacancies arose. In consequence, it alleges, two parties had arisen, supporters of Robert, who wanted preferment for 'strangers' and others who sought preferment 'for their friends'. It looks like a conflict between a court party, led by the bishop, and a country party composed of those who wanted local candidates.

As soon as Robert took possession of the See of Canterbury he investigated the condition of the estates belonging to the archdiocese and discovered that during Eadsige's time various estates, adjacent to lands held by the earl, had fallen into Godwine's hands. It is possible that this had been done with Eadsige's knowledge and consent, but it allowed Robert to accuse Godwine of 'invading' church lands, misappropriating them for his own use. He might well have been profiting by administering estates on behalf of Eadsige but the *Vita* author admits that there was some justice on Robert's side. Godwine could have been reluctant to return lands to the archdiocese. Strange things had happened during Eadsige's rule at Canterbury. In 1044 he had resigned his see, pleading 'incurable illness' and in a secret meeting with Edward and Earl Godwine arranged for Siward, Abbot of Abingdon, to become his suffragan or co-adjutor bishop (and so undertake all episcopal duties). The secrecy was insisted upon by Eadsige because he feared that some one he distrusted would secure the appointment, either by asking for it or purchasing it, that is by bribery. Then he resumed his functions again in 1048, because Siward had become ill and wished to return to Abingdon, where he promptly died. Yet it was later alleged that Siward had ill-treated Eadsige, depriving him of food, and that he was removed and given the See of Rochester in compensation.[14] This scarcely sounds credible in the light of the blunt statement in the Chronicles about his illness and death.

Archbishop Eadsige also seems to have surrendered secular control over Kent to Earl Godwine, so entitling the Earl to receive the third penny of the shire. A late eleventh century list of estates at Canterbury[15] reads, 'The Third Penny of the shire which the Archbishop who preceded Eadsige had. In the Time of Eadsige, King Edward gave it to Godwine.' No earl is named for Kent in Cnut's writs but Godwine is named as Earl in Kent in Edward's writs and 1044 looks like an appropriate date for the arrangement to have been made. It is evidence of co-operation between king and earl. Eadsige seems to have thought that bishoprics could be acquired for money or influence and they possibly were under the Danish kings. He cannot have thought he had to give Edward money (which would have meant simony) or he would not have approached him in this manner.

In 1051 Earl Godwine is, naturally, pictured as acting with restraint and preventing his own men from attacking the Archbishop. Robert used the dispute over the Canterbury lands to damage Godwine in the King's eyes and went on to revive the accusations made against the Earl alleging responsibility for the death of the King's brother, Alfred. Robert alleged that Godwine had actually advised Harold I to bring about Alfred's death and massacre his men, pointing out that the Earl had been King Harold's chief councillor.

Edward seems to have readily given the allegation 'more credence than was right'.[16] All this preceded the confrontation at Gloucester in 1051 following Godwine's refusal to obey the King's orders to ravage Dover. Both the *Vita* and the Chronicles agree that charges were laid against Earl Godwine at Gloucester, while disagreeing about the nature of them. The earl's refusal to obey must have led Edward to accept what Robert was saying. It is probable that the charge of complicity in Alfred's death was added to the other charges. To disobey a king's direct order could be interpreted as treason, and on this occasion it certainly was. The two versions then agree about the sequence of events leading to Godwine's condemnation.

Shortly after Archbishop Robert's return from Rome on 21 June 1051, Count Eustace of Boulogne, who had just married (or possibly was about to marry) the King's widowed sister Godgifu, arrived in England. Perhaps he came to seek approval for his marriage. No other reason is known. He saw the King, who was at Gloucester, 'talked over with him what he wished' and set out via Canterbury on his return to Boulogne. Having 'refreshed' himself and his men at Canterbury, the Count proceeded towards Dover. A short distance outside the town he and his men dressed themselves for battle, donning their armour. Eustace sent some of his men ahead to obtain billets and when one householder refused there was an affray.[17] The householder was wounded and in response killed his attacker. Eustace and his men mounted their horses and attacked and killed the injured householder 'on his own hearth' (which was a crime in Old English law).[18] The townsmen killed nineteen of Eustace's men and the count's men killed twenty householders. An unknown number, on both sides, were wounded.

Various conspiracy theories have been advanced to account for what happened. Eustace, it has been suggested, was acting on Edward's orders or with his agreement, to seize control of the 'Burh' or fortifications on the clifftop, or he had agreed to cause trouble in order to provoke Earl Godwine. There is really no evidence to support that kind of argument. Eustace and his men had acted in an arrogant manner and used violence against the citizens of Dover, who responded in kind. But Eustace now fled back to the King to get his version of events told first, blaming the townspeople for the affray, and Edward, perhaps influenced by Archbishop Robert, believed him. The Chronicle comments dryly 'but it was not so.' Edward gave credence to Eustace's account and put the Count and his men under his protection, summoning Earl Godwine to

Gloucester and issuing orders to ravage Kent, principally Dover. The Earl refused to inflict the punishment on his own people.

Such ravaging was the customary way used by kings to punish those who defied or injured them. Harthacnut had ordered the ravaging of Worcester and the whole shire when two of his men were killed while collecting his excessive taxes.[19]

Edward now summoned the *Witan* to Gloucester, shortly before 8 September, sending for the other Earls, Leofric and Siward and probably his nephew Ralph. Seeing the seriousness of the situation, and accompanied only by their household troops, they sent for reinforcements from their earldoms. Earl Godwine, at Beverstone (south west of Cirencester) put out a counter claim and demanded to appear to put his case to the *Witan*. His son, Swein, made his own complaint about the behaviour of those Frenchmen who had built castles in his earldom, accusing them of doing great harm to the King's men in Herefordshire. They also demanded that Eustace and his men be handed over to them. But Edward listened only to the 'foreigners' (later identified as Normans in late sources)[20] who had 'gained the King's ear' and who were alleging that the Godwines intended treason. The King refused to allow Godwine a hearing.

Two parties now formed. On the one hand, Leofric and Siward, and of course Archbishop Robert, taking the King's side, and on the other Earl Godwine and his sons, claiming that he wanted merely the opportunity to advise the King and resolve the dispute. He claimed that Edward had been insulted, presumably by both Eustace and the Frenchmen in the castles. The King affected impartiality, offering his peace and friendship to both sides yet refusing to hear Godwine's case. Civil war loomed as hot heads on both sides demanded action.

The Worcester Chronicle, drawing on its northern sources, declared that many began to say that 'it would be a great folly if they joined battle, because well-nigh all the nobles in England were present in the two companies and they were convinced they would be leaving the country open to the invasion of our enemies (meaning the Scandinavians) and be bringing utter ruin upon ourselves'. Earl Leofric took the lead here, counselling caution.[21] He and others advised that hostages be exchanged and the hearing postponed while a date was fixed to hear the case in London. Meanwhile, Leofric and Siward could raise more reinforcements. The King agreed to this course of action and negotiations were set to resume on 21 September.

Earl Godwine had, perforce, to agree to this but, as the days passed, his men began to have second thoughts, doubting the wisdom of defying the King. They began to desert Godwine in increasing numbers. Aware of this, Edward made his own move. He called up the Fyrd of Mercia and Northumbria, and, by implication, that of Wessex also. Men had to obey that summons on pain of forfeiting their lands. The King demanded that all of the thegns of Earl Godwine and Earl Harold find sureties for their good behaviour and transfer themselves to his service. He also outlawed Earl Swein who, in joining his father in opposition to the King, had probably broken the terms of his reinstatement.

The Earl was now summoned to appear before Edward, accompanied by only twelve men. He refused, demanding safe conduct and hostages and to be allowed to purge himself on oath of all charges. Edward refused that, giving him five days in which to leave the country or be treated like an outlaw. The *Vita* reports that, on being informed of this by Bishop Stigand, who was acting as intermediary, the Earl leapt to his feet, overturning the table, and fled with all his family, and as much portable wealth as they could carry with them, to Bosham. There the Earl and his wife, Gytha, and Earl Swein took ship from Thorney Island to Bruges and were given asylum by Count Baldwin who had always been a friend of the Godwines. Earl Harold, accompanied by his brother Leofwine, fled west to Bristol, and, in a ship left there by Swein, sailed for Dublin. Bishop Ealdred of Worcester, ordered by the King to intercept Harold, showed where his sympathies lay by failing to catch the Earl, 'because he could not or would not'.[22]

The Worcester Chronicle comments on how remarkable it would have seemed if anyone had predicted such an upset beforehand in the light of Earl Godwine's elevated position, his sons were earls and King's favourites, his daughter was married to the King, and he seemed 'to rule the King and all England'.

While Godwine wintered in Flanders, recruiting ships and men, the King made his own preparations. The great thegn Odda of Deerhurst was made Earl over south west Wessex from Somerset and Dorset to Cornwall, Leofric's son, Aelfgar was made Earl of East Anglia in place of Harold, and Ralph, possibly already holding the rank of an Earl, was put in charge of Herefordshire and probably the rest of Swein's earldom. Odda and Ralph were also appointed to command the fleet, based at Sandwich.

Edward now finally removed Spearhavoc from London and appointed his Norman chaplain, William, as bishop, evidence that Archbishop Robert's influence was paramount. Then, as the Chroniclers bluntly put it, Queen Edith was 'forsaken' by the King and deprived of all her lands and wealth. She was, they say, committed to the care of the King's sister, Abbess of Wherwell, whose name is unknown. The Worcester Chronicler stresses that Edith was 'married and espoused' to Edward, perhaps a hint that his action did not meet with approval everywhere. No attempt at separation could have been attempted earlier as Earl Godwine would not have agreed to her replacement. The Chronicles have no more to add until she is restored to her former position along with the rest of her family in September 1052. Florence of Worcester complains that she was sent 'very disrespectfully' to Wherwell, with only one female attendant (possibly her French lady-in-waiting, Matilda). He says she was 'repudiated', on account of the King's wrath against her father. In this he agrees with the account in the *Vita Edwardi*.

That document's writer, who must be taken seriously as his source is Edith herself, maintains not only that Archbishop Robert sent soldiers to pursue Earl Godwine, because 'he would have killed him if he could', but that he put pressure on the King to remove from court every member of the Earl's family and especially his daughter, Edith. He insisted that she be separated (*dissociaretur*) from Edward although this was 'against the law of the Christian Religion' (which forbade divorce). It is claimed, further, that it was to Wilton, where she had been brought up, that she went, not Wherwell. There, she was allowed 'royal honours and an imperial retinue' and remained for almost a year 'in prayers and tears'. The courtiers are described as distressed by this more than by the exiling of Earl Godwine, because she had been 'in all royal counsels' (as a queen was entitled to be) and that she strongly preferred the King's interests to power or riches.

The Latin of the *Vita* actually states that the King 'restrained the divorce proceedings' (*moderatus est tamen causam divortii*), that is, stayed their execution, giving the excuse that she was to await the subsidence of the storms over the kingdom, at Wilton. It would, therefore, seem that having been sent to Wherwell, possibly at Archbishop Robert's behest, she was moved to a more honourable captivity at Wilton. The word '*divortium*' itself means 'separation' and what would have been proposed was an annulment of the marriage by the Church, a ruling that the marriage itself was void and not a marriage at all. This could be done for a number of reasons: non-consummation of the marriage (by deliberate abstention from marital relations) the sterility of either party; or adultery. The obvious motive for such a move was to end the King's connection with Earl Godwine and, as there had not been any children in six years of marriage, to permit the King to marry again in the hope of producing an heir (who would not be a grandchild of Godwine). It would have made little sense for the Archbishop to press for divorce unless his purpose was to persuade the King to seek another wife.

Godwine's son Tostig had married Judith of Flanders, half-sister of Count Baldwin in October 1051, and Earl Godwine and his wife, in consequence, spent the winter and spring at Bruges. Diplomatic pressure was put on King Edward by Henry I of France and by

Baldwin, to no avail as 'the malice of evil men had shut up the merciful ears of the King'. Around 23 June 1052, Earl Godwine made a reconnaissance of the south coast of England, appearing off Dungeness. When Odda and Ralph sailed to confront him he headed for Pevensey and from there back to Bruges. Bad weather in the Channel prevented the King's fleet from making contact and the two commanders showed little competence and lost the confidence of the fleet. It was decided to move the fleet to London while the King found 'other earls and other rowers'. The move was in fact so long delayed that nothing happened and the crews all went home.

Godwine then sailed out again from Bruges towards the Isle of Wight and there seized ships and supplies, forcing the inhabitants to contribute to his war chest. At about the same time, Earl Harold returned from Ireland where he had recruited ships and men with the assistance of Diarmaid mac Mael na mbó, King of Leinster and Dublin. He raided Somerset, around Porlock near Minehead, seizing supplies and press-ganging local people for his crews. There was resistance and thirty 'good thegns' and some other men were killed. At about the same time the weakness of the King's position was illustrated when Gruffydd ap Llewelyn attacked Herefordshire, penetrating as far as Leominster and killing many men, both Englishmen and the Frenchmen from the castle. There is no record of any response being mounted by the English.

On his first raid, Earl Godwine had won over much support from the south coast ports. The Chronicle asserts that 'they all declared they would live and die with him'. He withdrew from the area when confronted by household troops from Sandwich. On his second sortie, the Earl was confronted by a fleet consisting of forty small vessels which was lying in wait for him. These were the light ships with crews of twenty-one men provided by towns like Dover (which with other towns later formed the Cinque Ports). The Earl withdrew, no doubt reluctant to attack men from his own earldom, and sailed west where he met Harold coming from

Land's End. The two then landed at various points along the coast, gathering supplies and winning over the inhabitants. They seized ships at Romney, Hythe and Folkestone along with their crews and so gathered a formidable force. Godwine then headed by way of the Kent Coast to London.

Rather extravagantly, the *Vita* claims that not only had all the people of the south east of England rallied to the earl's cause, 'like children to their long-awaited father', but that the whole city of London went out 'to help and protect the Earl'. He is said to have been urged to attack even the King, something from which he recoiled in horror. In practice the Earl's forces converged on Southwark and, with the connivance of the citizens, sailed with the tide through London Bridge, anchoring near the south bank but wheeling his ships round so that they seemed to threaten to encircle the King's fleet of fifty ships. While Godwine had been drawing nearer and nearer, the King had sent for reinforcements, which were slow to arrive, a great force of land levies. Once again, as in 1051, both sides were reluctant to come to blows because 'it was abhorrent to almost all of them that they should fight against men of their own race... and did not want that this country should be the more greatly laid open to foreign nations.'

Consequently a truce was arranged and the Earl and Harold were permitted to go ashore to a meeting of the *Witan* where he presented his case. The King still held back, unwilling to concede the demands being made of him and his delay caused those with Earl Godwine to become restless so that he could restrain them only with difficulty. The indefatigable Bishop Stigand enlisted the support of the cooler heads, advising an exchange of hostages, which saved the King's face, and this was done. At this the King's clerical support melted away and his Frenchmen fled. Archbishop Robert, accompanied by Bishops Ulf of Dorchester and William of London and their households fought their way out of London by way of the East Gate, injuring a number of young men who tried to stop them.

They made their way to 'Eadulf's Ness (the Naze, in Essex) and sailed for Normandy in an unseaworthy ship. The Canterbury account[23] almost gloatingly reports that the Archbishop abandoned his pallium in his haste 'and all Christendom here in this land' (that is, the Church in England) 'just as God wanted it.' Robert travelled on from Normandy to Rome where he complained bitterly to Pope Leo who accepted his, one-sided, account of events and sent him back with a letter demanding his reinstatement,[24] though the Archbishop never had the courage to present it to King Edward, retired to Jumièges and was dead by 1058. Bishop Stigand of Winchester was appointed by King Edward, to replace Robert Champart, retaining his See of Winchester while he was Archbishop. All the 'Frenchmen' fled, some west to Pentecost's castle and others north to Clavering in Essex where Robert FitzWimarc had built himself a castle. Most of them eventually took refuge in Scotland with King Macbeth, those in Herefordshire seeking permission from Earl Leofric to pass through his earldom in order to do so.

Earl Godwine was allowed to appear before the *Witan* and clear himself on oath of all charges against him. He is said by the *Vita* to have sought the King's consent for doing so by appearing before him and throwing himself at his feet, begging in the name of Christ for permission to purge himself of the charges. If he did, it was a smart move, like that of the Emperor Henry IV at Canossa, who appeared there for three days garbed as a penitent, imploring the Pope's forgiveness. Just as Gregory VII was unable to refuse a penitent emperor, so King Edward was unable to refuse a penitent earl.[25] The King 'was constrained both by his mercy and the satisfaction offered by the Earl' (who in fact 'appeared much superior in arms, if he chose to use them') and, deserted by the Archbishop and his men, and 'overcome by the prayers of the suppliants', gave Godwine the kiss of peace, condoned all his offences, 'and granted full favour both to him and all his sons.' (Except for Earl Swein who had already left on a pilgrimage to Jerusalem, from which he never returned, dying on the way back.)

So the Godwines were restored to their earldoms and all their estates and Queen Edith was duly sent for from Wilton with all honour and restored to her estates and 'to the king's bed-chamber'. Then the Earl set out his side of the case in full and as a result the Archbishop Robert and all the Frenchmen were declared outlawed as they were responsible for the discord between King and Earl in that they had 'promoted illegality and passed unjust judgements and counselled bad counsel'. A small number were permitted to stay, or, like Bishop William, to return because the King liked having them around him and they had been faithful to him and his people. Among those permitted to stay were Robert the Deacon and his son-in-law Richard FitzScrob, Alfred, the King's horse-thegn, and Ansfrid Cocksfoot.

Godwine's apparent triumph was not to last. Shortly after he had landed on 14 September, (the Feast of the Holy Cross), the Earl was taken ill, and, although he recovered in time to seek reconciliation, the Abingdon Chronicler comments that he did not show true repentance since he failed to make amends to the Church by restoring misappropriated church lands. That illness was his first warning. In the following year, while dining with Edward, at Winchester, on Easter Monday, he had a stroke; 'he suddenly sank down against a footstool, deprived of speech and all his strength'. His sons, Harold, Tostig and Gyrth, carried him into the King's chamber, and it was hoped that he would recover, as before. He did not, and on the Thursday after, 15 April, he died. His sons buried him in the Old Minster alongside his former master, Cnut. So the King was now without his premier earl and, since she had died on 6 March 1052, his mother Emma. He turned therefore to Godwine's surviving eldest son, Harold, and made him Earl of Wessex in succession to his father.[26]

Earl Harold was not yet as powerful as he later became. The whole of Wessex did not come into his hands until after the death of Earl Odda, nor did he obtain the lands of Earl Ralph's earldom in Herefordshire until after Ralph's death, and Harold had to give up his former earldom, East Anglia, to Leofric's son, Aelfgar. He gradually won a place under the King greater than that held by his father, but the rise was much slower than is often suggested. It would have taken Harold some time to establish himself in control of his new earldom and accept the commendation of its most prominent thegns. With Godwine's death, all sign of enmity between the King and the Godwines appears to come to an end, and the King, now about fifty years of age, began to retire somewhat from public life, amusing himself with his favourite pastimes of hunting and falconry, devoting himself to religious contemplation, the study of theology and, most importantly, supervising the construction of his great memorial, Westminster Abbey.

One more event during the King's brief period of rule in the absence of the Godwines needs to be considered. According to the Worcester version of the Chronicle, and confirmed by Florence of Worcester who must have drawn on the same source, early in 1052, and before 6 March when the Lady Emma died, 'Then soon Earl William came from beyond sea with a great troop of French men, and the King received him and as many of his companions as suited him, and let him go again.'

Florence adds that the Normans were 'laden with gifts'.

Much ink has been spilt over this visit and it has been linked to the post-Conquest Norman claims about William of Normandy's entitlement to the English throne. Some have even doubted that the visit took place, pointing to the fact that Duke William was at the critical time heavily engaged in warfare at the seiges of Alençon and Domfront, and would have found it difficult, though perhaps not impossible, to fit in a visit to England. Accepting that William did come, what can be made of it?

There is nothing to suggest that it had anything to do with any promise of the throne to William of Normandy. The Chronicle does not connect it to the question of the succession and neither does Florence of Worcester. But Florence, when recording the decision to recall Edward the Exile does connect that decision with the succession. The Norman writers themselves know nothing about any such visit and it must surely be accepted that had they known, they would have made great use of it. William of Poitiers actually puts a speech into his master's mouth (as was the convention in the eleventh and twelfth centuries) in which William, while claiming to have been made Edward's heir, asserts that Harold was sent to him in Normandy 'that he might personally take the oath which his father and others had sworn in my absence'. William of Jumièges also asserts that the message appointing the Duke as heir to the kingdom, was conveyed by Archbishop Robert, and again, that Earl Harold was sent to confirm it.[27] Neither ever claims that William received the promise directly from the lips of the Confessor.

William must have been invited to England; it is not credible to suggest that he visited King Edward of his own accord without an invitation. Duke William had not come to participate in the funeral of his great aunt, Queen Emma, which would have been a possible opportunity for Edward to make any intended offer of the succession. Instead, the visit in 1052 was a diplomatic mission of some sort. The language used points to it. The word used for 'received', is *underfeng*, from the verb *underfon* which has legal and political import. A lord who accepts the transfer of a man's service from another lord to himself is said to *underfeh* the man's service. When a king receives the submission of a conquered people, they accept him as their lord; '*underfengen to hlaford*'. When King Edward accepted William and some of (not all of) his men, he accepted them as his vassals. William of Poitiers makes William call Edward 'my lord and kinsman'. William had done homage and fealty to Edward, probably to seal a treaty of friendship or alliance between them. It has no connotations of making William the King's heir.[28] Perhaps Edward expected William to provide support against Earl Godwine (and the Earl's friend Baldwin of Flanders) in the event of his attempting a return to power. If he did, he was sadly disappointed. William did nothing. No use of this is made by those presenting the Norman case because they never show William as a petitioner seeking a favour. If Edward had made William his heir he would have done him a most tremendous favour. There is no independent evidence that he did any such thing.

11

The Politics of Succession

With Earl Godwine's death the Kingdom became more settled and relatively peaceful. King Edward now had no reason to be disturbed by distrustful thoughts about the loyalty of his leading earls. He had always remained suspicious of Earl Godwine and his motives and conduct because of his involvement in the death of the king's brother, Alfred. Almost any policy advocated by the Earl had met with rejection by the King, especially in the choice of bishops and in foreign policy. His loathing for the man he held responsible for his brother's death had surfaced in 1051, when the King had demanded that the Earl return to him his brother and all his men, alive and in possession of all their property.

This was seized upon by twelfth century writers who embroidered the tale of Godwine's death by alleging that it had been brought about not by a stroke, but by his reaction to a challenge by the King. Edward is alleged to have seized on a comment by Earl Godwine made when a passing waiter tripped and was prevented from falling, to remind him once more that he, Edward, no longer had a brother, thanks to Godwine. To this was added the improving tale hinging on the idea of ordeal by bread. Godwine is said to have called on God to permit him to swallow a mouthful of bread if he was aware of having done anything designed to endanger Alfred or harm Edward, and with these words choked on the morsel he had just put into his mouth and 'turned up his eyes in death'.[1]

The story is meant to illustrate the fate of those who tempt God. The sober narrative of the Chronicles gives no support for it, it is pure fiction. Godwine's death had been one of natural causes. He was already an old man by eleventh-century standards, born perhaps sometime towards the end of the tenth century, and probably in his sixties. He is described as an aged man[2] and as a venerable father figure[3] and the Chronicles indicate that he had fallen ill just as he landed at London on 14 September. He had no doubt been exhausted by his labours in securing the return of his family from exile.

However, with the promotion of Godwine's son, Harold, to the earldom of Wessex, the King's government returned to normality. Despite troubles on the Welsh borders arising from the ambitions of Gruffydd ap Llewelyn, King of north Wales, and the occasional forays by the Scots, together with the ever present menace from Viking raiders in the Irish Sea, the Kingdom enjoyed over the ensuing ten years an era of prosperity and progress under Edward's benign rule. Later writers were to look back upon his reign as a golden age under a second Solomon.

Agriculture improved as the climate began to change, emerging from several centuries of cold conditions into what is known as the 'medieval warm period', extending from Edward's time until the fourteenth century, when conditions rapidly became much colder. That period was one of the warmest and most favourable climatic phases in historical times.[4] There had been some hard winters early in the reign, notably in 1047 and 1048, but the climate improved as the reign progressed with increases in mean temperatures affecting plants and animals.

Increased prosperity favoured landlords and the population increased. The economy recovered with the end of the drain on resources of silver after Aethelred's reign and increased returns from land enabled Edward to abolish the heregeld when he got rid of the hired fleet. Higher rents could be demanded with increased services from tenants. The luxury trades benefited and foreign goods were imported. Prosperity among the thegns promoted political stability. The land produced food and drink in profusion. Home-produced cheese, wine, bread, honey, bacon, beef and lamb were plentiful. Men could afford to keep hawks and dogs and landowners could demand from their tenants the agricultural services they needed.

Winchester was the traditional seat of authority, while London remained predominantly commercial, so Edward divided much of his time between them. Winchester was the royal administrative centre and attracted lay and ecclesiastical magnates from throughout the kingdom.

It was an age of conspicuous expenditure on the part of the earls and richer thegns, with much use of gold thread and embroidery on clothing. Queen Edith saw to it that Edward shared in this fashion in order to maintain his royal dignity. Women did fancy needlework, using luxury fabrics, purple cloth, silk, jewels and gold, ivory and bronze. Men wore furs, marten skins for the King and sable, beaver or wolf for others. There were chests full of tapestries to serve as bedclothes or wall hangings. Rich gifts were made to churches of copes and other vestments, altar cloths, illustrated books and many other things. Earl Harold gave Waltham a chasuble called 'The Word spoke unto Me'.

The magnates joined the King and Queen in building or enlarging churches. Earl Harold rebuilt Waltham Holy Cross and Earl Leofric and his wife Godgifu (Lady Godiva) built the Church at Stow in Lincolnshire. That church had eighty-five foot transepts with arches and a central crossing thirty-three feet high. Waltham was embellished with elaborate and richly ornamented books and reliquaries, with silver and gold altar vessels and life-size figures of the twelve apostles. Others, like Earl Tostig, gave life-sized crucifixes and many gold and silver crosses to the churches of their choice.

The households of the great fed hundreds of servants and consumed the produce of their owner's estates. These thegnly estates
produced great wealth in both cash and kind; in 1066 Countess
Gytha could offer the Conqueror the weight of her son Harold's
body in gold for the release of that body for burial.

Earls had their own residences, as did king's thegns, comprising great aisled halls with separate private chambers called *cameras*.
These were located on a *setl* or enclosed area, with hedges or perhaps a ditch and palisade, enclosing an acre or more of land. Entry
might be by way of a 'burh-gate', a fortified entrance, and there
might be included a bell tower adjacent to an estate church, perhaps
like the round towers of Norfolk. Little of these residences can be
recovered by archaeologists as most of the building was in wood
and, one suspects, many must lie beneath the mottes built by the
Normans after the Conquest.

Men could improve their wealth and status by royal service in
shire and hundred or by service in the King's hall. Some 250 men
held estates, rated collectively at over forty hides (or carucates) of
land assessed to the *geld*, and at least one hundred held lands worth
more than £40 a year. Many held much more than that.

Bishop Herman of Ramsbury boasted to Pope Leo IX that
England was 'being filled everywhere with new churches which
daily were being added anew in new places.' That was the England
over which Edward now reigned.

Over a period of about five years, from 1053 to 1058, it became
necessary for Edward to fill the vacancies in the ranks of the magnates, as those who had attained office under Cnut and his sons, or
under Edward himself in his first ten years, died. He needed men
upon whom he could rely and was restricted to make his selection
from a very small pool of talent. It does not appear that the thegns
were at all disturbed by the King's preference for his kinsmen by
marriage, the sons of Earl Godwine.

Harold, now the eldest son, had been Edward's immediate choice
when Godwine died and there is no reason to suppose that it was

forced on him. Harold's succession to Wessex could easily have been agreed during the negotiations leading to reconciliation in 1052. The *Vita Edwardi*[5] stresses that Harold was chosen 'by the King's favour' and that he proceeded to deal with all 'disturbers of the peace, thieves and robbers'. The Chronicles mention the appointment in a very matter-of-fact way without comment. William of Malmesbury does not make any reference to it at all. No one seems to have regarded it as at all unexpected. Then the earldom of East Anglia was bestowed once more on Aelfgar, son of Earl Leofric. The Mercian Earl was still a force to be reckoned with in 1053.

The rest of the changes in the earldoms followed the same or a similar pattern. When Earl Siward died, the next son of Godwine, Tostig, was the King's choice rather than Siward's surviving son, Waltheof, who was rejected simply because he was too young. Earl Siward's eldest son, Osbern had been killed in the war in Scotland against Macbeth, otherwise Osbern would surely have been the natural choice and, like Aelfgar and Harold, been promoted to his father's earldom.

The death of Earl Ralph removed the last of Edward's kin by blood, son of his sister, Godgifu, and the King was left surrounded by his kin by marriage, the Godwines. On this occasion, no new earl was appointed, possibly because neither Gyrth nor Leofwine was yet considered old enough to be promoted, and because a strong hand was needed on the Welsh border. Earl Aelfgar's sons would also have been far too young. Instead, Earl Harold was given Ralph's lands in Herefordshire and incorporated them into the earldom of Wessex.

Wessex was nowhere near as large in the early 1050s as it was to become, or even as it had been under Earl Godwine before 1051. Odda of Deerhurst had been made Earl of the south-western shires of Wessex and appears to have retained his earldom until his death, perhaps as some sort of junior earl with special responsibilities there. Edward appears to have liked, or perhaps respected, Earl Harold. He had not been required to supply hostages in 1051.

Tostig was a necessary choice for Northumbria where the King had few known demesne lands and needed a capable lieutenant to keep order. The King expected to receive *geld* from Northumbria and had need of an earl who would be sure to collect it. In Northumbria the King was in some ways more of an overlord rather than their immediate sovereign. Much of the region lay outside the threefold division of Wessex, Mercia and the Danelaw;[6] even the Domesday survey was to stop at the Tees.

In the north, under Edward, some progress was made in Church affairs. The appointment of bishops there was now made by the King rather than the house of Bamburgh. There was no sign that Northumbria resented the overlordship of Wessex but the region still needed to be governed with care. Tostig's appointment marked a change of attitude towards Northumbria. His rule ended the custom of choosing earls with a connection to local Northumbrian families. Previous earls had been Anglo-Scandinavian but Tostig was Danish in name rather than attitude. He was to seek to integrate the area more firmly into the system of government and administration designed in the south.

Although the account of events over the period from 1053 to 1063 reads rather like the deeds of the house of Godwine, this is only an impression conveyed by the way in which the Chronicles record events. It is important that Harold was Edward's appointee, whereas his father had been appointed by Cnut. The Earl was to proceed to act as the King's loyal lieutenant, carrying out the decrees of the King and his *Witan*, collective decisions endorsed by the King himself, as Florence of Worcester insists. Earl Harold's position gradually grew stronger as the other and older earls died one by one. Siward, Leofric, Ralph and Odda were all gone by 1058, and even the King's great-nephew Edward the Exile. None of them left a sufficient number of sons old enough to fill the vacancies.

Aelfgar's appointment to East Anglia in 1053 had given Earl Leofric control over a vast swathe of territory stretching from the

East Anglian coast to the borders of Wales and from Chester to Ipswich, lying south of the Humber and north of the Thames.

Another characteristic of Edward's government after 1053 was the use he made of Church appointments to maintain the independent character of the English Church. Despite the uncanonical position of Archbishop Stigand, the Church in England did not become isolated or provincial and was never out of communion with Rome. The excommunication was applicable to Stigand personally and did not affect the rest of the hierarchy. There was no interdict applied to the whole English Church. There were abuses in need of correction, just as there were elsewhere in western Europe, but the accusations made later in Anglo-Norman times, to the effect that the church had been riddled with simony and pluralism are exaggerated, and the product of propaganda.

Sources such as the *Gesta Pontificum* of William of Malmesbury have little criticism of individual bishops, other than the Norman Ulf of Dorchester, of whom it was said 'he nothing bishoplike did so that it is a shame to tell of'[7] and Stigand who was accused of selling churches and subjected to a tirade of abuse[8] which ought to be rejected as exaggerated. The English bishops were accused, sometimes rightly, of pluralism, that is holding several ecclesiastical offices simultaneously. Thus Ealdred of York, who had not surrendered his See of Worcester when appointed in 1060, was forced to relinquish it by Pope Nicholas II in return for recognition as archbishop. But such multiple office holding had been customary for several generations. Only in the mid-eleventh century did the Papacy begin a campaign against it.

There is much evidence of apparent multiple office-holding during Edward's reign but there was often some justification for it. Archbishops of York had been accustomed, since Oswald of Worcester's time, to hold Worcester as well as York in order to compensate the archbishopric for the loss of estates during the Viking wars at a time when those estates could not be recovered. Other examples of plural office-holding may not be what they seem.

Ealdred, as Bishop of Worcester, is found administering several sees and more than one abbacy simultaneously and the Chronicles simply say that he was now abbot or bishop of a vacant see or abbacy. He held Worcester and Hereford jointly after 1055 until 1060 when he became Archbishop of York. But most of these arrangements appear to have been only temporary, made until a permanent replacement was found.

Hereford, where Leofgar had perished in battle against the Welsh, needed a strong hand in order to support Harold as Earl and keep out the Welsh. It resembles the situation in the south west of England where Lyfing, until his death in 1046 held, as the Chronicle puts it, 'three Sees, one in Devonshire, and in Cornwall and in Worcester', as had been the case since at least Cnut's time. He was succeeded at Worcester by Ealdred and the south western joint see was given to Leofric. He transferred the see to Exeter, with Edward's support and Papal consent. It seems that Edward simply moved bishops about from see to see, like chessmen, to suit his political purposes. But this pluralistic way of working was now under attack from the reformers.

The purpose of such ecclesiastical fiefdoms was largely a matter of military necessity. The King was recovering for the church parity of influence with the great earldoms and providing churchmen with a role in the defence of the kingdom. Ealdred's position enabled him to cover the southern marches and the Welsh border south of Mercia. Stigand's area of influence extended from Elmham, where his brother Aethelmaer was bishop, as far as Abingdon where Spearhavoc might have been the bishop's associate. Stigand also controlled Rochester from Canterbury, since no bishop is recorded for that see from 1046 to 1058. In fact Stigand was responsible for a vast area extending from the Wash to the Isle of Wight, excluding Essex. Sandwich, the King's naval base, was a manor belonging to Stigand. Unlike Ealdred, Stigand did not actually lead contingents of soldiers but he had responsibility and control over contingents of the fyrd and over burhs and bridges. These ecclesiastical dispositions were of far greater importance than the small number of estates on the south coast in Norman hands such as those of the Abbot of Fécamp.

There is little evidence for the allegation that Stigand engaged in simony, though it might well have been customary for grateful clerics who had won preferment to make gifts to those who had supported their promotion, just as the King and Queen expected men to show their gratitude. But the reformed Papacy was beginning to take a much stricter view of this time-honoured custom. That Rome judged some English bishops as guilty of simony or pluralism does not mean that they condemned the standards of the English church as a whole.

The church's reputation should be judged by the standards of the age and, when this is done, it compares well with churches elsewhere. Leofwine of Lichfield was apparently married and other clergy had wives or mistresses, but such conduct was widespread in the western Church and persisted well into the twelfth century. The reform campaign to require clerical celibacy went hand in hand with attempts to prevent bishops moving from see to see without Papal approval, and both were part of the drive to re-impose Papal authority which had declined since the fifth century.

The practice of pluralism in the case of abbacies did not attract the same disapproval. Leofric, nephew of Earl Leofric of Mercia, built up a veritable monastic empire constructed for him by Edward. He was primarily abbot of Peterborough but over the course of the reign acquired control over Coventry, Crowland and Thorney as well as Abingdon, Burton and Ely. The purpose could have been twofold. Politically it strengthened Earl Leofric's position, and that of the earldom of Mercia in general, especially in the Fens and it put a strong abbot in a position where he could improve the tone of several Benedictine houses.

It was not monastic reform on the continental pattern. Leofric was not really a grand abbot presiding over a number of daughter houses as was the case at Cluny. But Edward might have been feeling his way towards such a system. Leofric cannot have presided over each of these monasteries without representatives responsible for their day-to-day administration, and that would have meant a system of priors representing the sole abbot. Elsewhere there were improvements in cathedral chapters which were reorganised at Exeter, London and Wells and both Cynsige and Ealdred enriched and adorned the minsters of their diocese, especially York itself and both Ripon and Beverley.

King Edward was now becoming accustomed to ruling in a purely English political context, with no need to acknowledge the interests of any foreign dynasty. The Danish influence in his *Witan* had declined and the French or Norman influence had been removed. His rule now had unimpeachable legitimacy and the administration under Harold as premier Earl developed a markedly insular aspect, regarding any intruding outsider as a threat. It was remarkably successful in delivering peace and prosperity, and even the problem of Stigand's uncanonical position seemed to be solved, albeit all too briefly, in 1058 when Benedict X gave him a pallium. Unfortunately that Pope was rejected by the reforming majority among the Cardinals in January 1059 and the new Pope, Nicholas II, renewed Stigand's excommunication and annulled his own predecessor's acts.

To concentrate on tensions and divisions, such as the problem of Aelfgar, distracts attention from the co-operation between Edward and his earls. There were few cases of outlawry between 1053 and 1063, indeed Aelfgar and possibly Edric of Laxfield are the only recorded examples, to which perhaps that of Hereward the Lincolnshire thegn should be added.

Harold and his fellow earls operated with the King, imposing justice, collecting taxes and defending the kingdom, in contrast to the stormy history of Normandy with its wars and rebellions. Edward's rule was not weak nor was he a cipher or puppet in the hands of Harold Godwinson. A close relationship of interdependence between the King and his nobles was essential to effective rule and the themes of service and loyalty are the clue to the rise of the Godwines.

Edward might well have wanted to cut Earl Godwine himself down to size in 1051, but, unwisely, he had chosen to do so by accepting the counsels of Robert of Jumièges, who had his own schemes for personal aggrandisement. The archbishop had been over-ambitious and his hubris led inevitably to nemesis. The period 1051–52 had been one of high drama, with much violence, spectacular embassies and diplomatic revolutions. It was succeeded, as all such storms are, by a period of relative calm.

The new arrangements were, for a time, to give the king an even distribution of power among the great families, allowing him to play one off against another. Earl Harold would have been about twenty-seven and the King was now in his fifties with ten years of experience in kingship. His policies still remained something of a mystery which the *Vita Edwardi* does little to dispel.

One great issue now came to the fore. The King had been married for almost ten years with no sign of an heir. Concern over this could perhaps have begun to emerge in 1051 and might lie behind Archbishop Robert's attempt to persuade the King to abandon his marriage to Edith, so freeing himself to marry again and secure an heir. What is less clear is the cause of his childlessness.

The orthodox answer given after his death and hinted at in the ambiguous language of the *Vita Edwardi*, and which suited the medieval mind-set, was that the King from early youth had chosen a celibate lifestyle and therefore that the marriage had remained unconsummated. That case rests purely on the absence of children and on Edward's reputation for chastity. In Edward's case, unlike many nobles of the age, there are no stories, as there are for the Norman dukes for example, of mistresses or concubines and he had no bastard children.

But in this respect he was not alone. His half-brother, Harthacnut, never married and he also is not credited with illegitimate offspring. Earl Tostig's marriage was renowned for its chastity. The Earl was faithful to his wife Judith and never looked at another woman. No writer suggests either of these men was celibate.[9]

The charge is levelled at Edward principally because of the inclusion in the *Vita Edwardi* of Bishop Beorhtwold's vision. This venerable man, who died in 1045, was reported[10] to have dreamed that he saw St Peter 'consecrate the image of seemly man' (who remains unnamed) as king and dedicate him to a life of chastity. The chosen king then asked the saint who would reign after him and was sternly told that 'the Kingdom of the English is of God; and after you, he has already provided a king according to His will.' If, as is possible, the vision occurred sometime during the reigns of the Danish Kings, it is evidence of English aspirations for the return of their native dynasty.

The theme of chastity is repeated in the *Vita*[11] in the writer's sketch of the King's character. He is there said to have 'preserved with holy chastity the dignity of his consecration', living his life 'in true innocence dedicated to God'. This is part of the writer's view that Edward was a saintly man and a possible candidate for canonisation. It was used in the twelfth century to demonstrate Edward's devotion to what was now described as a celibate life.[12] Osbert of Clare, the advocate for Edward's canonisation insisted, for his own purposes, that Edward had remained a virgin.

The meaning of these passages hinges on the meaning of the language adopted in the *Vita Edwardi*. It is by no means a straightforward matter. Similar language is used of both Edward and Earl Tostig. Edward is to live a *vitam celibem* and Tostig is *celebs*. Both are translated as chastity in Barlow's edition of the *Vita Edwardi*. The *Vita* also writes of Edward's *castimonia* which means both purity of morals and chastity. *Celebs* as applied to both Edward and Tostig cannot mean 'celibate'. Tostig certainly was not celibate but a married man with two sons, Ketil and Skuli. That the author of the *Vita* says that Edward and Edith, when he knew them, lived like father and daughter is irrelevant. By the 1060s Edward was ageing and Edith still only in her forties and the marriage had become one of companionship. It is unfortunate that a few vital pages of the *Vita Edwardi* are missing. They contained the author's remarks on the subject of Edith's marriage and their content can only be partially recovered from the use made of the original text by William of Malmesbury and Osbert of Clare.

Malmesbury's claims that the king did not 'know her as a man should' (*virili more*; in manly fashion) is opinion not evidence. He bases his statement on what was 'very widely reported', that is, gossip.[13] Osbert simply adds his own spin to an original passage favourable to Edith's marriage, to bolster his claims that Edward retained his virginity. Nothing in these writers can be taken to prove that Edward remained celibate.

Osbert of Clare claims that some had tried to tempt the King, before his marriage so that 'his chastity should founder' and therefore that it was decided that he should marry and a suitable wife was found for him. Osbert has inserted his own interpretation into a passage similar to that quoted by William of Malmesbury about the choice of Edith as his wife. The original probably only stated that it was thought proper that he should marry.

There is a piece of neglected evidence in the *Vita Edwardi* which, if accepted, provides a solution. The *Vita* reports the rebuilding of the convent at Wilton by Queen Edith and its consecration.[14] The author then celebrates the ceremony with a metaphorical *epithalamium*, a poem celebrating a spiritual marriage. He sees the church of Wilton as 'a peerless mother' who will 'bear blessed babies' and at their birth it will 'feel no pangs'. He congratulates the church because it will have many children (the nuns who will come to the convent) and will never 'grieve at scanty progeny', or 'in slow time ... produce slow birth by ordered lapse of those long lazy months' and furthermore 'nor will one fashioned in your womb expire'.

The implication here is that the church at Wilton, mother of many (spiritual) children, is contrasted with the experience of someone, an unnamed woman, who has suffered a long pregnancy and extended labour and given birth to a stillborn child. The most obvious candidate for that role is Edith herself who has certainly failed to produce an heir because her child (even perhaps more than one) was born dead. If so, then Edward's lack of an heir is explained, and Archbishop Robert's desire that the King put away his wife.

Unable to produce children, Edith turned to ensuring that 'boys of royal blood' should be educated accordingly, meaning, it would appear, her younger brothers and, after 1058, the children of Edward the Exile and Ralph of Hereford. The Queen's 'ghostwriter', as he might well be termed, laments that he had 'thought to the last page of this devoted book to tell of blessed progeny', but instead finds himself writing about war and disaster.

Most of the rest of the 1050s was taken up with the English drive, inspired by Edward, who wished perhaps to emulate the achievements of his grandfather Edgar, to impose order on the Welsh and the Scots. This involved dealing with the activities of Aelfgar of Mercia, while the question of the succession to the throne concerned the *Witan* after 1054.

It was no doubt now recognised that Edith would never have children. She was in her forties and conception was doubtful or even impossible. A plan was therefore devised, not, as some have argued, to deflect the succession away from any foreign claimant (and certainly not William of Normandy), but to supply an English-born heir since Edward had no heir of the body. The King no doubt had accepted that it was God's will[15] that he would not have a direct heir. So a search was initiated to find the sons of Edmund Ironside.

Cnut the Great had sent them abroad to perish, and the King of Sweden, unwilling to do his dirty work for him, had sent them on to Hungary. The elder brother, Edmund, was dead by the 1050s. The surviving son, also called Edward (like the Confessor), had been well treated at the Hungarian Court and married Agatha, of Braunschweig, a daughter of Henry II of Germany's brother. It might have been known that the brothers were subject to ill health and so no effort had been made earlier until it was reported that the Exile now had a son, Edgar, (born perhaps circa 1052), who had survived his perilous early years, as well as the Exile's daughters, Margaret and Christina. So in 1054 Bishop Ealdred of Worcester was sent to find him and to sound out the German Emperor about the chances of bringing him back to England. This surely could not have been decided upon if it was known that the King had made a binding promise of the succession to Duke William of Normandy.

The Bishop was delayed for a year at Cologne to no avail, the time was not propitious. The Emperor was in dispute with Hungary over Magyar raids on the Empire and had no interest in raising his kinsman to the English throne.[16] Ealdred returned empty-handed although he did become acquainted with the latest trends in the Romano-Germanic *Ordo* and brought back ideas for the reform and improvement of the English Church.

The next opportunity came in 1056 with the death of Emperor Henry III. Earl Harold made a journey that year to Flanders, no doubt part of what the *Vita Edwardi* describes as his policy of making himself well acquainted with the various rulers of Europe.[17] He was accustomed to study the character, policies and strength of the various rulers and acquired an exhaustive knowledge of them so that 'he could get what he needed from them'.

In November 1056 the Earl was at St Omer where he witnessed a charter given by Count Baldwin to St Peter's Ghent.[18] He had, it is argued, arrived there either after a visit to Rome[19] or before going there via Cologne in the company of Pope Victor II. At St Omer he had the opportunity to negotiate with Agnes, Regent of the young Henry IV, for the return of the Exile. Hungary had been wracked with war in which Baldwin had been involved. It is possible that the *Aetheling* Edward was now open to the suggestion that he might visit England.

Bishop Ealdred was sent again to Europe to escort him back. The Bishop was well rewarded for his diplomacy. He received the bishopric of Hereford, after the unfortunate death of Leofgar, to hold in addition to Worcester.

The *Aetheling* returned in 1057[20] and, unfortunately, promptly died before he could even meet his relative King Edward. Florence of Worcester asserts categorically that it had been the King's intention to make the *Aetheling* his heir as does William of Malmesbury. The latter asserts that Edward 'having no children of his own' asked that Edward and his household be sent back to England so that 'either he or his sons, he said, should succeed to the hereditary throne of England' as 'his own lack of offspring ought to be made good by the support of his kinsfolk'.[21] There is no sign in this that anyone thought that God would provide a successor to Edward. The son of Edmund Ironside was much more closely related to Edward than was William of Normandy. The lament in the poem (recorded in the Chronicle and written then or shortly afterwards at Worcester) regrets the loss of the Exile but is not hinting at foul play so much as at the cruelty of fate. No one stood to gain as it was in the interest of all the magnates to have the succession question settled.

It is not completely clear whether his wife, Agatha, and his children, Edgar, Margaret and Christina, were with him in 1057, though the Chronicle implies it, but they certainly did arrive by 1058. Bishop Ealdred, the indefatigable, made a pilgrimage to Jerusalem that year, travelling by way of Hungary, and he might have escorted the widow and children to England then. At some point, Edgar was recognised as *Aetheling*, and is so referred to after the Conquest, so it was probably assumed that, should the King live long enough for him to grow up, he would be the heir.

But it is also from this time onwards that Earl Harold began to be singled out and treated as more than just another earl. His lands were vastly increased, and earldoms were found for his brothers. He was consulted on all decisions of importance. Hereford was annexed to his Earldom of Wessex on the death of Earl Ralph and he was associated very closely indeed with the King in treaties with the Welsh, made by 'consent of the King and the Earl'. The *Vita Edwardi* is remarkably fulsome about his role in government and that work seems, at least in part, designed to promote the claims of the Godwines, and especially Harold, in some sort of regency, on behalf of Edgar perhaps, after King Edward's death. Whatever the purpose of the *Vita* had been, that purpose was destroyed by the events of 1065–66 which made necessary a considerable amount of re-writing at the end of Book One, making it almost impossible to discern what the original purpose was.

12

The Glens of Desolation

After 1052 King Edward, faced with the problems posed by the Welsh and the Scots, decided that something had to be done. In Wales Gruffydd ap Llewelyn had made himself King, or at least overlord, of the whole country, while in Scotland Macbeth (mormaer: ruler or sub-regulus) of Moray had killed King Duncan, taken his throne, exiled Duncan's sons Malcolm and Donald, and recruited the Normans and other Frenchmen driven out of Herefordshire in 1052, to act as household cavalry.

Edward had inherited from his predecessors a policy of placing men with delegated royal authority in provinces requiring strong government. He was the King, and an anointed one at that, and had the last word in the appointment of earls. His actions can be interpreted as those of a man who preferred to conceal his iron hand in a velvet glove.

Earl Godwine was to defy him and fall from power, and was restored only because of the arrogance and incompetence of King Edward's choices to replace him and his sons, which turned the thegns against the King. Aelfgar of Mercia was to defy him and

suffered exile, eventually meeting what seems to have been an ignominious death. In Wales both Welsh kings were to lose their heads
and in Scotland Macbeth was to perish at the hands of Malcolm
after he was installed as king by Edward's viceroy, Earl Siward.

Wales

In Wales, Gruffydd, King of Gwynedd from 1039, had begun his
ascent to supremacy by engaging in warfare against English settlers near Welshpool (Rhd-y-Gros), killing Edwin, brother of Earl
Leofric, and other leading thegns, and defeating a Mercian army.[1]
He then spent some years securing control over the rest of Wales.[2]
The English had been putting pressure on Wales since the mid-
tenth century and there had been raids and ravaging to force Welsh
princes to pay tribute to the English kings in gold, silver and oxen.
Gruffydd now changed all that and English countermeasures had
proved inadequate.

Edward's first move, made shortly after his marriage to Edith,
had been to appoint Swein Godwinson to an earldom centred
mainly on Herefordshire but stretching across central England
north of the Thames. He had been placed on the Welsh border to
confront the ruling power in the area, Gruffydd ap Rhydderch of
South Wales (Gwent).

The border ran along Offa's Dyke, built to keep out the Welsh and
backed up by a chain of *burhs* from Chester to Glasbury-on-Wye,
with some eight centres such as Burghill. Edward was to settle the
men of his nephew, Ralph of Mantes (and afterwards of Hereford)
and to allow the construction of Norman-style motte and bailey
castles of a type unknown in England. The first was Pentecost's castle (renamed Ewias Harold for Ralph's son) and possibly another at
an unnamed location for Osbern Pentecost's associate, Hugh. There
is no evidence that any other castles were built before 1051. In that
year, after Earl Godwine's exile, more were built, at Hereford itself,

probably by Earl Ralph, and at Richard's Castle near Leominster by Richard FitzScrob. (The Breton staller Robert FitzWimarc also had one at Clavering in Essex).

Unwisely, Earl Swein made an alliance with the new power in south Wales, Gryffydd ap Llewelyn, so stimulating the Welshman's ambitions. As the Chronicle reports, Swein 'went into Wales and Gruffydd the northern king went with him; and they [the South Welsh] delivered hostages to him'.[3] Nothing more came of this because Swein then abducted the Abbess of Leominster and had to flee into exile. It is probable that it was during Swein's absence that the King licensed Ralph's men to build castles, as the Chronicle associates the castle-building with Swein's exile, saying 'Then had the foreigners erected a castle in Herefordshire among the retainers of Swein the earl, and wrought every kind of harm and disgrace to the King's men thereabout that they could'.[4]

The 'castle men' might have been sent to punish Swein's men for complicity in his crimes. It was these 'foreigners' (not Welshmen) who complained to King Edward in 1051. But King Gruffydd ap Rhydderch now took the opportunity during the confusion which ensued, caused by the appointment to Canterbury of Robert Champart and the consequences of Earl Swein's murder of his cousin Beorn, to join forces with an Irish fleet of thirty-six ships to attack the Usk.[5] Bishop Ealdred, who had been given charge of the area, raised the shire levies and attempted resistance but his forces were insufficient. The Welsh and their allies took them unawares 'at very early morning' and 'slew many good men while others escaped with the bishop'.

During the period of the exile of the Godwines, ap Rhydderch returned to the attack, and demonstrated the uselessness of 'Norman' tactics. The attack came on the anniversary of the occasion thirteen years earlier, when Edwin of Mercia had died at Welshpool. The Welsh harried Herefordshire as far as Leominster and when the local forces, reinforced by the 'Frenchmen in the castle,' many men, both English and French, were slain.[6] That it was Gruffydd ap

Rhydderch not ap Llewelyn is suggested by two points. Firstly ap Llewelyn had not yet defeated his south Welsh rival and secondly King Edward acted against the south Welsh in retaliation.

Edward must have been enraged. At the Christmas Court at Gloucester the decision was taken to send a small force to assassinate Rhys ap Rhydderch, Gruffydd's brother. It was successful and the victim's head was brought to King Edward as a trophy on 5 January 1053.[7] Edward might well have been venting on the Welsh his chagrin at having to restore the Godwines to their former position. The Welsh response seems to have been an attack on the English frontier at Westbury-on-Severn, killing a great number of guards.[8]

It is probable that the English had again been pushing westwards into Wales, as they had been doing for decades, but now they were meeting stiffening resistance, from Gruffydd ap Rhydderch in Gwent and from the ambitious Gruffydd ap Llewelyn in Gwynedd and Powys. From the English viewpoint the Welsh only kept the peace when obliged to do so. Walter Map was still complaining at the end of the twelfth century that 'while you hold the sword they beseech you, when they hold it, they will command'.[9] They were seen by the English as lovers of theft and plunder, swift to shed blood. Their kings embodied these characteristics. Edward was becoming increasingly alarmed at the frequency of Welsh attacks.

The death of Rhys ap Rhydderch might well have weakened his brother's position. In 1055 Gruffydd ap Llewelyn finally had him assassinated and took control of all Wales. At this news, Edward's reaction was to order the strengthening of defences. The Dyke remained a formidable obstacle and Earl Leofric of Mercia was well able to keep the Welsh out of his earldom, but further south, in the valleys of the Wye and the Severn, where the Dyke was weaker, it was a different matter.

Earl Harold now improved the defences of Hereford, restoring the older earthworks. The town of Hereford has to be distinguished from its castle (which the Welsh called the *gaer*).[10] Gruffydd ap Llewelyn when he counter-attacked in 1055 burnt down the town and destroyed the *gaer*. After seizing power, Gruffydd still kept clear of Mercia. Possibly this was because he felt Leofric was too strong, (he had the reputation of being the 'Hammer of the Welsh') but it might be that Gruffydd had hopes of an alliance with Aelfgar. Gruffydd's unification of Wales had made him a potent threat and a thorn in Edward's flesh. Although the English had been able to recruit Welsh troops, they now found them treacherous. Having promised fealty to the King they secretly sent messages to Gruffydd encouraging him to attack the English.

When Earl Siward died in 1055, the King chose as his successor Tostig Godwinson. Siward had left no heir old enough to succeed him (his son Osbern had died in Scotland, and the son of his second marriage, Waltheof, was too young). Aelfgar seems to have taken exception to Tostig's appointment. He might perhaps have felt that he should have been promoted rather than Tostig. After all, he Aelfgar, was Earl in East Anglia, which was possibly regarded as a sort of first step to a major earldom, and there was no sign as yet that his father Leofric would not live for some time.

Whatever actually transpired, Aelfgar was immediately outlawed for questioning the King's decision. The Chroniclers are divided over the issue. The Worcester annalist thought he had done 'almost' nothing to deserve it, while the Worcester writer thought him guiltless. The Peterborough text, which is based on another version written at Canterbury in the 1050s, says that 'he admitted his guilt before all the men there assembled, although the confession escaped him unawares'. It appears that he had muttered something in protest which was relayed to the King and to which Edward took exception. The King was noted for his outbursts of fury, as witness his cruel demand that Earl Godwine return to him his brother Alfred alive and well. Another story relates how the King, when crossed while hunting by a local peasant, was heard to say that he would do the man an injury some day if he could.

Aelfgar fled first to Ireland, and recruited eighteen ships and their men, to add to his own band of household troops, with which to follow the example of the Godwines and force the King to re-instate him, and then came into Wales where he allied himself with an all-too-willing Gruffydd who gave him his full protection.

Earl Ralph was commissioned to raise the border levies and pre-pare to repel them before Hereford. 'They came together there, but before a spear was thrown, the English fled, because they had been made to fight on horseback', reports the Abingdon annalist tartly. The casualties were heavy, some four or five hundred died, and Ralph permanently lost all military credibility and became known as 'the Timid'. Florence of Worcester calls him a coward and says that it was the Earl and his knights who were the first to flee. He says that the English levies had been forced to go into battle on horseback 'contrary to their custom'.

There is another explanation for Ralph's apparent cowardice. The Welsh method of opening battle was to 'shout and glower fiercely at the enemy and fill the air with fearsome clamour, making a high-pitched screech with their long trumpets'. Quite simply, the Welsh had successfully 'spooked' the horses which had panicked and run out of control.[11] The Welsh, contrary to English accounts, describe the affair in the *Chronicle of the Princes*, as a 'bit-ter struggle'.

The consequences for Hereford were terrible. The town was plundered and the cathedral burnt to the ground with its priests inside it. Many others were killed and all the treasures, relics and vestments of the Church were seized and carried off into Wales.

The King ordered out all the levies from the surrounding shires, under the command of Earl Harold, meeting at Gloucester. From there the Earl advanced a little way into Wales, putting up a defen-sive screen of men, while he ordered the repair of the city's defences. Overtures were made for peace, possibly from both sides, at the end of October; Harold wishing to avoid more fighting and Aelfgar seeking restoration. Florence of Worcester thought the Welsh were afraid to fight Harold. They met at Billingsley, 'and there peace and friendship was established between them'. Cooler heads had prevailed upon King Edward and Aelfgar was brought back. His Irish fleet went to Chester to await payment of their wages.

On 10 February the following year Bishop Aethelstan died, and, probably on Harold's recommendation, the Earl's chaplain or mass-priest, Leofgar, was appointed to Hereford. He proved to be an unwise choice, being both rash and warlike and having retained his warrior's moustaches after he became a priest, contrary to custom, until he became bishop.

Leofgar now decided to seek revenge on the Welsh for the attack on his cathedral; he 'abandoned his chrism, his rood and his spiritual weapons' and, taking up spear and sword, took the field against the Welsh. It proved a costly error. The bishop lost his life and the lives of all his priests with him, along with Athelnoth the Sheriff and his men whom he had taken with him. The Chronicle then laments the consequences and all the privations and suffering endured by the English with much 'marching and campaigning' and hard work, with the loss of men and horses. It clearly became necessary to fight a prolonged rearguard action until the *Witan* decided to intervene. Earls Harold and Leofric and Bishop Ealdred confronted the Welsh, probably in such force as to overawe them. Ealdred had been given charge of Hereford when news of Leofgar's death arrived. The three magnates now negotiated with Gruffydd and a treaty was arranged which, in part at least, saved Edward's face.

It was the same sort of stand-off agreement that had several times been arranged between English kings and their Celtic neighbours in the tenth century. Peace terms were negotiated and the Celtic princes, Gruffydd this time, swore oaths to be faithful under-kings to the English monarch. That was the conventional language used to signify a diplomatic détente in which the English king acknowledged the kingship of the Celtic ruler and that ruler in turn acknowledged a rather shadowy overlordship. Welsh gains of territory seem to have been accepted (land on the Dee estuary might have been sacrificed) and, if 'tribute' was paid, the Welsh probably saw it as restitution for the damage they had done.

The inveterate collector of curious tales, Walter Map, (author of *De nugis Curialium*) has a story which records an encounter between King Edward and Gruffydd ap Llewelyn when peace terms were about to be arranged between them. If it occurred, then 1056 could have been the occasion, allowing Gruffydd to perform his homage in person. The story goes that the two met on opposite banks of the river, probably the Severn and perhaps at the usual crossing point at Aust. A diplomatic problem of protocol arose as to which king should cross the river for the meeting. Both kings claimed precedence. Gruffydd on the grounds that his ancestors had conquered England from the giants of old and Edward claiming that his ancestors had taken it from the Welsh! As befitted a man who, when Walter wrote, was a canonised saint, Edward made the first move and began to wade across. Gruffydd, overcome by this display of humility, threw off his cloak, plunged into the river and proceeded to carry King Edward across to the Welsh side on his shoulders. Once there, Gruffydd duly did homage to the English king.[12]

The rival claims made do not ring true, though no doubt it was customary on these occasions to make face-saving boasts. If the Kings did meet it would most likely have been on a convenient island in the river or on a boat in midstream. Walter Map probably invented the details to illustrate the character of the rival monarchs; Gruffydd is obstinate and boastful and Edward becomingly humble.

A series of prominent deaths in those years cleared the way for a re-adjustment among the earldoms. Odda of Deerhurst died on 31 August 1056 and Earl Leofric, exhausted by his exertions in Wales, on 30 September 1057; then Earl Ralph on 21 December. Consequently, Odda's responsibility for the south-western shires ended and Harold resumed control over them. Ralph's earldom, as far as it affected Herefordshire, was annexed to the earldom of Wessex. Neither of these moves could have been made without Edward's consent and approval. Harold had proved to be a tower of strength and was rewarded accordingly.

The King was providing Harold with the sinews of war lest Aelfgar, and his ally Gruffydd, proved untrustworthy. As Aelfgar now became Earl of Mercia, in succession to his father, it was no doubt thought that his ambitions might thereby be satisfied. There is no indication that he was required to surrender East Anglia and was now rather more powerful than his father, and protected on his western flank by his Welsh alliance. But he did not regain for Mercia the lands taken from it to provide earldoms for Swein and Ralph. He could well have remained dissatisfied. Harold had emerged with an enhanced reputation for diplomacy and as a soldier, having achieved a strategic objective, and Edward had gained at least verbal recognition of his ancestral claim to be overlord of Wales.

Harold was certainly now the King's foremost counsellor[13] and, as the eulogy on Edward when he died has it, always faithfully obeyed the king and neglected nothing that was needful. He appears to have maintained his position by presenting his actions as carried out on behalf of the King, and that might have been his actual policy.

As for Aelfgar, he was again outlawed, in 1058, though no explanation is offered for it. Only the Worcester Chronicle and Florence mention it. The Abingdon Chronicle is blank for the rest of the reign until 1065 and the Peterborough Chronicle entries become brief and uninformative. Even the Worcester annalist was unwilling to give details, 'it is tedious to tell how it all happened' he says. It was a very much more serious affair than the Chronicle is prepared to admit. Aelfgar had to be 'driven out' and then returned 'with violence through the help of Gruffydd'. It was also associated with the arrival in the Irish Sea of a 'pirate host', from Norway. Its purpose was to make a raid and secure plunder. It was commanded by 'Maccus' (usually taken to be Magnus, son of Harald Hardrada, though he might have been too young in 1058). The Welsh annals saw it as significant but give no details.[14] The King held his court at Gloucester, as he usually did when concerned about Wales, but no actual fighting is recorded.

The Chronicles concentrate from 1056 on the return of the *Aetheling*, the activities of Bishop Ealdred, and Stigand's brief acquisition of recognition from Rome. Nothing significant is heard of from Aelfgar after his reinstatement. He is reported to have supported the nomination of Wulstan to Worcester in 1062[15] when Ealdred was forced by the Pope to surrender the see, and the Earl made a grant of land at Lapley, Staffordshire to the church of Rheims on the occasion of his son Burgheard's burial, probably in the same year.[16]

At some point he had married off his daughter, Ealdgyth, to King Gruffydd, no doubt to cement the alliance. They had a daughter, Nest, who became famous in Welsh folklore. It could have been because of that marriage alliance that Aelfgar was outlawed in 1058. Sometime after Gruffydd was killed in 1063, Earl Harold married her to ensure an alliance with her brothers Edwin and Morcar.

The situation in which an Earl of Mercia allied himself to a Celtic prince, probably in defiance of Edward's wishes, could not be tolerated indefinitely, and had Aelfgar survived it is likely that decisive action would have followed eventually. As it was he appears to have died by the end of the year 1062 (or just possibly a little later). In any event, at the Christmas Court of 1062 it was decided to act. The decision could have been triggered by news of Aelfgar's death. The Chroniclers are, unusually for them, silent about his death and it could be that there had been something shameful about it. Had it been another assassination it would certainly have been recorded, as also if he had died in battle or peacefully in his bed like Siward. Aelfgar's son Edwin only appears as Earl in 1065.[17]

Another trigger was the action of Gruffydd who, towards the end of 1062, and again possibly because Aelfgar was now dead and the treaty in which he was involved therefore a dead letter, raided Mercia. He never seems to have entirely held his men back from raiding into England and Florence of Worcester claims that King Edward had suffered 'many insults from him'. The King now dispatched a small force of men under the command of Earl Harold, possibly commissioned to do to him what was done to Rhys ap Rhydderch and assassinate him.

Gruffydd was apparently forewarned of Harold's coming and fled. The Earl and his men reached ap Llewelyn's 'royal' seat at Rhuddlan and there they burnt his residence and his ships and all their sails and returned to England. This had been done in the depths of winter when a full-scale campaign would not have been possible. It was now decided to launch a much bigger campaign and end this menace once and for all. The campaign began shortly before Rogation tide, which that year was at the end of May. It was decided that Harold would sail a fleet from Bristol, around the Welsh coast, no doubt raiding as it went, and forcing the lesser Welsh princes to submit and make peace. Meanwhile, in a sort of pincer movement, Earl Tostig invaded from the landward side, coming in from Northumbria. There is a Roman road from York to Chester that he could have used.

Gruffydd escaped into the mountains of Snowdonia and the earls combined their forces to harry him, devastating the valleys. Gerald of Wales reports that the path blazed by Harold was marked by a series of stones engraved with the words '*Hic fuit victor Heraldus*' (Here Harold was victor). Eventually support for Gruffydd ebbed away and the Welsh turned against him, blaming him for the harrying. On 5 August he was killed by his own men, led by Cynan son of Iago, and beheaded. The head was presented to Harold who took it to King Edward and gave it to him together with the prow of Gruffydd's ship and many other ornaments belonging to him.

The consequences for Wales were grave. The *Vita Edwardi*,[18] which might actually have been written at the time, attributes the planning to Edward because Gruffydd had done him a shameful injury by breaking his word. He had 'carried wrongful war across the Severn' and Edward was determined on revenge. Vast tracts of Welsh land were annexed; Wales again split in two under separate kings, and was to fall into further fragments. Maredudd and Rhys ap Owain seized power in Deheubarth (Carmarthen) and Cadwgan ap Meurig in

Morgannwg (Glamorgan). King Edward appointed Gruffydd's two brothers, Bleddyn and Rhiwallon as lords of Wales and they gave hostages to him and to Earl Harold. As was usual, they swore oaths to him to be loyal in all things and to be ready to serve him everywhere on sea and on land, and promised tribute of the same amount as had formerly been paid to Gruffydd. Florence implies that Gruffydd[19] had been keeping for himself tribute formerly paid to England.

The Welsh were forbidden to carry a spear beyond Offa's Dyke into England on pain of losing their right hand. So many Welshmen had been killed in the campaign that Edward gave permission, revoking a long-standing ban, permitting Welsh women to marry Englishmen. It might have been then that Harold decided to marry Ealdgyth. Such a marriage would have made Harold protector of her young brothers, Edwin and Morcar, and certainly their brother-in-law.[20]

There had now been a revival of English military power, carried out by Earl Harold and inspired by King Edward whose obituary lauds him as 'ruler of heroes, who greatly distinguished, ruled Welsh and Scots and Britons also'.[21]

Scotland

Macbeth, Lord of Moray, began his career at about the same time as Gruffydd ap Llewelyn, by killing King Duncan, not in any 'castle' but most likely in a skirmish or ambush at Bothgoganan near Elgin, probably in 1040 or possibly a little earlier. Macbeth had married Gruoch, a relation of King Malcolm II (Duncan's grandfather) widow of Gillacomgain, Lord of Moray (whose son was Lulach).

The opportunity presented itself to Macbeth to interfere because Malcolm II, who died in 1034, had attempted to alter the Scots laws of succession in favour of patrilinear rather than matrilinear descent and had been succeeded by his son Duncan.

Duncan had attacked Bamburgh and besieged Durham, probably in about 1039 but his attack came to grief and Scottish forces were destroyed.[22] This fatally weakened Duncan's authority.

His marriage had fired Macbeth's ambition and he now made himself King. He proved to be an able and satisfactory ruler for the next fifteen years, not the tyrant depicted by Shakespeare. But the supporters of the dynasty of Kenneth II were opposed to Macbeth's rule, seeking the return of Duncan's sons, Malcolm and Donald, who fled first to Cumberland and the Western Isles respectively, and then to England.

Crinan, abbot of Dunkeld, led a revolt in favour of Malcolm which failed, but in 1054 MacDuff, Lord of Fife, joined the rebellion aided by Earl Siward of Northumbria, whose sister had married Duncan. According to tradition the two sides met at Dunsinnan Hill in Angus, probably a defensible stronghold. Here Macbeth was defeated and routed but not killed. He retreated into northern Scotland. Over the next two years there was protracted skirmishing which ended at Lunmphanan in Aberdeenshire where Macbeth fought Malcolm and MacDuff on 5 December 1056. MacDuff is said to have killed Macbeth.

Macbeth's supporters rallied around Lulach, son of Gillacomgain, who was defeated and became a fugitive until killed by Malcolm on 3 April 1057 at Eassie in Angus. Malcolm was then crowned King of all Scotland at Scone on 25 April.

This civil war in Scotland had been of great assistance to King Edward. The Scots, heavily engaged in internecine warfare, were too preoccupied to attack northern England or give Earl Siward any trouble. Edward therefore adopted the policy of giving support to Malcolm, in order to overthrow Macbeth and put a client king on the throne of Scotland so demonstrating to Northumbria that the southern government had power in the north.

The sons of Duncan had ended up at the English court under Edward's protection. That gave Earl Siward the chance to destabilise Scotland, as King Edward no doubt desired. The English kings were looking for a way to recoup their losses due to the cession of parts of Lothian to Scotland in the tenth century. In fact Macbeth had been a better and more peaceful neighbour for England than Malcolm proved to be.

Internal strife in Northumbria had led to the thegn Karli, Hold of York, killing Ealdred of Bamburgh in 1038 (part of a longstanding feud) which had given Duncan the opportunity to attack. Siward put down Karli's rising but also killed Ealdred's brother Eadulf Cudel in 1041. Siward was still carrying out his commission by Cnut to pacify Northumbria and put an end to its feuds.

Siward never seems to have challenged the Scots control of Lothian but he was carrying out an extension of his earldom to the west. By the end of his life he had won back all the land between the Solway marshes and the Derwent under English rule.[23] His defeat of Macbeth made his acquisitions permanent.

When Edward became king, Siward ruled all of Northumbria from the Humber to the Tweed but the loss of Bernicia was a lost opportunity for Edward to rule a kingdom as extensive as that of Edgar. Nonetheless, he gave Siward his full support, endowing him with estates in the south and supplying men and ships. So in the early 1040s Siward extended his rule into Cumberland.[24] The Earl also invaded Scotland early in Edward's reign and supported Duncan's brother Maldred's bid for the throne.[25]

But his better known intervention came at Edward's behest in 1054 when it was decided to put Malcolm on his father's throne. Macbeth resisted, putting his trust in the Norman knights he had recruited in 1052 when they fled from England. But Siward slaughtered the knights while unfortunately suffering the loss of his son Osbeorn. Malcolm was nominated as King of Scotland while Macbeth fled and Siward retired, job done, to York. The casualties were reputed to have been heavy: some 8,000 Scots as against 1,500 Englishmen.[26]

The Earl, no doubt like Earl Godwine worn out by his labours, died at York in 1055 and was buried in his church, dedicated to

St Olaf, at Galmanho just outside the west wall of the city. He is said to have insisted on being dressed in full armour as he lay dying so that he could 'die with his boots on' so to speak. His recovery of Cumberland had gone some way towards redressing the balance between England and Scotland after the loss of Bernicia.

Edward's decision to send Siward to put Malcolm on the throne of Scotland was an act of aggression and should be attributed to the King, not his *Witan* led by Earl Harold. The Earl's instincts, as his actions in Wales had shown, were to use diplomacy rather than force. Some have suggested that Edward's aggression in Scotland allowed him to discharge his anger over his private problems. By 1054 he was no longer so ready to lead his armies himself.

On Siward's death, Tostig Godwinson was given the earldom of Northumbria. The intention was to put in place a strong man who would secure the frontier with Scotland as Siward had done. Had Tostig been as successful as Siward his rule in the north might have extended beyond 1065. But Tostig, unlike those who had preceded him as earl, was neither a Dane, like Siward, nor a member of the house of Bamburgh. In the end he proved unacceptable to the Northumbrians.

Siward's settlement of the Scottish problem proved much more short-lived than expected. Malcolm III's killing of both Macbeth, in 1057, and his successor, Lulach, in 1058, freed him in his own view from any debt to the English, especially as the earl who had put him on the throne was now dead. Malcolm now felt no debt of gratitude to King Edward and determined to recover Cumbria. Raiding began again almost immediately.

Tostig adopted a policy possibly modelled on that of his brother Harold in Wales. According to the *Vita Edwardi*,[27] in the face of Scots harassment and raids (rather than war), Tostig preferred to spare his own men and to wear down the Scots 'as much by cunning schemes as by martial courage and military campaigns.' No details of his methods are given, though one might suspect bribery played a part and, judging from his actions in 1065, some well-judged assassinations. In the end Malcolm was prevailed upon to visit King Edward at court, accompanied by the Earl himself, Cynsige, Archbishop of York, and Aethelwine, Bishop of Durham.[28]

It is usually accepted that the court was at Gloucester, which seems a long way for the Scots king to agree to come. The rather unreliable source, Geoffrey Gaimar[29] hints at a meeting much further north, saying that Edward went near Northumberland and that Malcolm came as far as the Tweed. The King could have held his court at York that year, and if so that would have been most unusual, as English Kings rarely travelled north of the Humber, but not impossible.[30]

As was usual on such occasions, a general peace was agreed and the Earl and King Malcolm became sworn brothers, the traditional northern custom signifying an alliance. Malcolm would have been expected to offer his thanks to Edward and to accept that he was Edward's vassal, and do homage. He possibly saw this as acknowledgement of the fact that he now held Lothian by agreement with Edward rather than that he held Scotland as a vassal. Orderic Vitalis puts words into Malcolm's mouth in his account of his invasion of Northumbria in 1091, and has Malcolm claim that King Edward gave him Lothian.[31] The death of Archbishop Cynsige on 22 December 1059 deprived Tostig of an ally with long experience of Northumbrian politics. He was replaced by Bishop Ealdred who brought political and diplomatic skills but lacked the northern experiences, contacts and connections of Cynsige.

Satisfied that all was well in his province, Earl Tostig decided to accompany Ealdred when he went to Rome for his pallium. That proved a serious mistake. Malcolm, believing perhaps that his peace agreement only operated when the Earl was in England, laid waste Northumberland and ravaged Lindisfarne. His depredations may have extended as far as Durham, but if this was an attempt to recover Cumbria, it failed.

On his return Tostig took no action against Malcolm, though his participation in Harold's Welsh campaign shows that he was not slow to fight when needful. If the *Vita* is right, he probably preferred to remind Malcolm of their sworn brotherhood and persuaded the Scottish King to 'confirm the peace by giving hostages'. Unfortunately the writer of the *Vita* did not fulfil his promise to give more details.[32]

Earl Tostig's policies with regard to Scotland might well have undermined his military reputation and credibility and encouraged opposition in Northumbria. His administrative changes there, and law enforcement, as well as heavy taxation, clashed with the interests of the thegns of York and the House of Bamburgh.

Northumbria

In England the King had always controlled ecclesiastical appointments and, in 1060, he did so again. Just as he had allowed Stigand in 1052 to retain Winchester when appointed to Canterbury, so he allowed Ealdred to retain Worcester when appointed to York. It was not an unexpected appointment; it had long been customary to permit York to be held in conjunction with Worcester since King Edgar had appointed Oswald. The purpose was to compensate York for the lands lost during the Viking wars which could not now be recovered from the descendants of the Danish invaders.

Ealdred was probably also appointed to provide Tostig with an ecclesiastical ally who had both political and diplomatic skills. But he proved less useful than had been hoped simply because he lacked any natural allies or contacts in Northumbria. Little is known of his predecessor Archbishop Cynsige but the even tenor of his episcopate suggests that he had acquired connections and won over the thegns, making himself familiar with the problems of local politics.

There was an ecclesiastical hurdle to be got over. The King could not afford to have two Archbishops out of communion with Rome and without a legitimate pallium. He had to have at least one to whom bishops and abbots could go for consecration. Stigand was never removed simply because he was too politically powerful and useful, but his position remained irregular. He had made no further effort to secure approval at Rome and would probably have been rejected if he had. He remained the loyal or at least obedient royal servant he had always been since his first promotion from Cnut's household to Elmham.

Edward needed a man of similar usefulness for York and appointed Ealdred who had been a firm ally of Earl Harold since 1051. Accordingly, Ealdred set out for Rome to secure a pallium and, to secure maximum chances of success, Tostig decided to accompany him, and a large embassy set out in 1060. In the party was a young man called Gospatric, a member of the House of Bamburgh (possibly as a hostage for the security of peace in Northumbria). The other ecclesiastics in the party included Wulfwig of Dorchester, and Giso and Walter, the new appointees to Wells and Hereford.[33] The object was to secure approval of their appointments also.

But there were immediate problems. Doubts were raised about the validity of the bishops' consecrations, and there were objections to reports of pluralism in England. The Pope, Nicholas II, in synod, confirmed and approved the two episcopal appointments and found in favour of Wulfwig of Dorchester in his claim that Lindsey came under the jurisdiction of Dorchester rather than York. Otherwise the mission was a shambles, since Nicholas rejected Ealdred, and the Earl and the Bishop began an ignominious return home.

Then fate intervened. A Tuscan 'nobleman', Gerard of Galleria, one of those who had brought about the election of Benedict X, was little more than a brigand. He now kidnapped a large part of Tostig's party in order to make the Pope a laughing stock who could not protect distinguished visitors to Rome. Gospatric, who was very finely dressed, distinguished himself. He allowed Gerard to believe that he was the Earl, while Tostig made good his escape. Fortunately for Gospatric the brigands, on discovering that they had been deceived, were overwhelmed by the young man's audacity and loyalty to his lord and released him unharmed.

Tostig, meanwhile, had stormed back to Rome and furiously confronted an embarrassed Pope. He insisted that the fact that his embassy had been attacked while under the Pope's protection was an outrage meriting withdrawal of the payment of 'Peter's Pence', the subsidy paid by the English to Rome. He berated the Pope for not securing the safety of travellers and declared that no one would fear excommunication by a Pope unable to control the surroundings of Rome itself. Nicholas and the cardinals, alarmed at the prospect of losing such a lucrative source of revenue, caved in. Tostig was invited to sit in synod with the Pope and a compromise was worked out to allow Ealdred his pallium.

The Pope excommunicated Gerard of Galleria, so speeding up the release of Gospatric and mollifying Tostig, but while granting a pallium, as desired, insisted that Ealdred surrender his lucrative See of Worcester, so saving the Pope's face. King Edward was to be advised to appoint someone else and to receive the Pope's legate to supervise the appointment and conduct an inspection of the English church. Ealdred probably suggested the name of his replacement, Wulfstan. Earl Tostig was further placated by splendid gifts and apostolic blessings.

Tostig's embassy had reached Rome in 1061 and the Papal synod had been held at Easter, 15 April. Ealdred had also been commissioned to secure Papal privileges for the King's new church at Westminster.[34] A papal bull was issued dated 3 May 1061 for Edward 'our friend'. Bulls were also issued for Giso and Walter; legates were sent to enforce the terms. Led by Ermenfrid, Bishop of Sion, the legates conducted a tour of inspection, accompanied by Ealdred, and allowed Stigand to sit in council with them. They expressed themselves satisfied with the state of the English Church.

After assisting his brother, Earl Harold, on campaign in Wales, Tostig was emboldened to tighten his hold on Northumbria, sure of Ealdred's support. It might have been at this time that he recruited the Anglo-Scandinavian thegn Copsige as his man of affairs, probably leaving him in charge of Northumbria while the Earl was in Rome and on campaign. Symeon of Durham records Earl Tostig's efforts to placate and enlist the support of the Community of the Canons of St Cuthbert, making elaborate gifts. Such generosity usually paid off but on this occasion it failed. The issue was their right of free election of the bishops of Durham. After Siward's death and the appointment of Tostig, the previous Bishop, Aethelric, put in place by Siward, had resigned his see and retired to Peterborough. The Community had been glad to be rid of him since he was the first non-Northerner to be appointed to Durham and lacked local support. The Community had even briefly driven him out of office in about 1045 but Siward had forcibly reinstated him.

Tostig further alienated the community by recommending Aethelwine as his brother's successor and overriding the Community's right of election. Nonetheless, and contradictorily, Symeon records warm tributes to Tostig, his wife Judith and to Copsige, for their generosity.[35] The Earl's prestige suffered further when the frontier with Scotland did not hold, though things did improve a little after Malcolm's visit to King Edward in 1059. Although Malcolm resumed raiding in 1060–61 during Tostig's absence in Rome, he did not do so during the campaign in Wales, which suggests a détente had been achieved.

But overall, Tostig's policies, emanating perhaps from decisions of the *Witan*, were threatening the reviving fortunes of the Bernician aristocracy as well as alarming the thegns of York. Nothing is known of what transpired during 1064 because the Chronicles are silent for that year, recording nothing. Even Florence of Worcester and the *Vita Edwardi* add nothing. But at the Christmas Court of 1064 (recorded under 1065), Queen Edith was believed to have brought about the death of Uhtred's last surviving son, Gospatric brother of Eadulf, sons of Uhtred's second wife, Sige. This is not the Gospatric who went to Rome (and was possibly a grandson of Aethelred).

Northumbria in Revolt

Tostig in 1063 murdered the key Yorkshire thegns Gamal son of Orm and Ulf son of Dolfin, who had come to see him in his hall at York under safe conduct.[36] The Earl either made a pre-emptive strike to rid himself of troublemakers or was embroiled in a feud. He was meeting increasing opposition to his harsh rule and heavy taxation. The murders left Tostig bereft of support in the north and isolated apart from his housecarls, and the households of Bishop Aethelwine and Archbishop Ealdred. A demonstration had been made by the Community of St Cuthbert in the spring of 1065. They had gone out of their way to display their most famous relics of King Oswine of Durham and this may indicate that the Yorkshiremen were attracting support in the north. Bishop Aethelwine had permitted the relics to be disinterred from their tomb in a monastery at the mouth of the Tyne (Jarrow and Wearmouth) and to be placed in a magnificent chest above ground.[37] They were now displayed and the gesture reminded everybody of the murder of Gospatric.[38]

Other sources blame the revolt on reaction to Tostig's law enforcement. Earl Siward had been greatly feared for his severity yet despite that, parties of even twenty or thirty men could be at risk of being killed or robbed because there were so many robbers. Of Tostig, it was claimed that he had reduced the number of robbers and cleared the country of them using mutilation or the death penalty and 'sparing no-one however noble who was caught in this crime' so that men could travel laden with goods without fear of attack.[39] The refusal to spare even members of the nobility explains the reaction. Tostig had not been prepared to accept the payment of wergild and substituted the sort of condign punishments introduced by King Edgar in southern England.

As the *Historia Dunelmensis* reveals, Tostig's enforcement of a West Saxon standard of law was less favourable to the continuation of feuds and lawlessness.[40] He ignored the right of sanctuary, as this story shows. A thegn named Alden-Hamel was pursued by Tostig's agent, Barkwith, and took sanctuary at the shrine of St Cuthbert. Barkwith is said to have been struck down by the saint for violating his sanctuary.[41] No doubt, in fact, Barkwith was attacked by the men of the canons. Yet Tostig in other respects had a good reputation at Durham for his generosity. His name is inscribed in letters of gold in the *Liber Vitae*. He is also named as a benefactor on the sundial at Kirkdale erected when St Gregory's Church was restored, 'in the days of King Edward and in the days of Earl Tostig'. The restoration itself is a sign of more settled and less lawless conditions.

Another possible cause, indicated in the Chronicle, was that he was accused of 'robbing God', that is despoiling the Church by heavy taxation. That he levied higher taxes than his predecessors seems certain.[42] Such an increase in taxation can only have been initiated by the King and his *Witan*, who set the levels for the collection of the *geld*. It is likely that Edward wanted Northumbria to pay *geld* at a level nearer to that paid south of the Humber. The King received two-thirds of all *gelds* as against the Earl's one third. But to do that was to challenge the status quo in the north which had existed since Edgar's time. It is possible that heavier *geld* had been levied to recover the costs of the Welsh war.

The suggestion is that there is evidence, in Domesday Book, that *geld* rates were lower in Northumbria than in Wessex or Mercia. Of the manor of West Derby it is recorded that 'in each hide are six carucates of land'.[43] This means that six carucates paid the same amount of *geld* as one hide. The system has been shown to have applied to all of Lancashire as well as parts of Cumberland and Westmorland and Durham. All these areas paid *geld* as part of Yorkshire at the rate of four pence on each carucate, so that six carucates produced two shillings (if *geld* was levied at two shillings on the hide).[44]

This system of reduced taxation had survived since Wessex annexed York in the mid-tenth century. Tostig, because of his unpopularity, would have required large amounts of money to support his armed household and to pay forces with which to resist the Scots. He had put pressure on the judicial system to produce fines and confiscations and, contrary to custom, levied higher levels of *geld*. The effect of any change can be demonstrated. He could, for instance, have levied the same sum, two shillings, on four rather than six carucates. That would still have been less than was levied south of the Humber, but would have been a fifty per cent increase in taxation. Applied to the three known leaders of the revolt, the result is as follows:[45] Gamal Barn holding about sixty carucates and paying a *geld* of twenty shillings, with the new levy would be expected to pay thirty shillings; Dunstan holding forty-eight carucates, paying sixteen shillings, would be expected to pay twenty-four; Gleniairnn having thirty-nine carucates, paying thirteen shillings, would be expected to pay nineteen shillings and sixpence.[46]

Even if the amount of *geld* demanded was levied only in pence not shillings, the thegns would still have faced a fifty per cent increase. The policy might have been that of the King and his *Witan*, but the Earl got the blame. It also suggests forcibly that King Edward did in fact levy the *geld* during his reign and after 1052.

Resistance to such changes had united the Anglo-Danes of Yorkshire and the English followers of the house of Bamburgh, despite the fact that they were traditional enemies. They made common cause against Earl Tostig and even after he had been outlawed and ejected, they compromised their rival claims by demanding recognition of their own man as earl: Morcar, brother of Earl Edwin, thus ensuring the support of Mercia. Waltheof was still too young to be useful; Gospatrick son of Maldred and Osulf son of Eadulf probably not acceptable to everybody. The latter two were almost certainly not acceptable at York. Only a candidate from the House of Leofric was acceptable to all parties, so Morcar's name was put to the King. Unlike Tostig he was not married and might be prepared to marry into the house of Bamburgh. Morcar probably had contacts at York as he held ten carucates at Fulford, nine and a half at Clifton and had a hall at Overton with another five carucates. He and his brother Edwin held land in several other places.

On 3 October 1065, while Earl Tostig was hunting near Britford in Wiltshire with the King, the Northumbrians, led by Gamal Barn, Dunstan son of Athelneth and Gleniairnn son of Heardulf entered York with two hundred men, seeking revenge for the deaths of the three Northumbrian thegns killed by Tostig and 'on account of the heavy tribute which he unjustly laid on the whole of Northumbria'.[47] They seized Tostig's leading housecarls, Amund and Ravensuart, and put them to death outside the walls of York. Next day they slaughtered more than two hundred of Tostig's tenants, broke open his treasury and carried off all his property.

That was a signal for all the men of the earldom to join them and march on Northampton looting and burning as they advanced, and carrying hundreds of men off into slavery. At Northampton they made their demands. Having already sent for Morcar, intending that he should be their earl, they advanced, still ravaging, into Nottinghamshire, Derbyshire and Lincolnshire.

At Northampton they were joined by Earl Edwin and the Mercian army, with many Welsh allies. The presence of Welshmen probably explains why the Chronicler, in reporting the attack on Harold's hunting lodge at Portskewett earlier in the year (24 August) by Caradoc son of Gruffydd ap Rhydderch, wonders whether there was a conspiracy in the offing.[48]

King Edward, at Britford, summoned his *Witan* and took counsel. There was a heated debate, some accusing Tostig of cruelty and punishing men out of a desire to confiscate their property while others suggested it was all got up by Earl Harold. Tostig even went so far as to charge Harold with plotting against him.[49] The *Vita* author in reporting this is careful to distance himself from such calumnies. Harold was forced to clear himself on oath of this allegation, though the *Vita* writer snidely remarks that he was 'too generous with oaths, alas!'. That was a general criticism of the Earl rather than a reference to the alleged oath at Bayeux.

The King sent messengers several times to the rebels, vainly trying to persuade them to see reason. Frustrated by their failure to obey him, Edward began to rage furiously, issuing orders for the *fyrd* to be called out and the rebellion to be crushed. But cooler heads, led perhaps by Earl Harold, counselled that it was inadvisable to attempt a campaign at that time of year as winter was fast approaching and the weather already changing. They stressed the difficulty of raising sufficient men in time. Most of all they expressed horror, as in 1051, at the prospect of civil war and 'strove to calm the raging spirit of the King' urging that no attack should be mounted but that negotiations should continue.

This contest of wills lasted for some days but eventually, and again as in 1051, the King gave in to the pressure exerted by his *Witan*. Earl Harold was commissioned to negotiate, as he had done in the past, and met the rebels at Northampton. They begged him to intercede for them with the king and secure his agreement to their demand that Morcar be their Earl. They said that they had unanimously outlawed Earl Tostig. Harold was unable to persuade the rebels to be reconciled with the Earl so on 27 October Harold returned to the King, who was now at Oxford, and relayed to him their insistence on having Morcar for Earl. The rebels had unanimously outlawed Tostig, with the support of Earl Edwin, on the grounds that he had 'robbed God and plundered all those over whom he had power as to life and land'.[50] Then on the following day the Earl announced at Northampton that the King had conceded their demands and would recognise Morcar as Earl of Northumbria. Harold also delivered the King's pledge to them that the 'Laws of Cnut' were renewed, perhaps displaying the King's writ and seal while doing so.

Edward could well have been reminded, by all this, of his previous pledge to observe the Laws of Cnut when he arrived back in England after his exile. The rebels, for their part, had advanced close to Oxford, or at least parties of them had, and maintained their pressure on the king. The rebellion had been the work of the men of two of the great earldoms, Northumbria and Mercia (revealing that Wessex could not really stand alone against the rest of the country without fighting). The situation was reminiscent of the accession of King Edgar with the combined support of the Mercians and the Northumbrians in 959. But this time it was a demand for their choice of earl and the renewal of the laws of Cnut.

The 'Law of Cnut' represented the whole pattern and essence of northern rule as undermined by Earl Tostig in bringing intensive southern government to the north. It stood for the concessions to Scandinavian customs maintained by Cnut's Codes.

Earl Tostig, either unable to bear the humiliation of his removal from office or in fear of his life, moved his wife Judith and his entire household to Flanders where they took refuge with Count Baldwin. There he spent the winter gathering support and planning his revenge, though those events fall outside the scope of this work.

The court, so it is claimed, went into mourning at the loss of the Earl and no doubt some were shocked and dismayed.[51] Edith was certainly distressed since Tostig appears to have been her favourite. Members of the household are said to have 'deduced future disasters from the signs of the present' and Edith, in tears, feared the worst, even open war between her brothers. Rich gifts were heaped on Tostig and he was allowed to go.

The King's health began to suffer and he fell ill. The *Vita Edwardi* claims that he had a sickness of mind, was plunged into deep sorrow, complaining to God in his prayers at being deprived of his men's obedience and calling down God's vengeance on them. No doubt he did mourn the loss of Tostig and was deeply unhappy and frustrated. But the *Vita* cannot be entirely trusted at this point and events are described from Edith's point of view. It suited her agenda to suggest that the King had been made ill by the frustration of his wishes. The text laments that the Queen had been 'bereft of all support by the powerlessness of her husband'. She was more concerned about the loss of her own influence than about anything else.

But winter had come, a particularly harsh one if the *Vita* is accurate, and Edward was now about 63 years old, an old man by the standards of the time. There had been no sign of ill health before these events developed; he was busy as usual hunting in

Wiltshire. Yet at Christmas that year he died quite suddenly just after midwinter. His resistance to illness might have been sapped by his bout of melancholia, possibly even depression. But melancholia and depression do not normally kill. He is described as taking to his bed as he perceived 'that the power of the disease was forcing him to his end' and prepared for death.

He was unable to attend the consecration of Westminster Abbey on 28 December. He was 'consumed by the fire of his illness'[52] and became 'drowsy because of his body's heaviness', with bouts of deep sleep. He began to have feverish dreams or even delirium and gave vent to rambling discourses which were taken as prophetic. Archbishop Stigand was heard to say that he was broken with age and disease and knew not what he said. Despite that, he rallied and had intervals of lucidity in which he gave instructions for his funeral and for the disposal of the kingdom after his death. His feet became icy cold and had to be warmed by Edith.[53] All of this sounds like the onset of pneumonia.

Having taken the *Viaticum*, his final Holy Communion (and no doubt having received all the other Last Rites of the Church) and leaving orders that he be buried in his great church at Westminster, he died, probably overnight on the eve of 4 January, and was declared dead on the morning of 5 January.[54] He was buried on the Feast of the Epiphany, 6 January 1066.

Until Edward took to his bed he had still been dealing with royal business. He left one legal case unsettled, intending to deal with it at his Christmas *Witan*. His discourses on the content of his dreams were taken to be the prophecies of a saintly man and became part of the account of his sanctity. But in what was his last lucid interval he dealt with the succession to the throne, and took care to ensure the protection of his wife, the Queen, and of his foreign servants in the royal household. In the presence of a number of people whom, when roused from sleep, he had ordered to be summoned, namely the Queen, Edith, her brother, Earl Harold, Robert FitzWymarc (described as steward of the palace) and Archbishop Stigand, and a few of his faithful foreign servants, the King made his final decision regarding the succession. Yet the *Vita Edwardi*, which stresses several times that the King's mind was disturbed, tries to obscure what was done, possibly in Edith's interest.

Edith's writer waters down the significance but does not dare to deny what had been done. The witnesses cannot be said to have been weighted in Earl Harold's favour and the Chroniclers seem satisfied with the result. Certainly the *Witan*, which had assembled in force for the consecration of Westminster and in the expectation of a Christmas council readily confirmed Harold's succession. In the chronicles it is plainly stated that:

> The wise King did entrust his kingdom to a man of high rank,
> To Harold himself, the noble earl, who ever faithfully
> obeyed his noble lord in words and deeds, neglecting
> nothing whereof the national king stood in need.[55]

The third Chronicler states simply; 'Earl Harold succeeded to the Kingdom as the king granted it to him and he was elected thereto.'[56] Florence of Worcester elaborates on this, saying 'The *sub-regulus* (under-king) Harold, son of Earl Godwine, whom the king had nominated as his successor, was elected king by the chief nobles of all England.' The *Vita* account should thus be understood in this context. It says that Edward stretched out his hand to his 'governor' (in the sense of protector), Harold and said:

> I commend this woman [Edith] and all the kingdom to your protection.
> Serve and honour her with faithful obedience as your lady and sister,
> Which she is, and do not despoil her, as long as she lives, of any due honour got from me.

The scene is faithfully rendered by the Bayeux Tapestry[57] with the same principal actors present and the King touching Harold's hand.

Even William of Poitiers was forced to admit that Harold had been bequeathed the throne.[58]

It rather looks as though the writer of the *Vita Edwardi* (whether he was Goscelin or Folcard or some other monk of St Bertin, there is no way of knowing) has re-ordered the '*verba novissima*' or testamentary last words of King Edward to suit Queen Edith's needs. She needed to be sure that her position as dowager queen, widow of King Edward, was recognised. She might have had visions of herself as a dominant figure like her mother-in-law, Queen Emma. The *Vita Edwardi* might in part have been intended to do for Edith what the *Encomium Emmae* had done for Queen Emma. Both documents are highly political. The King's deathbed scene in the *Vita* was most likely written after the Conquest when Edith needed to ensure good treatment by William the Bastard and could not afford to offend him by being too definite about Harold's claims.

If this be accepted, then it follows that King Edward had probably made three main statements, dealing with the position first of Earl Harold, then of Queen Edith, and finally that of his foreign household servants. The Bayeux Tapestry states simply that, in his last moments, he 'addressed his liegemen', his '*fideles*' or vassals. Edith is shown in the background behind figures representing Earl Harold, in the foreground, and Archbishop Stigand at his shoulder. The King is almost touching Harold's outstretched hand. The Earl is the most prominent vassal present.

A possible reconstruction of what was said would be that the King first addressed Earl Harold and said something like 'I commend all the Kingdom to your protection', thus entrusting the kingdom to him as the Chroniclers state. Then, still addressing Harold, he commended Edith to his protection also, and then thirdly said, 'Likewise, I commend those men who have left their native land for love of me and have up till now served me well'. Harold was asked either to accept from them an oath of fealty (as to a King) if they wished to serve him and he was willing to have them, or to allow them to return home under safe conduct. Finally the King ordered that he be buried in Westminster and that his death be announced so that all might pray for his soul. He then took Holy Communion and died. His words addressed personally to Edith preceded the '*verba novissima*', when he asked God to be gracious to her, so that she might 'obtain the reward of eternal happiness', because of her zealous service to Edward, as she had 'always stood close by my side like a beloved daughter'. This is quite separate from the address to Earl Harold.[59]

The Bayeux Tapestry conveys an impression of haste by depicting the King's burial and then showing his deathbed speech and actual death in two scenes one above the other. Following that, two men, representing the *Witan*, one bearing a ceremonial axe, point back to the dead King and present the crown to Earl Harold, and the title reads 'Here they gave the crown to Harold', who is then depicted crowned and enthroned in full regalia of orb and sceptre. To one side stand two nobles, one holding the Sword of State, and on the other stands Archbishop Stigand, robed and vested, addressing the unseen audience.

There was in fact no unseemly haste. It was purely a matter of expediency and convenience. The *Witan* had already assembled for the consecration of Westminster and the Christmas court and had remained in London when it became obvious that the King was dying. Harold was designated as Edward's successor and the *Witan* met and 'elected' him, confirming the nomination and consenting to it, and the coronation automatically followed. A change of dynasty required that the formalities be completed without unnecessary delay. It was surely recognised that Harold's succession would be contested, there were at least two Scandinavians who might challenge him, King Swein of Denmark, nephew of Cnut the Great, and King Harald Hardrada of Norway who might revive the sketchy claims of King Magnus. It is unlikely that anyone other than Harold thought of William of Normandy.

1 Cnut and Queen Emma. From the New Minster Register, Winchester.

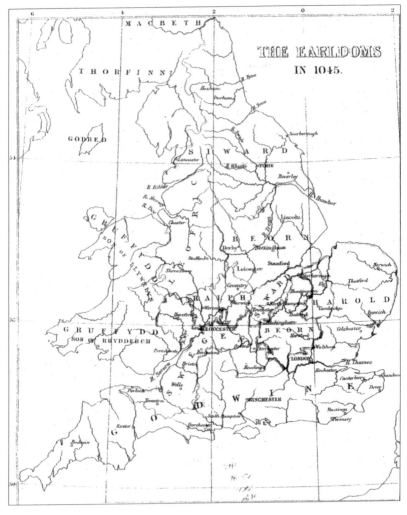

2 The earldoms in 1045.

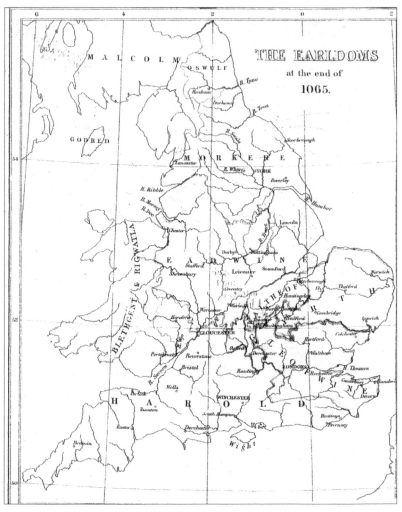

3 The earldoms in 1065.

REMAINS OF THE SHRINE OF EDWARD THE CONFESSOR, WESTMINSTER ABBEY.

4 The remains of King Edward's Shrine at Westminster.

5 Edward the Confessor's Chapel at Westminster; the only surviving remnant of the Anglo-Saxon building.

6 Dioceses of England under Edward the Confessor; showing many of the places referred to in the text.

7 View of the Tower of Bosham Church.

8 Hurst Point as seen from the Isle of Wight. Edward's landing place in 1041.

9 Bosham Harbour from which Earl Harold set sail in 1064.

Earl Siward
NORTHUMBRIA

Earl Leofric
MERCIA

Earl Harold

EAST ANGLIA

WALES

Earl Ralph

Earl Godwin

10 Map of England after Earl God-wine's return in 1052.

Earl Odda

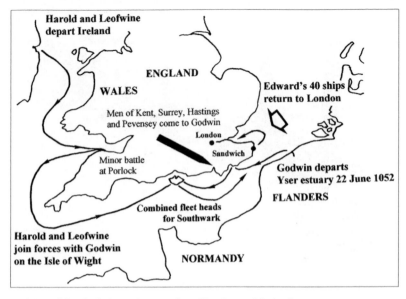

11 Map of the Godwinsons' return from Flanders and Ireland.

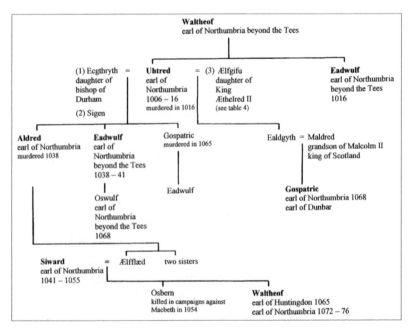

12 The House of Bamburgh: Descendants of Earl Waltheof I of Northumbria.

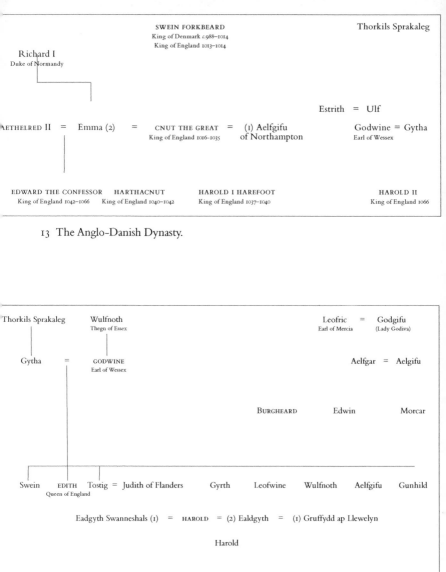

13 The Anglo-Danish Dynasty.

14 The House of Godwine.

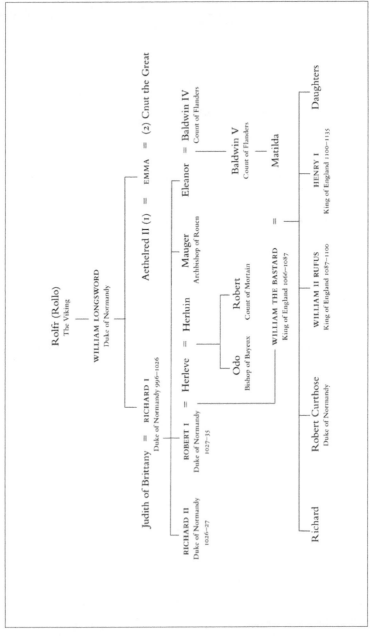

15 Descendants of King Aetheired II and Richard I of Normandy.

16 Impressions of King Edward's Great Seal.

17 Edward the
Confessor from a
painting at Ludham,
Norfolk.

18 King Edward and Earl Harold.

19 Bosham Church.

20 Earl Harold feasts at Bosham.

21 Earl Harold embarks at Bosham.

22 Earl Harold crosses the sea.

23 Duke William learns of the arrival of the Earl.

24 Earl Harold swears that oath.

25 Earl Harold returns to King Edward.

26 The Death and Burial of King Edward.

27 Westminster Abbey.

13

Succession and Subterfuge

Thus far little attention has been paid to the activities and claims of William the Bastard, Duke of Normandy. In truth, Normandy had made little impact on the course of events in England. Norman sources add little to what is known from English sources. They say really very little about the sojourn of the *Aethelings* in Normandy and what they do say consists of sweeping generalisations. Their doings made little impact on the affairs of Normandy. William of Malmesbury comments: 'For their restoration to their own country their uncle, Richard, took, I find, no steps; in fact he married his sister Emma to the enemy, the invader … who had harassed her husband and exiled her sons'.[1]

Only after Edward returned to England in 1041 do the Normans have much to say and then it is to make the dubious claim that Edward's accession to the throne owed much to the support and endorsement of the boy duke, a claim aimed more at enhancing William's prestige than explaining Edward's return.

Normans do figure in the crisis of 1051 but only Archbishop Robert played any significant part, and he was ignominiously driven out. The Duke plays no significant part in it and the sole reference to him in English sources is never used by Norman writers to enhance their case. Indeed William of Poitiers implies that his idol, Duke William, never received the promise of the succession in person. Always the promise is offered through intermediaries. Their accounts differ as to time and place and even the personnel involved and contradict one another quite freely. The actual year when the alleged promise was given is never specified and no context for it is provided. It is difficult to see when, in the course of events in England, such a promise could have been made.

No matter which year is selected the difficulties remain insuperable. Nor are the reasons given to explain why Edward should have made such a promise any better. It is alleged that the King was grateful for the 'sumptuous liberality' towards him displayed by Duke William and for the 'singular honour' bestowed on him. William is said to have shown him 'intimate affection', yet there was about twenty-four years' difference in age between them. Further, the Normans claim 'a long line of consanguinity' between the two rulers, though William was only Emma's great nephew and there were others, such as Ralph of Mantes, more closely related to Edward.

It is asserted that Duke William sustained Edward in his hope of a return from exile and that it was 'through his support and counsel that, on the death of Harthacnut, Edward was at last crowned and placed on his father's throne'. Accordingly, it is alleged that Edward 'wished to recognize him [William] in a way befitting his [Edward's] power and gratitude' and so 'determined by lawful donation to make him his heir to the crown which he had gained through his help'. None of this can be substantiated and there is no shred of evidence for it in English sources.

On the contrary, Edward's return was entirely the work of Queen Emma and her son Harthacnut, and his accession owed much to the support of Earl Godwine of Wessex and other English supporters. One account argues that Edward had been in two minds about accepting the crown and had to be persuaded to do so by

Earl Godwine on the grounds that it was better 'to live in glory on his throne than to die in obscurity in exile'.[2] He reminds Edward of 'his early privations' (in Normandy) which had taught him 'how to moderate the hardships of his subjects'. That paints a very different picture of what was known of Edward's life in exile. Edward is further described as being 'weary of his years of wandering' and so had been ready to accept Harthacnut's invitation to return.[3]

The young Duke William, born circa 1027/28, was much younger than Edward, and in 1042 only about fifteen. He was still at risk of losing his hold on Normandy and in fact gave Edward little help. He provided or permitted only a small escort of Normans to accompany the *Aetheling* in 1041. That was excused by Norman writers on the grounds that the English would only consent to a small entourage. William had scarcely any influence in England at all.

Nor is there any sign of the 'singular honours' or of any 'liberality' towards Edward on William's part, or that of his predecessors. William's father, Duke Robert the Magnificent, allowed the *Aethelings* to attend him at court and is alleged to have contemplated restoring Edward by force, though nothing came of it. But there is no evidence that the *Aethelings* were anything more than ducal pensioners, and useful pawns in diplomatic manoeuvres. No lands are recorded as having been bestowed on them and no-one claims that any were. Without lands of their own they would have been of little account in a feudal society.

That Edward had been so well treated in Normandy that he remained permanently grateful to the dukes and anxious to repay them for their generosity is a travesty of the truth. Exiles are notoriously fickle in their affections and liable to bite the hand that feeds them. (Consider the case of General de Gaulle; driven out of France and given refuge and aid in England, restored to France by Anglo-American force, he remained hostile to both England and America.)

Nor was there much sign of any connections between the Norman Court and those Normans who had followed Edward to England in the hope of making their fortunes. Few were men of substance in Normandy or the neighbouring states. The most high-ranking layman was in fact Edward's own nephew, Ralph of Mantes. Osbern Pentecost was given enough land to support a castle in Herefordshire, as possibly also his associate Hugh. Of other 'French' settlers little is known but the handful whose names survive were of little account.

The Norman clergy did somewhat better, but even they were mainly friends and supporters acquired by Edward while in Normandy and recruited to staff his clerical household. The most prominent of these, Robert Champart, former abbot of Jumièges, was an old friend, and was promoted first to London and then as Archbishop. His associate Ulf was made bishop of Dorchester (and did nothing bishoplike) and the third Norman bishop, William, only obtained London in 1051. None of these men, clerical or lay, had any real influence back in Normandy. Edward in fact promoted more Lotharingians than Normans to office in the Church and created no Norman abbots at all. After 1052 Norman influence declined even more than Danish influence had done, while Lotharingian influence continued.

Yet the Normans insist that William was designated heir to the English throne, a claim that appears to exist in a political and historical vacuum. Norman writers, for instance, know nothing of the crisis of 1051. When closely examined the Norman claims look increasingly dubious. The first attempt was made by William of Jumièges in Book Seven of his *Gesta Normannorum Ducum*.[4] He states quite unequivocally that Edward, because he had no heir, sent Robert, Archbishop of Canterbury, to Duke William 'with a message appointing him as heir to the kingdom which God had entrusted to him'. He adds further that the King, much later, sent Earl Harold so 'that he might guarantee the crown to the duke by his fealty and confirm the same [fealty or guarantee?] with an oath according to Christian usage'. He gives no indication of when or where these things were done nor advances any witnesses. He simply transforms Robert's flight into a mission to offer William the throne, so he must have known that the idea came to the Duke from the Archbishop. There is no supporting evidence for it. That William of Poitiers says something similar, and that he says Harold was sent 'to confirm his [Edward's] promise on oath', is mere repetition not independent verification. This writer has his own version of the promise which in many ways contradicts that of his predecessor. William of Malmesbury, with his customary scepticism, says only that 'some say' Harold was sent by the King, but others 'more familiar with his secret intentions maintain he was driven there against his will by the violence of the wind'.[5]

The most obvious occasion when the Archbishop might have conveyed such an offer would have been in 1050–51 when he went to Rome for his pallium. He could have passed through Normandy to do so. Yet this momentous decision had apparently been taken without reference to the *Witan* and no English source, neither the Anglo-Saxon Chronicle nor the *Vita Edwardi Regis*, makes any reference to it, nor is it raised in the context of the dispute with Earl Godwine despite the rejection of all Norman influence in 1052. If it had been done in 1050–51, then it ought to have been part of the quarrel between the King and the Earl. William of Poitiers raises more problems with his claim that the promise was agreed to by the three great earls and Archbishop Stigand, which points to 1052. The problem with that is that it could not then have been carried to William by Archbishop Robert. Nor was it done when William visited Edward in 1052 and no Norman suggests that it was. It is implicit in the Norman narratives that the Duke never set foot in England before the Conquest, though nothing would have better fitted their version of Anglo-Norman relations than the visit of 1052. 'It is little short of astonishing that they failed to record it'.[6] William of Poitiers relates the events of the sieges of Alençon and Domfront with no reference to any visit to England.[7]

In any case, King Edward's decision (and Florence of Worcester attributes the decision to the King) in 1054 to discover the whereabouts of his nephew, Edward, son of King Edmund Ironside, with a view to making him his heir, made with the consent of the *Witan* and recorded in the Chronicles, cancels any previous alleged decision.

The Norman accounts were written after the Conquest, and are set in the context of Earl Harold's sojourn in Normandy. Ultimately, what they say must derive from reports of what was said at that time. Neither writer appears to have been an eyewitness. William of Poitiers actually admits that he is relying on the testimony of the 'most truthful and most honourable men who were there present', none of whom he names. The only Norman magnates he does name are only named in the context of the decision of Duke William, in 1066, to 'regain his inheritance by war.' How could he 'regain' something he never had?

William of Poitiers presents a much fuller account[8] that differs significantly from that of William of Jumièges. As was the convention in writing 'history' at that time, Poitiers puts his attempts into the mouths of various participants. He says that Harold sent an envoy, after the Norman landing, to command Duke William to leave England and reports the envoy's words. They are, of course, the words of the writer and there is no evidence that they are verbatim. He wasn't there. So he has the envoy say that Harold admits that King Edward had sent him to confirm the promise to Duke William. This is a rhetorical device to allow the writer to state the claim. He then puts a speech into the mouth of William himself in which he asserts that he is Edward's heir and that Edward had chosen him 'because of the honours and rich benefits conferred upon him and his brother and their followers by me and by my magnates'. He has the duke add that Edward held him to be 'the best capable of supporting him during his life and giving just rule to the kingdom after his death'. Yet William had never been in a position to confer such benefits on either Edward or Alfred (the latter was killed in 1036) and there is no evidence of any benefits whatsoever given to Edward.

He also asserts that the offer had been made with the consent of the three earls and Archbishop Stigand. In that case it could not have been done in 1050-51 or earlier when Stigand was bishop of Winchester, not archbishop. If the date was early then Archbishop Robert should have been named, not Stigand. If it had been done when Stigand was bishop, there would have been no political force in naming him; he is named solely because he was an archbishop. But if the occasion was 1052, after the restoration of Godwine, there was no reason why the Earl should have agreed to it. The four magnates are also said to have sworn '*manibus junctis*', by placing their hands between those of Edward, to serve William as their lord after Edward's death. That is Norman custom. In England, men 'bowed' to a lord and swore oaths on the Gospels or relics, not in this subservient feudal manner.

In addition, Godwine was said to have been required to surrender a son and grandson as hostages (although if hostages were required, they ought to have been exchanged). He would never have done so in 1052. Nor does it make any sense that no hostages were required from the other magnates. Much of this is thus quite unacceptable and does not fit an English context. None of the statements given were the actual words of the duke but no doubt he was saying something like it. It is thought that William of Poitiers derived his statements from the brief presented at Rome to secure Pope Alexander II's blessing on the 'enterprise of England'. Poitiers claims that the Duke was given a Papal banner, and relics, as a pledge of the support of St Peter. Popes during this period of the eleventh century were in the habit of bestowing such banners on those whose actions they wished to endorse.

The Papal blessing was secured for Duke William through the influence of Archdeacon Hildebrand (later Pope Gregory VII) and was given after the case had been heard by Pope and Cardinals in King Harold's absence. The King might not even have been informed that Rome was considering the case.

None of the versions of the promise carries conviction. The other details related by William of Poitiers do not help his case. Yet Duke William was convinced, or had convinced himself, of the justice of his cause. On what, then, did he base his claim? He was apparently convinced that he had been informed that King Edward had chosen him to be his heir. The most straightforward version, that of William of Jumièges, simply maintains that he was told it was so by Archbishop Robert. Since the writer, William, and the Archbishop, Robert, were monks of Jumièges, and as Robert returned there after his visit to Rome in 1052 to complain about his expulsion from his See, and died there sometime before 1058, it seems likely that Robert Champart is the source of the story. He is also the most likely person to have handed over hostages to the Duke.

When he was driven out in September 1052, Archbishop Robert and his companions had to fight their way out of London and it is suggested that this was because he had abducted the hostages, the son, Wulfnoth, and grandson, Hacon, of Earl Godwine. It is possible, therefore, that, seeking to vent his rage at being driven out, Robert allowed William to conclude that he was King Edward's chosen successor, producing the hostages as evidence.[9] William of Poitiers declares that Robert was '*huius delegationis mediatorem*', the agent of this grant.[10]

Robert might well have actually tried to persuade Edward that he should offer the succession to the Duke, though his attempt to persuade the King to divorce his wife Edith (so permitting a second and possibly fruitful marriage) argues against it. The suggestion might have been put to the King by his other Norman favourites after the splendour of the duke's reception when he visited earlier in 1052 and Edward might not entirely have ruled it out. But the triumphant return of the Godwines certainly put paid to any such move. Robert, however, might have convinced himself that Edward did intend that the duke should succeed him, and so convinced the duke likewise.

But, if Edward had intended that William be his heir, he did nothing to make it happen. Instead he either chose to seek out his nephew, Edward the Exile, or allowed the *Witan* to do so. If Edward the Exile had lived he would have been the natural choice. He was a member of the royal kin, the *stirps regia* and would have been acceptable to the *Witan*. William of Malmesbury, aware of this, suggested that King Edward gave the succession to the Duke after the death of the Exile, but that is contradicted by the Norman writers themselves.[11] Had Edward intended Duke William to be his heir, then he ought to have been invited to England and put in possession of estates or even crowned or designated as the heir, but it never happened.

There is a much overlooked obstacle to the idea that Edward wanted William of Normandy for his heir: the Duke's bastardy. It would surely have done Edward no honour to nominate a bastard. There was a long-standing tradition in England that no bastard should be king. The Synod of Chelsea in 787, a legatine provincial synod, laid down that only legitimate kings were to be chosen and none resulting from 'adulterous or incestuous [*incestu* = unchaste] procreation'.[12] Orderic Vitalis linked William's bastardy to stories of wrongful seizure, thuggery and poisoning. He removes all of the rhetoric of praise in William of Jumièges' work.[13] He also mentions the attitude of the rebel baron, Roger of Tosny, in Normandy, who refused to obey William, saying that 'a bastard should not rule over him or other Normans'.[14] Orderic calls the Duke the son of a concubine and a bastard, '*utpote notus*' (as is commonly known).[15] Conan of Brittany rejected William's right to hold Breton territory; it was 'against all right because you are a bastard'.

The Normans also rested their case against King Harold on the events in Normandy, probably in the autumn of 1064. The problem is that there is no solid evidence, other than Norman assertions, that Harold was sent to Normandy by King Edward. That Harold set sail for the Continent is certainly the case, as the Bayeux Tapestry shows. He is shown seeking leave to depart from King Edward, though the Tapestry does not say, as it easily could have done, that Edward was sending him anywhere. He dines at Bosham then sets sail and a strong wind causes him to land in Ponthieu. The *Vita Edwardi* asserts that it was Harold's custom to travel on the continent to acquaint himself with the personalities and policies of its rulers so the natural interpretation is that he had set out once again to do so. He might well have been heading for Wissant, Boulogne or Bruges. There is no sign that he was specifically heading for Normandy. He ended up at the River Somme not the Seine.

Ponthieu was dangerous for travellers and a known haunt of 'wreckers' who robbed the unwary. Harold either managed to send for help himself or an agent of the Duke informed him of Harold's plight. Norman accounts maintain that Harold was 'rescued' from a dangerous situation and that the Duke demanded that he be surrendered to his care. It has even been suggested that it was a case of one gangster being trumped by a bigger one.

The details of Harold's sojourn need not be spelt out here. That he was prevailed upon, or compelled, to make a specious commitment to the Duke to support his ambition to succeed King Edward is clear enough. That he was sent specifically to confirm an earlier promise of the succession given by King Edward rests solely on the assertion of the two Norman writers. Whether he was also prevailed upon to become the Duke's vassal implies no justification for William's claim to the throne. It would, if true, have allowed William to depict him in the eyes of European contemporaries as a faithless vassal who had betrayed his lord. That ignored the fact that King Edward was Harold's lord and, as a King, his wishes took precedence over those of a bastard Duke.

Earl Harold probably did swear an oath which committed him to some sort of agreement with William. Most accounts of the matter, outside Normandy, state that Harold had agreed to marry a daughter of the Duke and that the quarrel between them was because he broke his word to do so. It was that and not an oath about the English succession that was widely known throughout western Europe.[16] William would certainly have been mortally offended by Harold's rejection of his daughter. Both an act of homage and an oath obliging Harold to accept a daughter of the Duke in marriage would, if broken, have allowed William to charge Harold with perjury, as he certainly did. He is accused of being a perjurer and oath-breaker and a faithless vassal. It was easy enough, when Harold accepted the crown in January 1066, to add the charge that he had usurped the throne.

Not everyone in Europe recognised William's right to the throne. Sigebert of Gembloux in his work uses the word 'invasit' of William's seizure of England, implying that he was a usurper.[17] An anonymous writer of Cambrai attributes the war to Harold having broken his promise to marry the Duke's daughter, as does the *De Inventione S. Crucis*: 'He was cunningly tricked by the perfidious Normans because he refused to marry the daughter of William of Normandy'.[18] Even Orderic Vitalis relates the tale of Gutmund of la Croix-Saint Lenfoi[19] who refused an endowment from William saying 'Read the Scriptures and see if there is any law that justifies the forcible imposition on a people of God of a shepherd chosen from among their enemies.' Orderic also refers to the promise to marry William's daughter, claiming that Harold had told King Edward that she was offered to him along with all of William's rights in the kingdom. One English source contradicts the Norman case completely by asserting that William usurped the kingdom and continuing to call Harold a king; that is the Chronicle of the Monastery of Abingdon.[20]

The embellishments on the oath alleged by William of Poitiers are quite unbelievable. Harold was supposed to have agreed to be William's 'vicar' (*vicarius*) at Edward's court, that is to act as a representative and press his claim, to have agreed to use his wealth and influence to secure the throne for him and to place a garrison in the (non-existent) castle at Dover and in other castles elsewhere in England. The other castles (about five) were already garrisoned by Norman settlers. All this is mere rhetorical decoration. Harold's oath had no effect on his subsequent conduct in England other than perhaps to make him aware that the crown might be within his grasp if Edward were to die in the immediate future.

No matter what Harold did or did not swear, the grant of the crown to him by King Edward on his death bed cancelled any previous commitments, confirmed as it was by the *Witan*. It was a *verba novissima* grant and so superseded any other promise, even to Edgar the *Aetheling*, let alone William of Normandy. English wills in the eleventh century were of two kinds, either a *post obitum* bequest, which would take effect after death or a *verba novissima* made orally on the testator's deathbed, declared before a priest and preferably in the presence of the beneficiary.[21] (A third form, called a *cwide* was a declaration before witnesses and could be revoked.)

Duke William was claiming some sort of *cwide* or possibly a *post obitum* bequest, but the *verba novissima* form was regarded as binding and cancelled either of the other forms. William of Poitiers confirms the account in the *Vita Edwardi* since he has Harold claim the gift of the crown by King Edward in his last moments and that such a bequest was regarded by the English as inviolable. He cannot deny the claim, so the writer simply tries to assert that the Duke had a better one and invokes feudal ideas to depict Harold as in breach of the obligations of a vassal. Archbishop Robert might have persuaded the Duke that Edward had willed the throne to him, by *cwide* or *post obitum* bequest, but that, in any case, had been cancelled out by the recall of Edward the Exile.

The throne could be the subject of such a bequest since the kingship was seen as hereditary within the royal kin, as their property, and a king was expected to designate his successor.

There had been, and were, other claimants to the throne besides William of Normandy. Magnus of Norway was reported to have written to Edward waiving his claim, derived from a bargain struck with Harthacnut, and reserving his right to reassert it if Edward died.[22] King Swein of Denmark claimed to have been named because he was the nearest blood relative of Cnut the Great.[23] Part of Edward's foreign policy had been to drop hints to rivals when seeking to make treaties with them. It seems to have been a regular part of treaty-making for a king to claim the right to bid for his opposite number's throne should he die first. Another possible heir was Edward's sister's son, Walter of Mantes, who did not die until

1064, and then it was while in Duke William's custody. Edward would not have intended his promises to be taken seriously; they were a lure to attract kinsmen and a diplomatic gambit. Florence of Worcester said that Edward had 'decreed' that Edward the Exile would be his heir, though it is more credible that he only intended to do so if he proved suitable.

Part of the *Aetheling*'s claim to the throne rested on the probability that he was Edmund Ironside's son by Ealdgyth, widow of Sigeferth son of Arngrim, and so acceptable to the thegns of the Danelaw. His son, Edgar *Aetheling*, was thus Ealdgyth's grandson. Orderic Vitalis was to claim that Edward raised the Exile's children as his own.[24]

But in 1066 Harold was the most obvious choice given the threat posed by Earl Tostig who would have been expected to seek allies and try to return to power by force, as indeed he did. Harold's power and authority had been steadily increasing for fifteen years, with alliances with influential churchmen like Ealdred and his military household augmented by the grants of estates by the King so that he could effectively carry out his military duties. Much Godwinson land lay in areas threatened by Viking attack: Eastern England, the Isle of Wight, the Welsh Marches, even Northumbria. Some historians see Harold's family as having reached the greatest height and dignity a subject could reach. He held close to 2,500 hides or carucates of land and his commended men also held a great deal. All of Harold's lands became royal demesne when he ascended to the throne (and were retained by the Conqueror in due course).

Could it be that, after the death of Edward the Exile, Edward consciously set out to construct a supporting framework for the monarchy based on his kin by marriage, the Godwines, in the absence of any kin by blood other than Edgar *Aetheling*, who had few resources and no natural supporters? The *Vita Edwardi* saw the brothers as the pillars of the State. King Edward might not have planned to transfer the dynasty to the Godwines but rather was making them the natural supporters for it and Harold, as the eldest, an English 'Mayor of the Palace' in Carolingian mode.[25] He might even have thought it possible that one of them might, if it were God's Will, even become King. Accordingly, on his death bed, seeing his realm in jeopardy, he designated Harold as his successor.

It is possible that the family was being groomed for kingship, as the *Vita Edwardi* implies, or at least to be of crucial importance to a new king.[26] The *Vita Edwardi* is in this respect similar to the *Encomium Emmae*, which advocated Harthacnut's rights to the throne. Other historians, more cynically, think Harold was increasing his power in order to acquire the crown. The power of the Godwines actually increased the stability of Edward's monarchy.

There was certainly a sea change in Harold's position after the death of Edward the Exile.[27] It can be suggested that Englishmen began to expect his succession and many of them, as Domesday Book shows, became commended to him. It can even be said that had Edward died before 1064, only Harald Hardrada could have challenged Earl Harold.

The Earl became so pre-eminent that only the lack of (English) royal blood seemed to stand between him and the throne.[28] He did have royal blood, as a descendant of Harald Bluetooth. Edward, as Florence of Worcester states, allowed him the status of 'sub-regulus', implying a tacit assumption of a right to the succession. His name was coupled in a significant fashion with that of the King in dealings with the Welsh princes who swore oaths to both the King and the Earl. To foreigners he was a *dux*, that is duke, and the Bayeux tapestry labels him '*Dux Anglorum*' in opposition to the *Dux Normannorum*.[29] It is important to grasp that in England all public authority derived from the crown and even an earl came to his authority by royal grant.[30]

Edward's reign had demonstrated that England could be independent and avoid belonging to either a Scandinavian or a Norman empire. Edward presided over a national renewal of confidence in the royal house. There is no reason why a king sustained by his faithful men, born of an ancient house, should have betrayed that by looking for a foreign successor. Harold I, Harefoot's alleged bastardy (his mother Aelfgifu of Northampton was 'married' to Cnut only '*more Danico*') had discredited him in the eyes of the Church. Archbishop Aethelnoth refused to hand over the royal regalia to him and forbade any one to remove them. Harold I was not a consecrated king.[31] Had Edward died shortly after 1052 the *Witan* would certainly have conducted a search for an heir while a Regent ruled the realm.

No foreign heir would have been wanted. As the Chronicle accounts for 1051 show there was a constant fear of leaving the country the 'more open to foreigners'.

PART THREE

The Saint

14

Character and Appearance

Only a conventional description of Edward's physical appearance and mode of behaviour can be deduced from the available evidence. There are no realistic portraits of the man. The images on his coins are symbolic not naturalistic, as are the images of him in old age on the Bayeux Tapestry.[1] The latter are derived from traditional conventional images of an ageing kingly figure. However, it is known that he was tall and handsome in middle age, a fine figure of a man, 'the most fair and noble of English Kings.'[2] He was said to be majestic in public and dignified in private; the picture of the ideal of kingship in accordance with the expectations of his coronation service.

Embodying, by convention, the royal attributes of justice and piety he fits the picture of Christian King presented in Archbishop Wulfstan's Institutes of Polity:

A King is father and protector of his people, cherishes religion and the Church, establishes peace and gives good justice. He is

well-intentioned and punishes evil-doers, especially robbers and
bandits and enemies of God.

This picture of a King provides the template for the account of his
character and behaviour in the *Vita Edwardi Regis*. In that work he
is the justiciar and corrector of people's sins and offers leadership
and protection. The fact that he spent time every year recounting
the saga of Olaf Tryggvason and insisting that it was right to do this
on Easter Sunday because Olaf was as much superior to other kings
as Easter Day was to other days of the year, suggests that he modelled himself on that king.

The *Vita Edwardi* contains a description of his appearance
towards the end of his life, when the author might well have seen
him. He was nobly fine in limbs and mind, with locks of snowy
(or milky) white hair and a similar beard. He had rosy cheeks, long
white hands with translucent fingers and had no physical blem-
ishes on his body. In death his face 'blushed like a rose' (perhaps
meaning flushed with the effects of a fever), his beard gleaming
lily white, his hands straight and whitened, looking more asleep
than dead.[3]

Whereas a tyrant like Harthacnut was depicted as cruel and
wicked, Edward the Christian King is 'claene and milde', that[4] is,
clean-living and merciful. To the Chroniclers he was '*craeftig raeda*'
strong in counsel (where his father, Aethelred, had been 'unraede',
without counsel). In the *Encomium Emmae* he is a man among
men, conspicuous by strength of mind in council.[5] He has all the
royal virtues.

He was more warlike and bellicose than the usual idea of him.
The *Vita Edwardi* describes his actions in 1052 in the following
terms:

When the King heard of this hostile and unlicensed entry into the
kingdom, although he did not believe his informants, he came with
such military force as he could muster to London and, as he was

of passionate temper and a man of prompt and vigorous action, he tried to deny them entry into the city where he was encamped.

He had a terrible temper, though not given to ranting and raving. He was eager to fight Earl Godwine in 1051, commanding his fleet at sea against pirates and in the blockade of Flanders. Like his grandfather King Edgar he might well have held an annual review of the fleet, at Sandwich. He led a small army in person in 1043 to remove Queen Emma from her control of the treasury at Winchester. He could be ruthless towards political enemies, exiling them whenever the opportunity arose. A Dane called Svein, friend apparently of Bishop Hereman, entered the country without prior leave sometime between 1055 and 1058, only to be arrested and bound as a spy on the king's orders.[6] On another occasion a *ceorl* happened to obstruct the King while hunting, upsetting the fences which directed the stags into nets, and Edward cursed him, saying 'By God and His Mother, I will hurt you as much if I can some day.'[7] Swein Godwinson was advised to leave the country so as to placate the King's anger.

He could take harsh political decisions, ordering the assassination of Rhys ap Rhydderch in 1053 and probably that of Gruffydd ap Llewelyn in 1063, having only grudgingly pardoned him in 1056. It is these vignettes which bring the King to life rather than the rhetoric of the *Vita Edwardi*.

King Edward was certainly strongly religious, taking a keen interest in his duty to govern the church, pious in his behaviour at Mass, fond of converse with monks and priests to discuss theological matters. He devoted much time and thought to his construction of a Romanesque church for Westminster. But he could be violently secular in other contexts. He appointed a kinsman, Wulfric, as abbot of Ely and his personal doctor, Baldwin, as abbot of Bury St Edmunds, as well as the Norman friend of his youth, Robert Champart, to the archbishopric of Canterbury and made his own nephew an Earl. He chose, unwisely, his own goldsmith, Spearhavoc, as Bishop of London. Some might call that nepotism.

The *Liber Eliensis* reveals how he could be careless and self-interested. When Aesgar the Staller appropriated to his own use the *vill* called Easter, allegedly the property of Ely Abbey, the brethren appealed to the King, who either did nothing or rejected the appeal since it had no effect and Aesgar ignored all efforts to persuade him to return the estate. Allegedly, the King, after the monks had excommunicated Aesgar, had the Staller arrested and compelled to reach agreement with the monks. In the end it was agreed that Aesgar should retain the estate for his lifetime on the understanding that it be returned to Ely when he died. This rather dramatic tale, if one reads between the lines, actually suggests that the King merely mediated between the disputants and allowed his Staller to retain the benefit of the estate.

The monks show that they had little respect for Edward's choice of Wulfric for abbot. The abbot is accused of leasing monastery lands to his own brother, Gutmund, (so that he could have sufficient land to justify his marriage to a nobleman's daughter). The monks saw this as criminal behaviour for which the abbot was punished by an unexpected death.[8] Edward is usually seen as a benefactor of churches, especially Westminster, but Peterborough thought differently. Hugh Candidus accused him of trying to rob the monastery.[9]

Edward's court was anything but dull. His habit of relating the sagas to his household has already been mentioned. Another story relates how a court held at Bury St Edmunds, before 1046, was a joyful one attended by many English and Danish nobles. Osgod Clapa, the Staller, said in this source to have been Edward's '*major domo*' was seen swaggering about in full Danish armour, but that Edward preferred to sit 'in Chapter' with the monks and entered into confraternity with them (becoming, as would be the case today, a lay associate of the Order of St Benedict, or member of a Third Order.) His favourite relaxation was to go hunting or hawking. That was something Canon law forbade the clergy to do.

Legend and hagiography have covered up much of Edward's wilfulness and passion. In life he could be hasty and ill-tempered and was capable of great wrong, but he seems to have mellowed as he grew older and devoted more of his time to thoughts of religion. His sanctity, emphasised in the second part of the *Vita Edwardi*, was largely unrecognised. In the earlier part of the *Vita* he is seen as 'the glass of fashion', and as a man who could be misguided and misled by ambitious men, yet also capable of piety and good works. Only towards the end of his life can he be said to have 'lived like an angel in the squalor of this world, devoted to God'. So he was believed to have been 'joyfully taken up to live with God' (as all good Christians would hope to be). Yet other sources give no hint of obvious holiness. He is seen as most pious, a lover of justice, and generous to those in need.[10]

Too much must not be made of assertions that he had been a good Christian King. Dudo of St Quentin could describe Richard I of Normandy, ('the duke of the pirates'), as *dux sanctissimus*, the most holy duke, claiming he was blessed and holy and even a 'confessor'; then go on to describe his fondness for concubines![11]

Edward, then, had his faults. He mistrusted Earl Godwine, even perhaps on occasion finding it difficult to forgive him, though it was Archbishop Robert rather than the King who sent men to pursue Godwine in 1051 so that they might kill him if they caught him. Edward readily exiled Earl Aelfgar for daring to question his decisions. He could be devious and ambiguous, wrathful when crossed, yet would, if persistently opposed, reluctantly give way. But there is no real evidence that he was easily controlled by his counsellors, especially Earl Godwine, who was more often on the losing than the winning side in disputes over policy. The allegation that he was over-influenced by Archbishop Robert, so that if Robert said a black crow was white the King would believe it, is a late and unauthoritative gloss on the assertion in the *Vita* that 'the malice of evil men had shut up the merciful ears of the king'.[13]

As King he performed remarkably well for a man who had arrived back after over twenty years in exile, without a natural 'affinity' to support him in England. At first he recruited Bretons,

Lotharingians and Normans to his household, but promoted few to any position of high authority. He had recruited support because Cnut had stripped England of Edward's English relatives. His generosity, after 1053, towards Harold and his brothers was realism rather than favouritism. Edward was manufacturing a new family for himself. There is little to show that he had any better alternatives as counsellors. The policy was a success and his reign remained largely one of internal peace, especially after the expulsion of ambitious foreigners in 1052. There had been no actual civil war, which says something about Edward's prudence and good sense.

He was never a pious nincompoop but rather an intelligent ruler, balancing the disparate forces within his kingdom with remarkable finesse, while maintaining a balance of power against rival states which prevented any attempt at invasion while he still lived. There is no evidence that any weakness in Edward or his conduct of affairs encouraged any tendencies towards anarchy. His government maintained the continuity of Old English administration, even developing some aspects of it, and promoted social growth.

If support for the idea of his sanctity is sought, then the language of the *Vita Edwardi* is ambiguous. He is there pious, benign, generous, religious-minded, showing more than common devotion to God. He was thought of after death as of holy memory, seen as a devout worshipper at mass and enjoying the company of clerics, the most educated class in that era.

Yet the first part of the *Vita* is over-quick to reveal what it considers to be his faults (while glossing over them in the second part when it was desirable to emphasis his better qualities). So he is presented not only as warlike in aspect but also as quick to anger. He threatens war but leaves the fighting to his subordinates. He can, according to the *Vita*, be emotional, rash and misguided, mainly because he is seen as endangering the kingdom by listening to his favourites (rather than to Earl Godwine). He is unjust and merciless, with a cynical, even malicious, sense of humour.

On the other hand, he was nobly fine in limb and mind and a golden age dawned at his coming. In personal behaviour he was '*claene*', that is clean-living and not known to indulge himself with concubines. To William of Malmesbury his mind and spirit were 'simplex', that is frank and open and straight forward in his dealings. In the twelfth century, but no earlier, he was, to the monks of Westminster, a saint.

As a man he had remarkable physical strength and a high degree of courage, facing adversity with determination and vigour of mind. To the author of the *Encomium Emmae* he was '*vir virium*', a man among men, distinguished by the strength of his intellect in council, gifted with a lively temperament who achieved the height of distinction in all things worth striving for.

The claim that he was a perpetual virgin is hagiography not fact. It does not appear until Osbert of Clare wrote his own life of the King, using as a basis parts of the *Vita Edwardi*, but enhancing the language and adding his own views. The language of the *Vita*, applying, in its version of Bishop Brihtwold's Vision, the word '*celebs*' (from the classical Latin *caelebs*) is too ambiguous to justify the claim that his marriage was a celibate one. The word is used of Earl Tostig and the account spells out that it means that 'he renounced desire for all women except his wife' and 'governed the use of his body and tongue chastely [*celebs*]'. The author could hardly have dared to write so plainly about his royal master.

Much is made of the content of Bishop Brihtwold's Vision but it is not certain that it has survived in its original form. The main point of the vision is that God, not man, would provide an heir to the (unidentified) king chosen by St Peter. William of Malmesbury presents it in the context of the almost complete destruction of the royal line of England, which had distressed the good bishop who then dreamed ('was rapt up to heaven') and saw St Peter consecrate a king, later identified as Edward (who was then in exile), and lay down for him a life of chastity (*celibe vita*). One suspects that the original merely stressed that Edward was not yet married and had no prospect of ever being so and that St Peter assured him that God would see to that. The primary meaning of *celebs* was unmarried.[14]

That the word *celebs* was not sufficient to prove the case for Edward's alleged celibacy is demonstrated by Osbert himself since he has to insist that Edward was a virgin. In fact it appears that Edward, like Earl Tostig, avoided the common practice among many nobles, including the Dukes of Normandy and Cnut the Great himself, of taking a concubine. There is no evidence to suggest that Edward had any illegitimate children. The whole idea that Edward's marriage was a celibate one hinges on the plain fact that he was childless, but there are several other possible explanations for that.

A married couple may have no children simply because one of them is infertile, and infertility can arise for a number of reasons quite unconnected with abstention from marital relations. It is also possible, as has been argued earlier, that the truth was that Edith had proved incapable of bearing a child, that she had tried and that the child (or even more than one) had been stillborn. Edith disappears from witness lists in the late 1040s until the mid 1050s. She could have been quite seriously ill. That also would explain the attempt to persuade the King to divorce her, something quite unnecessary if it were known that the King had opted for a celibate marriage. He might well have decided at some point to cease any attempts to father a child to spare Edith the trauma of further failure. There is a tendency to avoid acceptance of the idea that Edward and Edith might well have been a devoted couple and might have grown closer after the death of her father. Such a view is supported by the text of the *Vita*.

To Edith, Edward is 'nobly fine in limb and mind' and the couple are 'one person dwelling in a double form'; it is Archbishop Robert and not the king who seeks a divorce, and Edward readily receives Edith back to his bed. Edith is said to prefer the king's interests to power and riches. On his deathbed he took care to ensure that Earl Harold would protect her.[15]

In any case, the *Vita* also maintains that Edward 'preserved with holy chastity [*castimonia*] the dignity of his consecration and lived his whole life dedicated to God in true innocence'. *Castimonia* means primarily purity of morals and, by extension, chastity. It does not mean celibacy. Nor does a man have to be celibate in order to 'live in true innocence'. Osbert of Clare again had to add his own spin by saying that Edward avoided 'carnal copulation'.[16] If the meaning had been so obvious, Osbert would not have needed to embellish the original text.

The weakness of Osbert's case is demonstrated by his repeated efforts to enhance the impact of what he was claiming. So he insists that Edward 'preserved the purity of his flesh', like St Alexius the Virgin, and exploits the *Vita*'s remark that (when the author knew them) Edward and Edith lived more like father and daughter than man and wife. In the mid 1060s Edward was in his sixties and Edith about twenty years younger, young enough to be his daughter.

That part of the *Vita Edwardi* which would have described Edith's marriage to Edward is missing and only fragments are known from the writings of William of Malmesbury and Osbert. What is known is that Edith was 'delivered to the bridal apartments with ceremonial rejoicing' as part of the wedding ceremonies and that in 1052 she was 'restored to the King's bedchamber'. The natural meaning of such phrases is that the marriage was seen to be a perfectly normal one.[17] William of Malmesbury simply says that the king took her to wife.[18] The Church's stance on matrimony was that where there was no sexual intercourse there could be no marriage.[19] Other remarks by Osbert are his own, unfounded additions. His purpose was to achieve, by whatever means he could, the canonistion of King Edward. In the twelfth century claims of miracles, of a holy life, and that the body of the candidate for sainthood was found to be incorrupt were not quite enough. The acceptable test was that he should have lived a celibate life. Osbert had to insist that Edward was celibate.

Much of the case rested on interpretation of Bishop Brihtwold's Vision. The versions of it presented by William of Malmesbury and

Osbert both paraphrase it to some extent and add their own details. As there is no version of this 'vision' or prophecy earlier than that provided by the text of the *Vita Edwardi*[20], the account of the bishop's prediction could already have been altered before it was used by William of Malmesbury and Osbert of Clare. Much of what was in the *Vita* had already become unacceptable shortly after the Conquest, containing far too much praise for the family of Earl Godwine.[21] There had been a copy at Westminster in 1085, seen by Sulcard, and William of Malmesbury had a copy in 1124. The present copy is thought not to be either of these and both of them had already been 'improved'. Even Osbert's version can be shown to be later than the probable date the original was completed, circa 1067.[22] The text which has survived is of that of the author who wrote it for Queen Edith.

The themes of the *Vita* can be summarised as: the greatness of Edith and her family; that her husband was divinely chosen to be king; that God would choose his successor; that Edith hoped to survive the Conquest as a queen. Christian ideas of marriage are presented and Brihtwold predicts a chaste marriage.[23] That theme of chastity was continued by William of Malmesbury, as regards Edith. He alleges that both during Edward's life and afterwards she was 'not free from suspicions of misconduct' (a charge frequently levelled, out of jealousy, at previous queens) but that, on her deathbed, she satisfied those around her 'on oath at her own suggestion' of her '*perpetua integritate*'. *Integritas* can be translated as purity, innocence, integrity or, of a woman, chastity. One might also suspect that there has been some confusion between Queen Edith and her famous namesake, King Edgar's daughter, St Edith of Wilton, of whom William of Malmesbury states that 'she earned God's favour by ever-incorrupt virginity', using the word '*virginitate*' not '*integritate*' which he uses of the Queen.[24]

It is only William of Malmesbury's report, for which he produces no evidence, which says that Edward never knew her as a man should. He admits that it was 'very widely reported, that he never broke his chastity [*pudicitia*] by consorting with any woman'.[25] This is rumour not fact. When this particular writer does this he is distancing himself from what is said and does not vouch for its truth. The rumour had been spread by William of Jumièges; 'as they say, the pair preserved perpetual virginity'.[26] Consider the contradiction. Edith is simultaneously accused of (marital) misconduct and yet said to have been a perpetual virgin.[27] It has been well said that the further medieval writers were from the events they were describing, the more they claimed to know about them. It was Edward's subsequent reputation for sanctity, proved by the incorrupt state of his body when viewed in 1102 that encouraged speculation that he was a virgin king. Bodily incorruptibility was taken [in those days] as evidence of a celibate life.

15

The Cult of Edward's Sanctity

The author of the *Vita Edwardi*, having had the main purpose of his work destroyed by the events of 1065–66, proceeded in part two of his work to attempt to salvage what he could for his patroness, Queen Edith. He seems to have expanded his account of the King's death to emphasise his prophetic powers, introducing the King's vision of two monks whom he had known when a youth in Normandy, who prophesy woe and disaster. They are said to have condemned all the Earls and the entire English hierarchy of bishops and abbots as being 'servants of the devil' and that a year and a day after the king dies 'God had delivered all this kingdom, cursed by Him, into the hands of the enemy, and devils shall come through all this land with fire and sword and havoc of war'. Edward protests that he can persuade the people to repent but is told that they will not.[1]

The two monks then tell the king the legend of the Green Tree, which, being cut in two, and one part carried three furlongs away, if it be made whole again without human intervention and brings forth leaves and fruit, only then will the evils cease. The author also claims

that the Pope and his legates had frequently complained about the
state of the English church, which seems to refer more to the issue
of general admonitions to reform emanating from the reformed
papacy. Whatever the King's vision actually said, this account bears
clear signs of having been 'improved' after the Conquest. No doubt
Edward had dreamed that God was angry with his people following the Northern Rebellion, and that He would punish them. The
Green Tree is a vision of something impossible, rather like Edward's
grim jest aimed at Earl Godwine, that he could hope for the King's
forgiveness if he restored to him his brother Alfred and his men,
alive and well with all their possessions. The original meaning of
his prophecy has been distorted to fit what happened and was further altered in the twelfth century and various interpretations were
made of it. They add nothing to the facts about King Edward.

The King's claim to sanctity is then enhanced by the relating of a
number of miracle stories not all of which are thought to have been
in the original text of 1067. An unknown young woman is cured of
scrofula (known even then as 'the king's evil' or '*morbus regis*') when
her diseased glands are anointed by the King with water into which
he has dipped his hands. A similar cure is said to have been affected
by Robert II, the Pious, of France. Subsequently, the young woman,
who up to then had been barren, became pregnant. Edward's French
servants are then said to have claimed that Edward had often performed cures in this manner as a youth in Normandy. William of
Malmesbury, who adds the detail that the young woman later had
twins, goes out of his way to ascribe this to Edward's sanctity, deny-
ing that it was due to 'hereditary virtue in the royal blood'.[2] In his
other writings he insists that the disease is cured by the intervention
of the saints. He was countering French claims that it was a power
inherent in royal blood.

Similarly Edward is said to have cured a blind man whose
face was washed, by servants, with the water in which the king
had washed himself. These are the only two miracles found in the
form in which they were recorded in 1067, the rest, because of a

gap in the manuscript, are only found mentioned in the writings of William of Malmesbury, Osbert of Clare and Sulcard of Westminster. Between them they record the cure of a blind man from Lincoln, the building worker on the royal palace at Brill, Buckinghamshire, named Wulfwi Spillecorn (son of Wulfmaer of Ludgershall) both by Edward himself, and three blind beggars and a one-eyed man washed by a courtier with the king's washing water. By the standards of most medieval saints, this is a very modest total.

The story is told of how the King had a vision, allegedly in the year 1060, of the 'Seven Sleepers of Ephesus' and burst out laughing because he saw them turn from their right to their left side while asleep. He then prophesied seventy-four years of disasters like those foretold in the Gospel. The King's vision is alleged to have been confirmed by men sent to investigate. Since they visited the area in the time of George Maniaces, a famous Byzantine soldier, who died in 1043, the alleged proof is somewhat doubtful.[3] The tale is not in the original text of the *Vita* and was added later. It is intended to enhance Edward's claim to prophetic powers. William of Malmesbury relates only the King's prophecies, his early miracles and the story of the Seven Sleepers.[4]

It therefore seems, since nothing is recorded of any devotion to King Edward between 1067 until after 1075, when King William I wrote to Abbot John of Fécamp to secure the monk Vitalis as abbot of Westminster, which was venerated as the burial place of 'his lord, King Edward and his illustrious wife', that there was no public cult. Sulcard of Westminster, who describes the abbey in 1080, making use in part of the description in the *Vita*, makes no reference to any cult devoted to Edward in the monastery. The Mortuary Roll of Abbot Vitalis, circa 1121, lists prayers for Edward along with prayers for the abbot and the monks. But when attention to Edward did begin, in 1102, when his tomb was opened, it appears that some people, described as 'holy and religious men' (but not necessarily priests or monks) still remembered him and desired to look upon his face once more. It is thought that a few men, possibly surviving members of his household both French and English, had kept his memory alive and they might have believed in his sanctity.[5] The *Vita* suggests that some of his household thought him capable of miracles. It was less than forty years after his death and some then alive still lived.

In 1102 the time was becoming ripe for the development of a cult. Belief in the King's sanctity seems to have been strong enough, perhaps among Londoners looking back to the 'golden age' before the Conquest, to cause the text of the *Vita Edwardi* to develop a more positive tone, emphasising both his sanctity and chastity. He had two sanctified ancestors, his half-uncle St Edward the Martyr and his aunt, St Edith of Wilton, though the cult of his murdered brother Alfred at Ely did not develop. Belief in his moral purity of life had been fostered after 1066 by the suggestion that his interest in religion had deepened with advancing age. There were stories of his almsgiving and generosity towards the poor and infirm. Perhaps reports of his healing powers had begun to circulate and the circle of his foreign favourites might have tried to encourage belief in his royal power to effect miraculous cures.

There was a change in attitude towards all things English with the accession of Henry I. He had referred to King Edward's laws in his *Charter of Liberties* and during his reign new lives of English saints were produced. Miracles were reported in 1112 even at the tomb of the executed Earl Waltheof. The King married Edith-Matilda daughter of St Margaret of Scotland, sister of Edgar the *Aetheling*. There were vague hints that Henry himself could 'touch for the King's Evil'. That in itself developed from the fact that Kings were consecrated and anointed with Holy Oil. Furthermore, in 1102, Archbishop Anselm of Canterbury, in Synod at Westminster, ruled that reverence should not be paid to the dead without episcopal approval.[6] That might have moved Abbot Gilbert Crispin to investigate any signs of a cult for King Edward and to discover the exact whereabouts of his tomb. Sulcard in 1080 made no reference to it in his description of the abbey. The Abbot might have decided to see if episcopal approval was desirable since, if Westminster did possess the tomb of a saint, it would prove beneficial to the abbey.

Not everyone in the monastery approved, which might reflect the known Norman hostility towards English saints. Some snobbery might have been involved, since Ailred of Rievaulx in his revised life of the King in Henry II's time was to claim that the 'rustic multitude' had always revered Edward.

The tomb was located and opened in the presence of Bishop Gundulf of Rochester, probably in the expectation of seeing a decayed corpse. The bishop's presence was vital as it provided the monks with an independent and presumably impartial witness. To everyone's astonishment the body was found to be incorrupt and complete with the royal regalia, crown, sceptre and ring. This was to play a major part in the development of Edward's cult. Westminster was to claim possession of these objects and they appear, except for the ring, to have been removed from the tomb in 1102.

The body was intact and in no way decomposed and a fragrant smell filled the church. The King's hands were found to be soft and flexible, as were his joints. His sandals showed no signs of the stain of corruption. A pall still covered his face and had to be moved to reveal it. His beard was white and curled. The clothing he wore was whole, clean and unfaded. Those present having verified the presence of the King's body and that it was incorrupt, the tomb was closed and remained so until after he had been canonised. It does, however, appear to have been 'translated', as the tomb was moved to a location in front of the High Altar. Osbert later claimed that miracles occurred at the time but as he gives no details his claim adds nothing to the cause.[7]

The liturgical practices of the abbey now kept Edward's memory fresh and there was an annual revival of interest in him every 5 January. A mass was said in his honour on the anniversary of his burial. His tomb became a place of sanctuary for accused criminals, as the writs of Abbot Gilbert show, though that might in part have been due to its position before the High Altar.

In 1117 the office of abbot fell vacant and no abbot was appointed until 1121. During that time Osbert, who came from Clare in Suffolk, achieved some prominence and might perhaps have been a candidate for the office. It is possible that it was during this period that interest in the *Vita Edwardi* increased and it was felt to be inadequate to serve as a saint's *Vita*. It was revised to expand the account of the miracles and to include the story of the Seven Sleepers, to produce a version which was used by William of Malmesbury. That prompted the collection of other stories about Edward, such as his vision of the death of King Swein, junior, of Denmark who drowned before he could invade England and a number of improbable wonder tales which were eventually added to the *Vita* by Ailred of Rievaulx. But in 1121 the almoner, Herbert, was elected abbot and the Mortuary List had the names of Kings Offa and Edgar and Queen Matilda added to it.

Osbert proved to be a vexatious monk and soon quarrelled with the new abbot and as a result was banished for a time. On his return in 1134 when Herbert had become old and possibly infirm, he took the lead of a group of monks who wished to use Edward's claim to be a saint as part of the drive to defend the privileges of the abbey. Osbert, now prior, used the poor state of the abbey's archives as a weapon with which to oppose Abbot Herbert, pointing out the lack of written evidence for the grant of lands and privileges. That led to the wholesale 'reconstruction' of missing charters, some perhaps based on genuine writs and other genuine claims. But many of them are clumsy forgeries. One, an alleged writ of King William, begins 'I, William, surnamed the Bastard'. But charters in King Edward's name, if he became a saint, would have been unassailable.

Osbert founded a house of Canonesses at Kilburn, whose principal duty was to pray for King Edward's soul and for the abbey and its brethren. Herbert died in 1136 and for two years Osbert had a free hand. Some sort of popular cult of the King had increased among the lower classes in London, and in 1137 Osbert decided to preach on the anniversary of the King's death. He himself had previously fallen sick of the 'quartain fever' during the mass being said for 'the glorious Prince Edward', so Osbert prayed fervently to him and recovered from his fever.[8] In his sermon during the vigil on 4 January Osbert stressed Edward's humility, patience and chastity and demonstrated the King's sanctity by reference to his miracles, including Osbert's own recovery from fever. The keeper of the royal palace at Westminster, a knight called Gerin, also suffering from the fever, was inspired to spend the night in a vigil at the tomb, and he also recovered. As Osbert reported, 'Edward heard Gerin and Christ heard Edward'.

Although he had not instituted the vigil and the mass, which were already an annual event attended by a large congregation, Osbert was certainly trying to convert the occasion into a saint's feast day. His efforts seem to have been rewarded by a resumption of miracles at the tomb. Osbert records the cure of a cripple called Ralf and of six blind men led by a one-eyed man during the month of prayers for the deceased King. Desperate for 'signs' he added the story of Abbot Aelfwine of Ramsey's prediction of victory for Harold Godwinson and the cure of a blind bell-ringer at Westminster. He then added the story (possibly fabricated) of how Archbishop Lanfranc tried to depose Bishop Wulfstan of Worcester. The Bishop defied Lanfranc and insisted on surrendering his staff to King Edward, from whom he had received it, by striking the stone over the tomb. The staff sank into the stone and could not be removed from it until Lanfranc reinstated the bishop.

Osbert then rewrote the *Vita Edwardi*, omitting the political and historical content, so that it was now a saint's Life, *Vita beati Eadwardi Regis Anglorum*. He also composed three charters for the abbey in Edward's name. He stressed the King's humility, chastity and patience and cited his miracles as proof of sanctity. Then Herbert's successor was chosen, Gervase of Blois, an illegitimate son of King Stephen, during a legatine council at Westminster held by Alberic, legate of Innocent II on 13 December 1138. Osbert seized his opportunity to present a copy of his new *Vita* to the legate and a letter in which he asked that Edward, God's anointed, incorrupt in body, should be canonised.[9] The legate was the right man to approach, he held the office of '*Exaltatio Sanctorum*', the elevation of saints.

There was no set procedure as yet for canonisation. Cults were often the result of popular religion and some survived while others did not. John XV in the tenth century had begun to impose some ecclesiastical control over the process. He canonized St Udalric at a council in Rome in 993, and in the process stressed that the honour paid to the saints, both martyrs and confessors, was ultimately referred to God Himself because Christ had said 'He who receives you receives me'.[10]

Osbert also influenced the new abbot who wrote to his uncle, Bishop Henry of Winchester, stressing Edward's miracles and his relationship to the bishop (and his brother, the King), and gained his support. Osbert and several companions were sent to Rome but crucially lacked sufficient support from the English hierarchy. He had letters from King Stephen, from Bishop Henry and the Chapter of St Paul's (in the absence of a bishop of London). Only Stephen was at all enthusiastic, seeking honour for England and its monarchy. He stressed the English loyalty to Rome, the payment of Peter's Pence and the piety of English kings. He also mentioned that Edward, benefactor of Westminster, was his relation. Unfortunately for Osbert, he acted too late.

The legate, Alberic, consecrated Theobald of Bec as Archbishop of Canterbury, 8 January 1139, and he was no supporter of King Stephen. At the Lateran Council of spring 1139 the Angevin supporters of Henry I's daughter Matilda, denounced Stephen as a perjured usurper. The Pope was not impressed. In summer Stephen quarrelled with the Church, by breaking Bishop Roger of Salisbury (who controlled the royal administration as '*Regis procurator*') and other members of his family (Roger le Poer, his son, the Chancellor, Bishop Nigel of Ely, his nephew, the Treasurer and another nephew, Alexander, Bishop of Lincoln), and in October Matilda, accompanied by Earl Robert of Gloucester invaded England. If, as seems likely, Osbert reached Rome by December 1139, it was too late. The Pope had every reason to postpone a decision. His letter to Abbot Gervase said that Osbert had made a good impression but lacked sufficient testimonials to support the cause. Something which would redound to the honour of the whole kingdom ought to be supported by the whole kingdom. But the kingdom was divided and there was no chance of a wholehearted approach.[11] The Abbot and monks must provide the necessary testimonials to add to Osbert's three essential elements for canonisation: a saint's *Vita*, miracles and the suggestion of the king's chastity (now enhanced by Osbert as a claim to celibacy). The Pope also ordered that the 'most glorious' King Edward's regalia should be carefully preserved by Westminster.

The cause had apparently been rejected as defective in form not content. It was also politically inopportune. Osbert had made a good impression but could do no more. However, his version of the *Vita* had named Edward *beati Edwardi*, 'Blessed Edward', and his work had met with papal approval. Although the present process of canonisation was not then in use, by which a new saint is, on proof of a first miracle, given the title 'Blessed' and devotion to the new saint is permitted on a local basis (with full canonisation on proof of a second miracle), it does look as though Innocent had foreshadowed that development. He did not forbid Westminster from further devotion and he specifically said that he would have canonised Edward had there been sufficient testimonials from the rest of England and left it to the community at Westminster to decide whether to collect the necessary testimonials and renew the petition.

There followed a gap of twenty years during which there were no further developments. Osbert quarrelled with Abbot Gervase and lost his office of prior and seems again to have been exiled. In his absence his supporters did nothing and no miracles were recorded. Ailred of Rievaulx wrote his *Genealogy of the Kings of England* in 1153–4 and his chapter on Edward ignores his claims to sanctity. Nonetheless the work had some impact. It hailed Matilda's son Henry as having united the English and the Normans, a sign that the political atmosphere was changing. Stephen had accepted that Henry would be his heir. Osbert wrote a flattering poem in Henry's honour.[12]

Abbot Gervase, as a supporter of Stephen, was deposed in about 1158 and replaced by Master Lawrence of Durham, a monk of St Albans who had studied at Paris. He discussed Edward's claims with his senior monks and it was agreed to press the claim once more. The books written about Edward were inspected and read and his cause approved.[13] In 1139 there had been disunity in England which had ruined the attempt, now there was division in the Church. There had been a double election to the Papacy, with French and English cardinals favouring Alexander III and the Empire choosing Victor IV. Imperial councils pressed the claims of Victor but councils in England, Normandy and France supported Alexander. Henry II therefore used his royal prerogative and recognized Alexander who was also accepted by King Louis VII of France. That tipped the balance and Alexander was accepted universally as Pope.

Abbot Lawrence saw his chance. The abbey had Pope Innocent's instructions about what was needed. This time a thorough campaign was launched and a petition of the whole kingdom organized. Both Archbishops and the Bishop of London were recruited to the cause and a circular was sent to all bishops and abbots.[14] This was done in summer 1160. Even if it had been done earlier, nothing could have happened until Alexander had been recognised as Pope. Thirteen of the letters of the bishops have survived, copied into a book. They are a selection only. Westminster's own petition (and all the associated documents) is missing.

Lawrence enlisted King Henry's support, visiting him personally, and, at Paris, obtained the backing of the legates Henry and Otto.[15] He showed them Edward's vestment, removed from his tomb in 1102, to prove Edward's incorruption; it was still whole, clean and unfaded. The King, full of himself after his success in bringing about Alexander's recognition as Pope, approved of the plan and the legates were suitably grateful for Henry's support. A delegation from Westminster then travelled to Anagni to see the Pope. The party included the infirmarer, Roger, who could give evidence about cures, and the sacristan, Walter, who could testify to any signs seen in the Church. The Abbot did not accompany them as it was then winter; and it is unlikely that the aged Osbert was there either.

In a private audience they presented Innocent's letter and the other proofs including Osbert's book of miracles, together with the necessary testimonials. In response the Pope, in consultation with his cardinals, issued the Bulls of Canonization.[16] He chose to dispense with the usual procedure of calling a solemn council and acted with the consent of the cardinals. The action is not unlike the issue in modern times of a '*Motu Proprio*', a personal act of the Pope. Alexander sent a brief letter, dated 7 February 1161, to the Abbot and Church of Westminster and the whole Church in England. Edward was thus added to the 'Canon' or catalogue of saints and so enrolled among the saints and confessors (that is, those who have achieved sainthood without martyrdom). A Cardinal was authorised to say the first Mass of St Edward the Confessor. In acting so promptly, the Pope had repaid his debt to King Henry.

Back at Westminster the abbot held a great assembly at which the Bull was read and the second Mass in honour of Saint Edward was said. The next step would be to raise the King Saint's tomb above ground so that it could be seen or even touched and properly revered by the faithful, and offerings could be made for the benefit of the monks. But King Henry II was still overseas and the move to a new tomb, the Translation, had to await his return. That gave ample time for the work to be done. Osbert's *Vita* was largely an old-fashioned collection of miracles, prophecies and stories rather than a full saint's Life and the *Vita Edwardi* was unsuitable, even unedifying, so Ailred of Rievaulx was commissioned to produce an appropriate *Vita*.

Ailred brought the whole account up to date and strengthened the historical context, adding matter from reputable Chronicles.

His work, *Vita Sancti Edwardi Regis* became the standard medieval life of the king. But everything now hinged on the availability of King Henry. Then in 1163 Henry held a council at Westminster concerning an ecclesiastical lawsuit, at which Ailred was present, and it seems that the matter of the translation was discussed. Abbot Lawrence was advised to make a secret preliminary inspection of the tomb, in case there were any unexpected snags, and, after some hesitation, did so. It might have proved awkward if the body had been found to have decayed.

So the Abbot, the prior and a few chosen monks vested themselves in albs one night after matins, and cautiously and with due reverence, opened the tomb. They found the saint wrapped in cloth of gold, purple shoes on his feet, and a pair of precious slippers. His head and face were covered by a round mitre embroidered with gold, his beard was white and still curly and he had a ring on his finger. To everyone's relief nothing had changed, the body was still intact and the vestments only a little dulled and soiled by the mortar and dust of the tomb. The body was lifted out, laid on a carpet and wrapped in silk cloth. It was then placed in a wooden coffin, a 'feretory' which could be carried, and transferred to the new shrine, intact except for the ring which was removed to be kept as a memorial. It is also alleged that three cloths were removed and incorporated into embroidered copes.[17]

During another council on 1 October 1163, held to deal with the 'ancestral customs' of the realm (and ending with the disgrace of Archbishop Thomas Becket), it appears that final arrangements were made for Edward's Translation, the King no doubt seeking to capitalise on this to strengthen his position with respect to Becket. The Council, so seriously divided on 1 October, met on 13 October at the abbey. Only Archbishop Becket and his suffragans of the southern province were present, possibly because of the long-running dispute over primacy between Canterbury and York, along with three Norman bishops, four major abbots, eight earls and, of course, the King.

The feretory was opened to allow the King and others to see the Saint (and, if they dared, touch him) and was then carried in procession through the cloisters by the King and his leading magnates. It was placed in the shrine, which allegedly incorporated metalwork placed there by William I. Ailred presented his new Life to the King and preached on the text usual on such occasions, that a 'glorious lantern had been placed on a candlestick in the House of the Lord'.

Everyone benefited. Edward had received his due honour, the monks who had supported Osbert had won through at last, Abbot Lawrence had acquired a valuable cult for his church and Henry II had scored a valuable point in his quarrel with Becket. He had an 'antecessor' who was a saint. The Archbishop contented himself with asking for and receiving the stone in which Bishop Wulfstan's staff had been stuck.[18] No doubt he hoped the relic, and the support of good King Edward, would protect him against Henry. It did not.

Although the timing of the canonisation of Saint Edward in 1161 owed much to politico-ecclesiastical diplomacy, Edward's cause had met the requirements for canonisation as then in force. These were twofold: proof of a pious life and virtue of morals and confirmation by miracles or signs. He was alleged to have been chosen to be a king before birth, consecrated as it were by Providence, and designated king in his childhood. He preserved his chastity and dedicated the latter part of his life to the service of God, a model of Christian Kingship. His chastity is emphasised because the theology of the reformers at Rome was endeavouring to get all priests to give up marriage and, more importantly, the use of concubines, and live a chaste life. By the end of the eleventh century this had become a demand for complete celibacy and the theme of Edward's chastity was transformed by Osbert into a claim that he had been celibate.

Edward's cures would have seemed sufficiently miraculous in that age and the fact that the cures followed his intervention, and later followed prayers to him, were seen as proof of his sanctity. His cult was never to be as popular as that of several other saints and was quite overshadowed by the cult of the 'holy blissful martyr' Thomas Becket.

As for Edward's posthumous reputation, some still see his reign as a failure or as a prelude to the Norman Conquest, yet he ruled without real challenge to his position or even his authority for twenty-four years. He was never at serious risk of losing his throne to either internal or external enemies. The country enjoyed a period of increasing prosperity which, for the English at least, came to an abrupt end after the Conquest. Other judgements made of King Edward depend upon unsubstantiated assumptions and his real achievements have often been ignored. The achievements even of weak rulers are nonetheless achievements and Edward was not weak.

In his reign the borders of the country were strengthened and more clearly defined; the English claim to hegemony over the Island of Britain was more definitely enforced. Edward's reign was not a mere provisional interlude and his contribution was as essential to the development of the eventual Anglo-Norman State, as it would also have been to the future growth of the Old English State had the Norman Conquest never been accomplished.

The Danes had been integrated into English society; there were far reaching developments in local government and the overall pattern of society. Edward consolidated changes made by his predecessors and was never an arbitrary ruler unlike William I and his successors. Edward had recovered and preserved the rights of the English monarchy, and the machinery of government became so robust that it survived the shock of the Conquest intact. The King successfully transferred the crown to Earl Harold and it was perhaps only the unfortunate advent of a double invasion that deprived him of it.

It is also somewhat difficult to see how the cult of Edward's sanctity got started. He was not an obviously saintly character, and was given to bursts of intense wrath. He could be acid-tongued and it was sometimes difficult to make him see reason. But the more extreme judgements which suggest he was paranoid or neurotic must be rejected for lack of real evidence. His exile and separation from his mother might well have left their mark on him but what that effect was is now impossible to decipher.

It is certainly wrong to accept Norman claims that Edward was eternally grateful to the dukes for having harboured him. Exiles are as likely to resent having to accept the charity of others as to be grateful for it. His reputation for sanctity encouraged much speculation in the Anglo-Norman period, especially as his married life with Queen Edith had been portrayed (as it might well have been in his declining years after 1060) as one of father and daughter rather than man and wife, which led to the belief that he was a virgin king devoted to celibacy. Yet, of the contemporary sources, only the *Vita Edwardi* attributes a chaste life the King. Book One hints at it and Book Two, written after his death, is more definite. But he should be compared to Henry II of Germany and his wife Kunigunda. They were a healthy and devoted couple yet remained childless and were both canonised as Confessors, yet neither was ever portrayed as celibate.

Belief in Edward's power to work miracles, both in life and in death, was perhaps strengthened by the widespread belief in the thaumaturgical powers of kings, and the development of belief in 'touching for the Kings Evil'. That latter belief became so deep-rooted that it survived right down to the reign of Queen Anne who 'touched' Dr Johnson for scrofula.[19]

Henry III rebuilt the Abbey in Edward's honour (and his own) and again the body was translated to a new resting place, behind the high altar. Its exact location was found by radar imaging in December 2005.[20]

As a canonised saint Edward was entitled to seven honours: his name was added to the catalogue of saints so that he received public recognition; his intercession could now be invoked in public (as opposed to private) prayers; churches could be dedicated to God and to the new saint's memory; the Eucharist and Divine office could be celebrated in his honour; his feast day could be observed; pictorial images of him, surrounded by 'heavenly' light, could be exhibited; his relics were enclosed in precious vessels and publicly honoured.[21] He received papal canonisation rather than the approval of his cult by a local bishop because the Papacy was now beginning to insist on its right to approve all cases of canonisation. The political aspect of his canonisation lies only in the fact that it suited the purposes of King Henry II to lend his support to Edward's 'cause' and that the Pope found it opportune to decide the case in a manner which rewarded Henry for his support. Without that aspect of the affair, Edward might have had to wait until Rome decided to take notice of Westminster's request. King Henry got involved because no approach could have been made to Rome without his consent.

As Innocent III laid down in January 1199[22] in the case of Saint Homoborous, canonisation requires proof of a pious life, that is virtue of morals, and confirmation by miracles, that is virtue of signs, and Edward had both. His cult after his death had been just strong enough to intensify the praise meted out to him by the author of the *Vita Edwardi Regis*. Later writers had ignored the historical content and progressively enhanced his claims to sanctity. There had been increasing emphasis on his moral 'purity of life' justified by evidence that his interest in religion had deepened as he grew older. He had maintained the poor and infirm at court and elsewhere (works of Christian charity) and reports of persons being healed by his intervention began to circulate at an early stage. He was not a martyr, nor did he fall into the class of saintly bishops and abbots, therefore he became a 'Confessor', that is someone who has demonstrated sanctity of life greater than that demanded of an ordinary pious Christian. He thus became known as Saint Edward the Confessor.

Appendix One

Westminster Abbey

dward's church at Westminster stood until Henry II's reign. Henry decided to rebuild the abbey in the current Gothic style and so destroyed Edward's work, allegedly in order to give him greater honour. The original is shown on the Bayeux Tapestry[1] and described in the *Vita Edwardi Regis*.[2] It was a Romanesque building following the example set by William of Volpiano and his pupils in Normandy and is generally accepted to have been modelled on the church of Jumièges. Whether the fact that Robert Champart, Edward's choice as Archbishop of Canterbury, had been abbot there had influenced the style of the Church at Westminster cannot be established. Notre Dame at Jumièges was being built during Edward's reign and was consecrated in 1067. It is difficult to see how a building then under construction could have served as a model for another under construction at the same time. The west front of Jumièges has a central façade with a pointed gable end, with two much higher towers on each side; it looks nothing like the picture of Westminster in the Bayeux Tapestry which shows a high tower with a dome at the west end. On each side there are two pointed turrets of almost the same height, with two smaller turrets, one on each side of the larger ones. Jumièges was more like Southwell. What can be suggested is that Edward's choice of the Romanesque style could well have been influenced by the opinions of his friends, Archbishop Robert and John, Abbot of Fécamp after 1052. Jumièges was begun in the 1020s by Abbot Thierry and was not completed until the abbacy of Abbot Robert II (1048–78).

Romanesque architecture appeared in Europe during the second quarter of the eleventh century and was not a single homogenous style but consisted of several regional styles of which 'Norman' was one. England had not participated in the movement and Edward's church was the first building in the new style in England. The most that can be said is that it drew on early Romanesque style in Normandy, transposed onto a scale not paralleled in the Duchy and so might itself have influenced the Norman abbey of Jumièges. Architectural style was already beginning to evolve from Early to High Romanesque.[3]

Edward had a 'church-wright' called Teinfrith,[4] who was German, and two master masons, Leofsi Duddesone and Godwine Gretsith, both English. These men were the nearest medieval equivalent to what would now be called an architect. They worked by rule of thumb rather than by preparing detailed scale drawings in advance. It was architecture of volume and form but equally of texture, colour and light. So much has now been destroyed that it is difficult to appreciate this as the wall paintings and coloured glass that was used are no longer there. What is visible is only a ghost of the original work of art. The fragments of painting remaining at Ely (which also has a group of sculptured portals leading from the church into the cloister) provide some indication of what the decoration at Westminster might have been like. As William of Malmesbury says of Canterbury:

> In the many-coloured pictures remarkable artistic skill, enticing the splendour of the pigments, quite carried the heart away; and the charm of beauty aroused the eyes towards the panelled ceiling.[5]

Some idea of what these paintings looked like can be gained from surviving illustrations in manuscripts. Sulcard, in his *History of Westminster*, accepted that the *Vita* description was accurate and made use of it in his Prologue on the construction of Westminster. There is also some archaeological evidence from excavations.

The building was dressed in Reigate stone. The nave was long with six double bays on each side and a lantern tower over the crossing. Beyond that there was a chancel with another two bays and possibly a porch which connected the new church to the old until the work was completed. A later poem suggests that it had two towers at the west end.

The nave was one hundred and forty feet long. The rows of arches separating the aisles supported a further six bays. Support for this was given by great compound pillars which supported pairs of rounded arches on cylindrical columns. Above that level there was a gallery over the aisles and above that a clerestory of upper windows. The roof was timbered and covered with lead.[6]

The transepts each had their own chapels, and above them at triforium level there was a large gallery which permitted access from the nave gallery into the chancel and provided further space for chapels. All these chapels were consecrated to apostles, martyrs and virgin saints, among them the Apostles Peter and Paul and Saints Nicholas and Benedict.[7]

The tower over the crossing rested on arches at the clerestory level. Such a feature, a lantern, was apt to dominate the church. A lantern tower is open to view from below and illuminated by windows. The chancel had bays which continued the line of the nave arcading. The chancel was surrounded by an ambulatory, the passageway around the choir, (as at Jumièges, Rouen and Fécamp). The nave was longer than that of Jumièges.

The *Vita Edwardi* says of the tower that it was 'reaching up with spiralling stairs in artistic profusion and then with plain walls climbing to a wooden roof carefully covered with lead'. The Bayeux Tapestry shows a cluster of turrets around the tower. The overall impression could have been somewhat like Ely cathedral.[8] The idea could have been to create a monumental vaulted basilica. Of Edward's original building, only the vaults of the College building, which were used as the Pyx Office (a repository for gold and silver coins) until 1855, remain, previously known as St Edward's Chapel.

Romanesque influence is also detectable elsewhere in England, at Wittering, Northamptonshire, Wareham in Dorset and Great Paxton, Cambridgeshire. Goscelin of St Bertin was reported to have told the English clergy that 'If you want to build something better, you have to start by tearing down what is already there'. He came to England in 1058 and said of the buildings he saw that they were 'magnificent, marvellous, extremely long and spacious, full of light and also quite beautiful'.[9]

Appendix Two

The Sources

The essential sources for a life of King Edward are primarily the texts of the Anglo-Saxon Chronicles and that of the *Vita Edwardi Regis*. Much can be learned also from Anglo-Norman writers such as William, the monk of Malmesbury, and something can be gained from a study of the writings of the Normans, William of Jumièges, William of Poitiers and Orderic Vitalis. More information can be derived from the Conqueror's great survey of the realm called Domesday Book and from the writs and charters of King Edward and others. Some account of the nature of these sources and their strengths and weaknesses may help in evaluating the relative evidential value of each source.

The Chronicles

In form they were books laid out solely for the recording of annals year by year and dated by the Year of the Lord or Anno Domini (AD). For the chronicles in Edward's reign the year began at Christmas, called 'The Nativity', though a few entries in the eleventh century were based on a year beginning on 25 March, the Annunciation. For Edward's reign the three manuscripts labelled by convention 'C', 'D' and 'E' provide the bulk of the information. The alphabetical labelling was the work of Charles Plummer who published an edition of the Chronicles in 1892–9. By the eleventh century the annalists who wrote the Chronicles had ceased to record simple annals, that is, a one- or two-line entry recording a significant event such as the death of a king or a battle which helped men distinguish one year from another. They wrote thumbnail sketches of the events of the year, often in a personal and colloquial narrative. Accusations are thrown at prominent individuals and use is made of rhetoric. The writers often display a bias towards one side or the other in a dispute.

The three manuscripts are, for 'C', the Abingdon Manuscript (MS),[10] for 'D', the Worcester MS,[11] and for 'E', the Peterborough MS.[12] There is also a bilingual epitome, 'F', from Canterbury.[13]

The Abingdon MS is a mid-eleventh century text using West Saxon sources and ends with the battle of Stamford Bridge in 1066. The Worcester MS, also written out in the mid-eleventh century, was well informed about events in the north of England and on Anglo-Scandinavian affairs, pointing to the connection between York and Worcester in this period; it ends in 1079. The Peterborough MS is a copy of an older MS made at Peterborough after 1116. In that year the monastery was destroyed by fire and the contents of its library were lost In the process of restocking the library after the fire, the monks borrowed a manuscript from a Kentish library, thought to be probably St Augustine's, Canterbury. The text was copied up to date and continued for another fifty years. The text of the copy had additions made to it based on local sources and knowledge. The bilingual, Latin/English, epitome was written about the year 1100 at Christ Church, Canterbury and is an abridgement of the text which was used at Peterborough. It ends in 1158.

Of the three texts, that of 'C' is the most original and authoritative. 'D' is well informed especially for the period after 1040 when Archbishop Aelfric of York was Bishop of Worcester. 'E' develops a degree of original-ity after 1023 and has a great deal of 'inside information' and detailed local knowledge of the events at Dover in 1051. Other, later, chroniclers were indebted to these texts for much of their information. As for the question of bias or partiality, 'C' tends to be hostile towards the House of Earl Godwine. This may not be unconnected with the fact that the Abbot of Abingdon after 1056 was a certain 'Rodulf', a Norman 'relative' of King Edward. 'D' tends to display impartiality concerning the politics of the period and is mildly sympathetic towards the Godwines. 'E' is strongly biased in favour of Earl Godwine and his family as a Canterbury source might be expected to be.

The next source to consider is the 'Chronicle of Chronicles' usually attributed to the monk Florence, though its most recent editors attribute it to another writer, John, who explicitly continues the Chronicle after the death of Florence in July 1118. It is argued that after Florence's death, John continued the work under his own name. Possibly Florence had been master of the Scriptorium or the Library and his assistance and consent had been vital to the production of the work.

The book is based on the *Chronicle of Marianus Scotus* with a great deal of information from English sources interwoven into it. In particular it uses a version of the Anglo-Saxon Chronicle which has since been lost The edition used for Florence of Worcester is a translation of Benjamin Thorpe's edition of 1848–9 by Joseph Stevenson and published in his *Church Historians of England*, Vol. II. 1853. The author of the Chronicle was an accurate but somewhat pedestrian writer but supplements the Anglo-Saxon Chronicles in a most useful manner.

The last of the principal English sources is William of Malmesbury and his *Deeds of the Kings of the English (Gesta Regum Anglorum)*. His *Deeds of the Bishops of England (Gesta Pontificum)* is also useful. The *Gesta Regum* was written in the first quarter of the twelfth century and finished in 1125; this applies to the *Gesta Pontificum* also. William is a skilled narrator and a genuine historian who admits his ignorance and distances himself from reports that he cannot verify. He deals with an impressive mass of material very competently. He seeks not only to record facts but to explain them, stressing cause and effect. He was the son of a French knight and an English mother.

The monk Orderic Vitalis wrote a monumental *Ecclesiastical History* of Normandy (and England) between 1123 and 1141 at St Evroul monastery in Normandy. The work is actually a general history of England and Normandy under the Norman dynasty. He himself was of Anglo-Norman parentage, born in Shropshire in 1075. He is critical of the flattery embedded in the work of William of Jumièges which he revised and extended.

The first of the Norman writers is William Caillou of Jumièges, a monk of that abbey and author of the *Deeds of the Dukes of Normandy* (*Gesta Normannorum Ducum*), written in or shortly after 1070 (though some argue that the earlier part of the work could have been written in the 1050s). He had little detailed information at his disposal and what he writes reflects Norman opinion and sentiments about significant events. He was the first writer to insist that King Edward had bequeathed the crown to Duke William. His description of events is authoritative but marred by the interpretation he puts upon them.

William, Archdeacon of Lisieux, had studied at Poitiers and been a soldier. He became chaplain to Duke William. His work is *The Deeds of William, duke of the Normans and king of the English* (*Gesta Willelmi*). He writes in a highly rhetorical style, largely coloured by prejudice and repellently boastful in tone.

An enigmatic source is the work known as the Bayeux Tapestry. This is not a tapestry at all but a roll of stitchwork some twenty-three feet long on which is embroidered the story, from a strictly Norman perspective, of the personal relations between William the Bastard and Earl Harold Godwinson. Since at least 1476 it has been among the possessions of the cathedral of Bayeux, hence its name. It is thought to have been created, probably in England and in Kent, at the behest of Odo, Bishop of Bayeux and half-brother of Duke William.

The suggestion is that it was the work of English needlewomen. It makes use of English letters and a number of place names seem to derive from English forms. Some have argued that the text which accompanies it (most of the scenes have short headings in Latin) is studiously non-commital and capable of more than one interpretation. To a Norman observer it tells a straightforward version of Harold's sojourn in Normandy which appears to confirm the accounts given by William of Jumièges and William of Poitiers. To English eyes there are significant omissions. No reason is given for Harold's journey. Nothing is said to indicate what the Earl and the Duke discussed when they met. Harold is said to have made an oath to William at Bayeux (other sources name different locations) but there is no indication of the content of the oath. Lastly Harold's return to England shows him before King Edward in an attitude of shame and dejection, as though he has let the King down. For these and other reasons the Tapestry remains a fascinating enigma.

The *Vita Edwardi Regis*, or *Life of King Edward who lies at Westminster*, is an anonymous work surviving in a single mutilated manuscript of c. 1100. Most, but not all, historians accept that it was most probably written, by an unknown monk from the monastery of St Bertin, during the last years of the Confessor's reign and completed not only after his death but after the Conquest. The text as it stands has no title. It is in two books; book one is an historical essay divided into a series of episodes connected by sets of verses.

The author claims that it is intended as a work in honour of Queen Edith in the form of an account of the great deeds of her family, that is, her husband, the King, her father, Earl Godwine, and her brothers, especially Harold and Tostig. Pages which might have said more about the other brothers are missing as is the account of Edith's marriage in 1045. Some of what is missing can be recovered from quotations in the works of William of Malmesbury and Osbert of Clare. Book Two is about the religious life of King Edward. It contains also a lament that the author's work has been in vain because all the heroes in it are dead. He turns instead to describe King Edward's miracles and the story of his death and burial. Much of Book One is highly political.

The *Encomium Emmae Reginae, In Praise of Queen Emma*, is also an anonymous text and by an unknown monk from St Bertin, and like the *Vita Edwardi* has no title. It is a manuscript of the eleventh century and ends with the return of the *Aetheling* Edward to England at the invitation of his half-brother, King Harthacnut, in 1041. The work covers Swein

Forkbeard's invasion of England, Cnut's Conquest and his marriage to the Lady Emma and culminates in the triumph of her son Harthacnut. It is a work of propaganda on behalf of Queen Emma and justifies many of her actions. It is greatly concerned with the rights of the Danish line of succession to the throne of England.

There are also non-narrative sources to be considered. There are the codes of law issued by various Kings, notably for this period by King Aethelred II and Cnut the Great. They are indispensable for knowledge of the rights of the King, the position of the *Witan*, the shire and hundred courts and the boroughs; the machinery of central and local government. Then there are the charters. They fill in many gaps left by the Laws. They were issued only by Kings, the Church and very great men and contain grants of land and privileges, leases and mortgages, and show the law of the land in operation. They reveal the powers of the King and the influence of the Church. In Edward's reign, they began to be replaced for many purposes by Writs; short peremptory written commands of the King addressed usually to the Earl, Bishop and Sheriff of the shire requiring action on some specific matter. Their use could have originated earlier but it is in Edward's reign that they become an ordinary instrument of government.

Then there is William I's Great Survey: the Domesday Book. Compiled at the Conqueror's behest in 1086 (ordered to be made at the Christmas Court of 1085) and completed just before his death in 1087, it consists of two parts: Volume I, or Great Domesday, covering thirty-one shires from the Channel to the Tees River; and Volume II, Little Domesday, covering Norfolk, Suffolk and Essex. The second volume is actually larger than the first since it has been less tightly abbreviated and contains a wide range of information which seems to have been excluded from Volume I. It is of the greatest importance for the study of pre-Conquest England as it contains information about land holdings, customary dues and rights (especially those of the king) as they were *Tempore Regis Edwardi*, in the time of King Edward. There are also documents relating to the material in Domesday Book which provide evidence about the way in which it was compiled; notably a Survey of Cambridgeshire, the

Inquisitio Comitatus Cantabrigensis, another of the lands of the monastery of Ely, the *Inquisitio Eliensis*, and the *Exon Domesday*, a digest of the survey returns for the south western shires preserved at Exeter Cathedral.

Appendix Three

The Members of the *Witan*

A clearer grasp of the identities and careers of those members of the King's Council, his *Witan* or men of wisdom (the Sapientes or Wise) may be helpful in sorting out the implications of their actions.

A *Witan* comprised all those who, by wealth, influence or office-holding, were felt (or felt themselves) to have the right to be consulted or whom the King himself felt it desirable to consult. They included, naturally, all the earls, the archbishops, bishops and abbots, principal members of the royal household, known in Edward's reign as 'stallers', that is placemen, and prominent King's thegns (of whom some were of national importance while others were only important locally, attending when the council met in their region). In addition, his queen and his mother might also wield influence. In the background there were also a number of influential women, notably the wives of the great earls and possibly some influential abbesses. Not all of these people can be sufficiently identified to allow much comment about them but something is known about the more important of them.

The Earls

An earl can be defined, for the Old English period, as a provincial governor appointed by the king and presiding in the king's name over a number of shires, perhaps as many as ten.

The most influential and probably the wealthiest and most powerful of Edward's earls was Earl Godwine of Wessex. He was in all probability the son of a prominent thegn in Sussex called Wulfnoth Cild who lost his lands under King Aethelred (for rebellion). His son won back most of his father's lands by faithful and assiduous service to Cnut the Great, marrying the King's sister-in-law, Gytha (whose brother, Ulf, had married Cnut's sister Estrith). Cnut made Godwine Earl of Wessex and, in effect, his viceroy in southern England.

After Cnut's death, during the disputed succession (between the sons of Cnut, by different mothers, Harold Harefoot and Harthacnut), Earl Godwine skilfully supported first Harthacnut (and his mother Emma) and then, when Harthacnut failed to return from Denmark, transferred his support to Harold. He was instrumental in facilitating the arrest of the *Aetheling* Alfred and his men, which led to the *Aetheling*'s murder at the hands of King Harold's men. When King Harold died in 1040, Godwine swiftly changed sides again and supported Harthacnut. He was instrumental in organising the return from Normandy of the *Aetheling* Edward when he was invited to return by Harthacnut and helped to ensure a smooth transfer of power to Edward in 1042 when Harthacnut died of a heart attack.

His reward for his efforts came when King Edward married the earl's daughter, Edith, and that resulted in the grant of Earldoms to his two elder sons, Swein and Harold. Earl Godwine was also the recipient of many grants of land which enhanced his considerable wealth and power. Tensions developed between the King's Courtiers, led by the Norman Archbishop Robert, and the Earl which resulted in an open quarrel and the outlawry of the Earl and his family in 1051. Godwine won his way back by a display of immense force, and a series of piratical raids on coastal towns, and was restored to power in 1052. He did not live long to enjoy his success, dying of a stroke on 15 April 1053.

The second most powerful earl was Leofric of Mercia, son of the Ealdorman Leofwine (governor of the area known as the land of the Hwicce – who gave their name to Wychwood in Worcestershire). He, like Earl Godwine, rose to power under Cnut the Great. His family might have been related by marriage to Aelfgifu of Northampton, Cnut's wife '*more Danico*' and mother of Harold Harefoot. He certainly supported Harold against Harthacnut. He also threw his weight behind the accession of King Edward in 1042. In the great quarrel of 1051 he supported the King but, on Godwine's return helped to arrange reconciliation between the Earl and the King. He governed his earldom in a capable manner, defending it against the Welsh, and was a notable benefactor of the Church. His wife was Godgifu (in Latin, Godiva) who was most likely the daughter of an influential Mercian family. Leofric died on 31 August 1057 and was succeeded by his son, Aelfgar, who had been made Earl of East Anglia by King Edward.

The third most powerful earl, and the most enigmatic, was Earl Siward of Northumbria. Most of what is known of him is a matter of legend rather than fact. Unlike the other two earls he was a warrior rather than a statesman. He had been given, by Cnut, the task of defending the northern frontier of England and imposing some sort of order on Northumbria, the most disorderly province. The area had previously been ruled by various members of the Northumbrian family based at Bamburgh, descendants of an Earl with the Scandinavian name of Waltheof.

Siward at some point succeeded Cnut's first Earl of Northumbria, Eric of Norway, and it was Siward, rather than Eric or Cnut, who restored English rule in the north. He had governed in York from about 1033 and was undisputed Earl of Northumbria after Earl Eric fell out with Cnut. Siward married twice. His first wife's name is unknown but she was mother of the earl's eldest son, Osbeorn, who died at the battle of Dunsinnan in 1054. Siward's second wife was Aelffleda, daughter of Ealdred, of the House of Bamburgh. She was mother of Waltheof who was made Earl of Northampton, probably in 1065 by King Edward, and later Earl of Northumberland under the Conqueror.

Siward supported King Edward in 1051 in conjunction with Leofric, whose lead in political matters he appears to have followed. Siward defeated Macbeth, in 1054, and put Malcolm III on the throne of Scotland. He died in 1055 at York.

After the death of Earl Godwine in 1053, King Edward promoted the earl's second son, Harold, as Earl of Wessex, rather than the eldest son, Swein who had been outlawed. Harold served King Edward well as ruler of Wessex and, in consequence, became the richest man in the country after the King. He played a major role in resisting the ambitions of Gruffydd, King of North Wales, and especially that King's support for Earl Aelfgar of Mercia in his two exiles. Harold, with the assistance of his brother Tostig (created Earl of Northumbria on the death of Earl Siward) defeated the Welsh King in 1063 and brought about his death. He had also been instrumental in securing the return of Edward the Exile from Hungary in 1057. His capture, by William of Normandy, put him in an embarrassing position which had unfortunate consequences in 1066 as it enabled William to convince his own men, and the rest of Europe, that he was justified in invading England. Harold was killed, along with his brothers Gyrth and Leofwine and the flower of the English army, at Hastings on 14 October 1066.

Swein Godwinson, Earl Godwine's eldest son, created Earl in the West Midlands and Herefordshire after the King married Edith, was an acute embarrassment to his father. He denied his own parentage, alleging that he was the son of Cnut, he abducted and either raped or seduced the Abbess of Leominster (for which he was outlawed for a time) and murdered his own cousin, Earl Beorn, brother of Swein of Denmark, incurring a second and final outlawry. Driven out with the rest of his family in 1051, he was sent to do penance by making a pilgrimage to Jerusalem from which he never returned, dying near Constantinople on 29 September 1052.

The third son, Tostig, was created Earl of Northumbria on the death of Earl Siward, largely because the earl's son, Osbeorn, had been killed in the war in Scotland and the surviving son, Waltheof, was too young. He ruled Northumbria with a firm hand until 1065. He successfully reduced the threat to English interests represented by King Malcolm III. He visited Rome in 1062 where he was enabled by circumstances to secure a pallium for Archbishop Ealdred of York. In 1063 he cooperated with Harold in the successful invasion of Wales. His rule in Northumbria became progressively harsher and perhaps even tyrannical and he provoked a rising in 1065 which led to his ejection from power. He chose exile rather than acquiescing in his demotion, stirred up trouble for his brother, King Harold, and allied himself with King Harald Hardrada of Norway. He died with his ally at the battle of Stamford Bridge on 25 September 1066.

Little is known of the younger Godwinsons. Gyrth was given an earldom comprising Norfolk and Suffolk in the early 1060s. He visited Rome with Earl Tostig in 1062 and was killed at Hastings in 1066. His brother, Leofwine, who had an earldom covering Essex and the southern bank of the Thames estuary, also in the early 1060s, had accompanied Earl Harold in 1051 when he went to recruit warriors in Ireland to support his father's return in 1052. He too died at Hastings.

King Edward's remaining earls were Earl Ralph, of Hereford, Odda, of Deerhurst and Beorn, brother of King Swein. Of Beorn little can be said other than to note that his murder by Swein Godwinson damaged the interests of Earl Godwine. Beorn held an earldom in the East Midlands. Odda of Deerhurst was a prominent thegn, related in some manner to the King, who was created Earl over the South-Western shires in 1051 which he held until his death in 1056. He commanded part of the King's fleet against Earl Godwine in 1052.

Earl Ralph was the son of King Edward's sister, Godgifu, who married Drogo (or Dreux), Count of Mantes in the Vexin, a contested region between Normandy and the Île de France. The Earl was given Herefordshire as an earldom, probably in about 1051, where he had already begun encouraging Norman and French knights to settle and construct motte and bailey castles. Ralph supported the King against Earl Godwine in 1051–52, commanding, not very successfully, a contingent of the royal fleet. In 1055 he attempted to confront the outlawed Earl Aelfgar and his Welsh and Irish allies near Hereford. As he commanded his English levies to fight on horseback, contrary to custom, his attempt failed. The whole force fled in disorder before making real contact with the enemy. Possibly the horses had taken fright at the noise created by the battle hardened Welshmen, but English opinion blamed the earl, accusing him of cowardice and of being the first to flee. Thereafter he was known as Ralph the Timid. He died on 21 December 1057 and is buried at Peterborough.

Of the other lay members of the *Witan* little can be said except for those known to have held office as stallers. Of those whose identity is known, three were Danish, Osgod Clapa and Tofig the Proud and his grandson, Ansger, and two were at least part Breton, Robert FitzWymarc and Ralf, known only as 'the *staller*'.

Tofig occurs in Edward's story only as the bridegroom at a wedding at Lambeth on 8 June 1042 at which he married Gytha, daughter of Osgod Clapa. During the wedding feast, King Harthacnut had a seizure and dropped dead, so enabling Edward to become king, much to the latter's surprise and possibly dismay. Tofig was a survivor of the reign of Cnut (under whom he held an estate in Reading) who had survived the reigns of his sons. He also figures in the history of Waltham Abbey. According to the abbey's Chronicle, Tofig had founded the original church at Waltham after he discovered a wonderful miracle-working image of Christ on the Cross carved from either black marble or polished blue lias. That was why the Church was that of the Holy Cross.

Osgod Clapa (his cognomen means 'the Ruffian'), was another survival from the reign of Cnut, holding land in East Anglia. Osgod possibly caused trouble for Earl Harold of East Anglia, because King Edward exiled Osgod in 1046, but it might also have been part of the King's policy of eliminating Danes from his administration. Osgod Clapa caused some trouble over the next few years, planning attacks on England from a base in Flanders and raiding Essex. He died suddenly, in his bed, in 1054.

Tofig's grandson, Aesgar, became a staller sometime towards the end of the reign. His only known exploit was to defend London against the Conqueror after the Battle of Hastings.

Robert FitzWymarc was probably part Norman, part Breton and named for his mother. He is described as a kinsman of the King and as his steward of the palace or procurator. William of Poitiers says his mother was a Norman relative of the Duke, called Guimara, but modern historians think her name is of Breton origin. He might just possibly be the

Robert the Deacon given a prebend in Bromfield, Shropshire, by King Edward in 1065. He was one of those present at the King Edward's side when he died in 1066. Robert's son, Swein, became sheriff of Essex under the Conqueror and held a castle at Clavering.

Ralf the Staller was a Breton and father of Ralf de Gael, King William's Earl of Norfolk. He appears to have entered Edward's service in 1050. He survived the Conquest and died before April, 1070. His son was also Lord of Gael in Brittany. If, as William of Poitiers claims, he too, like Robert FitzWimarc, was Norman, then Ralf Staller was probably Norman-Breton; but the Peterborough Chronicle claims he was English and born in Norfolk, so he is more likely to have been Anglo-Breton. He is 'Ralph *Anglicus*', Ralf the Englishman, on a charter of Alan, Duke of Brittany. Other sources call him Breton. He could have been called English because he was born in England. William of Poitiers would have been only too keen to claim that men close to King Edward were Normans.

The Bishops and Other Clergy

King Edward had three archbishops of Canterbury: Eadsige, Robert Champart, and Stigand.

Eadsige (1038–1050) was appointed by Cnut and served his sons and Edward. He is described as an ally of Earl Godwine, but that could be mere deduction from the fact that he performed Edward's coronation. But he did allow Earl Godwine to hold and administer some of the estates of Canterbury. In the 1040s he resigned his see for a time on grounds of ill health and then resumed it when his assistant bishop proved unworthy. He finally died on 29 October 1050.

Eadsige was succeeded by Robert Champart, former prior and abbot of Jumièges. Robert was appointed by Edward as bishop of London, taking office by 1044, and promoted to Canterbury in 1050, because they had been friends during Edward's exile. He appears to have had a great deal of personal influence over the king which led to conflict with Earl Godwine as they struggled for control over events. Expelled from his see in 1052, on

Godwine's return to power and influence, he went to Rome to complain. That resulted in Rome's refusal to acknowledge the legitimacy of Bishop Stigand's transfer to Canterbury. Robert could have been the person who planted the idea in Duke William's mind that King Edward had chosen him as his successor on the throne of England. The former Archbishop retired to his abbey in Jumièges after his return from Rome and died sometime before 1058.

Stigand, who replaced Archbishop Robert after his expulsion, was never recognised at Rome as legitimate archbishop. This was partly because of the way in which Archbishop Robert had been removed, and partly because Stigand transferred from his See of Winchester without surrendering his bishopric. He was also criticised for holding simultaneously a number of other clerical offices, including abbacies, and so guilty of pluralism. Another charge laid against him was the sin of simony, the purchase of clerical office. He could well have been guilty but there is no direct evidence. He had been a royal chaplain in Cnut's time, and had held the See of Elmham, in East Anglia (which he passed to his brother Aethelmaer after becoming Bishop of Winchester). He was also a confidant of Queen Emma. He was briefly recognized as Archbishop in 1058 by the anti-pope Benedict X. A wily and astute politician rather than a holy churchman, Stigand was an able if somewhat devious and cynical operator. He survived the Conquest and retained his see under the Conqueror (who did not allow him to perform the coronation) until deposed by the Papal Legates in 1070. His family came from Norwich and he had extensive lands in East Anglia.

The Archbishops of York

Again there were three during the reign: Aelfric 'Puttoc', Cynsige and Ealdred.

Aelfric Puttoc, 1023–51. A former provost of Winchester and servant of Cnut, his knowledge of the Winchester liturgical tradition contributed to the ceremonies of King Edward's coronation. He was notorious for participation in the desecration of Harold Harefoot's body on the orders of King Harthacnut; the body had been disinterred and thrown into the Thames.

Cynsige, 1051–60. A royal clerk in King Edward's service, he began the adornment and enrichment of the four Yorkshire minsters and consecrated Waltham Holy Cross for Earl Harold. Cynsige was English and his appointment in 1051 balances that of the Norman Robert as Archbishop of Canterbury.

Ealdred, 1061–69. A Devonshire man, abbot of Tavistock and kinsman of his predecessor, Lyfing, as bishop of Worcester, he became Archbishop of York on the death of Cynsige. He was almost deprived of his promotion by the Pope in 1062 but saved by the embarrassment caused by the attack on Earl Tostig's entourage. He was Bishop of Worcester from 1046 until 1062 when he had to surrender the bishopric as the price of being confirmed as Archbishop. He allowed Earl Harold to escape in 1051 and seems to have been a supporter of that earl. He performed Harold's coronation in 1066. A diplomat as well as a churchman, he was sent on embassies to Rome and to Germany by King Edward and was responsible for the return of Edward the Exile in 1057.

The Bishops

Of the Bishops, only two were Norman, the rest either English or Lotharingian. The Normans were Ulf, of Dorchester (on Thames), 1049–52, and William, of London, 1051–75. Of their antecedents nothing is known. Ulf was a most unbishoplike bishop, almost unfrocked, for simony, by the Pope at the Synod of Vercelli. He was a former royal clerk in the household, like so many others, but his appointment was seen as scandalous and probably reflects the influence of Robert of Jumièges. William lost his see briefly in 1052 but, as he was held blameless, was restored to office and remained in place for the rest of the reign into that of the Conqueror. He ruled his see competently but without great distinction. Ulf was expelled in 1052 along with the archbishop, upon the return to office of the Godwinsons.

The other appointees were almost all former royal clerks. There was Herman, a Lotharingian, appointed to Wiltshire in 1045; Leofric, an Englishman educated in Lorraine, appointed to Devon and Cornwall in 1046; Heca, another Englishman, given Sussex in 1047; and Aethelmaer, brother of Bishop Stigand, who was given Elmham in 1052. The appointment of these men reflects the need to placate local opinion rather than some conscious design intended to balance the appointment of a couple of Normans. In fact, of the eleven bishops who witness charters between 1049 and 1050, all except the two archbishops had been appointed by King Edward. He had certainly stamped his own choice on the Church.

In the 1060s there were a few more bishoprics to be filled, notably by Walter, another Lotharingian, given Hereford. He was a chaplain to Queen Edith, and yet another from Lorraine, Giso, a royal clerk, received 'Somerset', that is, Wells. Both went to Rome, with Earl Tostig and Ealdred, and were accepted there by Nicholas II. Giso was the successor of the long-lived Dudoc of Wells, another Lotharingian but appointed by Cnut in 1033. Lastly, among the foreign clergy, was the King's '*cancellarius*' Regenbald, who was probably either German or Lotharingian. He survived the Conquest and served the Conqueror as chancellor. He served Edward from 1050 onwards as *cancellarius* and as *sigillarius* (keeper of the Seal). He had all the rights of a diocesan bishop without actually being one.

Abbreviations

A.N.S.   Anglo Norman Studies.

A.S.E.   Anglo Saxon England.

D.B.   Domesday Book.

E.H.D.   English Historical Documents.

E.H.R.   English Historical Review.

G.G.   Gesta Guillelmi. Poitiers.

G.N.D.   Gesta Normannorum Ducum. Jumièges.

G.P.   Gesta Pontificum. Malmesbury.

G.R.   Gesta Regum Anglorum. Malmesbury.

H.Y.C.   Historians of the Church of York.

LE.   *Liber Eliensis*.

N.C.M.H. New Cambridge Medieval History.

R.A.D.N. Recueil des Actes de Ducs de Normandie.

T.R.H.S. Transactions of the Royal Historical Society.

Bibliography

'The Aetheling; a study in Anglo-Saxon constitutional history.' D.N. Dumville. A.S.E. 5 1976.

The Aethelings in Normandy. S. Keynes, *Anglo-Norman Studies* (cited as A.N.S.) 13.1991.

Aethelred the Unready: the Ill-Counselled King. Ann Williams. London 2003.

'Edward the Confessor and the Celibate Life.' E. John. Analecta Bollandiana 97. 1979.

The Anglo-Saxon Age c. 400-1042. D.J.V. Fisher. Longman 1973.

The Anglo-Saxons. G. Hindley. London 2006.

Anglo-Saxon Charters. A.J. Robertson. Cambridge 1939.

Anglo-Saxon Charters. P. Sawyer. London 1968.

The Anglo-Saxon Chronicles. Everyman Edition. G.N. Garmonsway. London 1955.

The Anglo-Saxon Chronicles. Ed. & Trans. J. Stevenson. London 1853.

The Anglo-Saxon Chronicles. M. Swanton. London 2000.

Anglo-Saxon England. Sir Frank Stenton. Oxford 1988.

Anglo-Saxon England and the Norman Conquest. H.R. Loyn. London 1962.

Anglo-Saxon Wills. Ed. and Trans. D. Whitelock. Cambridge 1930.

The Anglo-Saxons. Ed. J. Campbell. Oxford 1982.

The Anglo-Saxons. Ed. P. Clemoes. London 1959.

The Anglo-Saxon State. Ed. J. Campbell. London and N.Y. 2000.

Annales Cambriae. Ed. J.W. ab Ithel. R.S. 1869.

'A Pre-Conquest Occupation of England?' M.W. Campbell. *Speculum.* 46 1971.

The Archaeology of Anglo-Saxon England. D.M. Wilson. London 1976.

Authority and Interpretation of the Bayeux Tapestry. N.P. Brookes and H.E. Walker. A.N.S.1 1978.

'Baldwin, Abbot of Bury St. Edmunds.' A. Gransden. A.N.S. 4 1982.

The Blackwell Encyclopaedia of Anglo-Saxon England. Ed. M. Lapidge 2001.

Basic readings in Anglo-Saxon History, Vol.6. M. Clunes Ross 2000.

The Bayeux Tapestry. D.M. Wilson. London 1985.

The Bayeux Tapestry and Schools of Illumination. C.R. Hart. A.N.S. 21 1998.

'The Bayeux Tapestry: Invisible seams and visible boundaries.' G.R. Owen-Crocker. *Anglo-Saxon England* 31 2002.

Blood Feud: Murder and Revenge in Anglo-Saxon England. R. Fletcher. Penguin 2002.

'Bookland and Fyrd Service in Late Saxon England'. R. Abels. A.N.S. 7 1984.

Brut y Twysogion: The Chronicle of the Princes. T. Jones. Cardiff 1955.

Canonization and Authority in the Western Church. E.W. Kemp. Oxford 1948.

Change and Continuity in Eleventh Century Mercia. Emma Mason A.N.S. 8 1985.

The Changing Climate; Selected papers. H.H. Lamb. London 1966.

'Changing Thegns; Knut's Conquest of the English Aristocracy'. K. Mack. *Albion* 16 1984.

Chronicle of Florence of Worcester. Ed. And Trans. J. Stevenson. London 1853.

Chronicon Monasterii de Abingdon. Ed. J. Stevenson 2 Vols. R.S. 1858.

'Clio's legal Cosmetics; Law and Custom in the work of Medieval Historians.' M. Chibnall. A.N.S. 20. 1997.

Cnut: the Danes in England in the Early Eleventh Century. M.K. Lawson. Harlow. 1993.

Codex Diplomatici Aevi Saxonici. J. M. Kemble. London 1939-48.

'The collection of danegeld and heregeld in the reigns of Aethelred II and Cnut.' M.K. Lawson. E.H.R. 99 1984.

Conquest, Co-Existence and Change: Wales 1063-1415. R. Davies. Oxford 1987.

The Constitutional History of Medieval England. J.E.A. Jolliffe. London 1937.

'Coronation and Propaganda. Some implications of the Norman claim to the throne of England in 1066.' G. Garnett. T.R.H.S. 5th Ser.36, 1986.

The Cultivation of Saga in Anglo-Saxon England. C.E. Wright. London 1939.

De moribus et actis primorum Normanniae ducum. Dudo of St Quentin. Ed. J. Lair. Caen 1865.

The Diplomas of Aethelred, 'the Unready', 978-1016. S. Keynes. Cambridge 1980.

Domesday Book. Ed. And Trans. Ann Williams and G.H. Martin. Penguin 1992.

Domesday Book and Beyond. F.W. Maitland. Cambridge 1887. 1965 Ed.

'The Domesday Estates of the King and the Godwins. A Study in late Saxon Politics. Robin Fleming. *Speculum.* 58, 1983.

The Dukes of Normandy and their Origin. Rt. Hon. The Earl of Onslow. London 1945.

Encomium Emmae Regina. Ed. And Trans. A Campbell. Cambridge 1998.

'Ealdred of York; the Worcester Years.' Vanessa King. A.N.S. 18. 1995.

'Earl Godwine of Wessex and his political loyalties.' D.G. Raraty. *History.* 74, 1989.

Early Medieval Kingship. Ed. I.N. Wood and P.H. Sawyer. Leeds 1977.

The Ecclesiastical History. Orderic Vitalis. Ed. and trans. Margery Chibnall. Oxford 1969-80.

Edward the Confessor. F. Barlow. London 1979.

'Edward the Confessor and the Norman Succession.' E. John. E.H.R. 04 1979.

'Edward the Confessor, Duke William of Normandy and the English Succession.' D.C. Douglas. E.H.R. 68 1953.

'Edward the Confessor; Early Life, Character and Attitudes.' F. Barlow. E.H.R. 79 1965.

'Edward the Confessor's Promise of the Throne to Duke William of Normandy.'T.J. Oleson. E.H.R. 72, 1957.

'Edward the Confessor's return to England in 1041.' J.R. Maddicott. E.H.R. 118, 2004.

Encheiridion Symbolorum. Denzinger H. Cologne 1920.

England before the Norman Conquest. R.W. Chambers. London 1928.

England before the Norman Conquest. P. Clemoes and K. Hughes. Cambridge 1971.

England before the Norman Conquest. Sir Charles Oman. London 1921.

English and Norse Documents relating to the reign of Ethelred the Unready. M. Ashdown. Cambridge 1930.

The English Church and the Papacy. N. Brooke. Cambridge 1972.

English Historical Documents. Vol.1 Ed. D. Whitelock. London 1979.

English Historical Documents. Vol.2 Ed. D.C. Douglas and G.W. Greenaway. London 1953. (Cited as E.H.D.)

The English Nobility under Edward the Confessor. P.A. Clarke. Oxford 1994.

English Romanesque Art 1066-1200. Arts Council of Great Britain. 1984.

Essays in Anglo-Saxon History. J. Campbell. London 1986.

Fear and Faith in Anglo-Saxon England. P. Cavill. London 2001.

Feudalism. F.L. Ganshof. London 1966.

The Feudal Kingdom of England. F. Barlow. London 1961.

The Foundations of Medieval England. G.O. Sayles. London 1947.

'The French in England before the Norman Conquest.' C.P. Lewis A.N.S. 17, 1995.

From Roman Britain to Norman England. P. Sawyer. London 1978.

Geoffrey Gaimar; L'Estorie des Engles. Ed. and Trans. J. Stevenson. London 1854.

Gerald of Wales; Journey through Wales and Description of Wales. Trans. L. Thorpe. Penguin. 1978.

Gesta Normannorum Ducum. William of Jumièges. Ed. J.Marx. Rouen-Paris 1914.

'Gesta Normannorum Ducum'. A history without an end. E. Van Houts. A.N.S. 2, 1979.

Gesta Regum Anglorum. William of Malmesbury. Ed. and Trans. Mynors et al. Oxford. 2006.

Gesta Willelmi, ducis Normannorum et Regis Anglorum. William of Poitiers. Ed. Foreville. Paris 1952.

Giso of Wells. S. Keynes. A.N.S. 19, 1996.

The Godwins; the Rise and fall of a noble dynasty. F. Barlow. Harlow. 2001.

The Governance of Anglo-Saxon England 500-1087. H.R. Loyn. London 1984.

Guillaume le Conquérant. Michel de Boüard. Librairie Arthème Fayard, 1984.

Handlist of Anglo-Saxon and Runic Inscriptions. E. Okasha. Cambridge 1971.

Harold, the last Anglo-Saxon King. Ian W. Walker. Stroud 1997.

Harold II The Doomed Saxon King. P. Rex. Tempus 2005.

Historia Novorum in Anglia. Eadmer. Ed. M. Rule. Rolls Series. London 1884.

'Historiography and Hagiography at St Wandrille' (*Inventio et Miracula Sancti Vlfranni*) E. Van Houts A.N.S. 12 1990.

Historians of the Church of York. Ed. J. Raine. R.S. 3 Vols. 1879-94.

History of the Archbishops of Hamburg-Bremen. Adam of Bremen. Trans. F.J. Tschan. New York 1959.

History of the Norman Conquest. 6 Vols. E.A. Freeman. Oxford 1862.

A History of Wales from earliest Times to the Edwardian Conquest. J.E. Lloyd. 2 Vols. London 1939.

'The Housecarl in England in the Eleventh Century'. N. Hooper. A.N.S. 7 1984.

The House of Godwine; The History of a Dynasty. Emma Mason. London and N.Y. 2004.

In Search of the Dark Ages. M. Wood. B.B.C. Books 2005.

An Introduction to Anglo-Saxon England .P. Hunter Blair. Cambridge 1956.

An Introduction to the History of England. D. Jerrold. London 1949.

'Keeping up with the Godwinsons; in pursuit of aristocratic status in late Anglo-Saxon England'. C. Senecal. A.N.S. 23 2000.

The Kings and Queens of England. W.M. Ormrod. Tempus 2004.

'Kings and Thegns; aristocratic participation in the governance of Anglo-Saxon England.' K. Mack. Unpublished research paper, University of California at Santa Barbara, 1982.

The Kingdom of Northumbria. A.D. 350-1100. N.J. Higham. Stroud 1996.

King Harald's Saga. M. Magnusson and H Pálson. Penguin 1966.

Kingship and Government in Pre-Conquest England, c. 500-1066. Ann Williams. Macmillan Press 1999.

'Land and Power in the Eleventh Century; the estates of Harold Godwinson'. Ann Williams. A.N.S. 3. 1980.

'The Lands and Revenues of Edward the Confessor'. J.L. Grassi. E.H.R. 117. 2002.

'The Lands of Harold son of Godwine'. R.H. Davies. Unpub. Ph.D. Thesis, Cardiff 1967.

'The Language of the Bayeux Tapestry'. I. Short. A.N.S. 23 2000.

La Tapisserie de Bayeux. Lucien Musset. 2nd Ed. Zodiaque Paris 2002 (Trans. Richard Rex 2005).

The Laws of the Kings of England. A.J. Robertson. Cambridge 1925.

Le Mémorial des Siècles: XI Siècle, les evénments. La Conquête de l'Angleterre par les Normands. André Maurois. Éditions Albin Michel. 1968.

Letters of Osbert of Clare. Ed. E.W. Williamson. Oxford 1929.

Liber Eliensis. A History of the Isle of Ely. Trans. Janet Fairweather. Boydell Press 2005.

Lordship and Military Obligation in Anglo-Saxon England. R. Abels London and Los Angeles. 1988.

The Making of English Law. King Alfred to the Twelfth Century. Vol. 1. P. Wormald. Blackwell. 2000

The Medieval Foundations of England. G.O. Sayles. London 1948.

The New Cambridge Medieval History. IV. Parts I and II. Ed. D. Luscombe and J. Riley-Smith. Cambridge 2004.

'The New Wealth, the New Rich and the new Political Style in late Anglo-Saxon England'. Robin Fleming. A.N.S. 23 2000.

The Norman Conquest. D.J.A. Matthew. London 1966.

The Norman Conquest and Beyond. F. Barlow. London 1983.

The Norman Conquest of the North; the region and its transformation 1000-1135. W.E. Kapelle. London 1979.

'The Norman Conquest through European Eyes'. E. Van Houts. E. H.R. 110 1995.

The Normans and their Histories; Propaganda, Myth and Subversion. E. Albu. Woodbridge 2001.

The Normans in England before Edward the Confessor. R.L.G. Ritchie. Exeter 1948.

The Norman Monasteries and their English Possessions. D.J.A. Matthew. Oxford 1962.

The Origins of English Feudalism. R.A. Brown. New York 1973.

The Papal Monarchy: the Western Church from 1050 to 1250. C. Morris. Oxford 1989.

Politics and Ritual in Early Medieval Europe. Janet Nelson. London 1986.

'Problems connected with the English Royal Succession 800-1066'. Ann Williams. A.N.S. 2 1979.

Queen Emma and the Vikings. Harriet O'Brien. London 2006.

Queens and Queenship in Europe. Ed. A.J. Duggan. Woodbridge 1997.

Queens, Concubines and Dowagers. Pauline Stafford. London 1983.

Queen Emma and Queen Edith; Queenship and Women's Power in the Eleventh Century. Pauline Stafford. Oxford 1997.

Reassessing Anglo-Saxon England. E. John. Manchester 1996.

'Regenbald the Chancellor [sic]' S. Keynes. A.N.S. 10 1988.

'The relation between England and Flanders before the Norman Conquest.' P. Grierson. T.R.H.S. 4th Ser. 23 1941.

'The Rites of the Conqueror'. Janet Nelson. A.N.S. 4. 1981.

Romanesque. Ed. Rolf Toman. Trans. F. Hulse & I. Macmillan. Cambridge 2004.

Ruling England 1042-1217. R. Huscroft. Pearson Longman. 2005.

Saxo Grammaticus Gesta Danorum. Ed. E. Christianson. BAR International Series. 84. 1980.

Select Charters. Ed. W. Stubbs. 8th Ed. Oxford 1900.

Shorter Cambridge Medieval History. Vol. 1. Ed. C. W. Previté – Orton. Cambridge 1952.

Simeon of Durham. Ed. T. Arnold. R.S. 2 vols. 1882-5.

'Some Notes and Considerations on problems connected with the English Royal Succession 860-1066'. Ann Williams A.N.S. 1 1978.

'The Stallers; an administrative innovation in the reign of Edward the Confessor'. K. Mack. J.M.H. 12 1986.

'Thegnly Piety and Ecclesiastical Patronage in the late Old English Kingdom'. Robin Fleming. *Speculum* 58 1983.

Time and the Hour. D. C. Douglas. London 1977.

'Towards an Interpretation of the Bayeux Tapestry'. H. E. J. Cowley. A.N.S. 9 1986.

Unification and Conquest; A political and social history of England in the tenth and eleventh centuries.' Pauline Stafford. London 1989.

'A visit of Earl Harold to Flanders in 1056'. P. Grierson. E.H.R. 51 1936.

Vita Edwardi Regis: the Life of King Edward who lies at Westminster. Ed. and Trans. F. Barlow Oxford 1992.

'Wales and the coming of the Normans 1039-93.' J. E. Lloyd Trans. of Hon. Soc. of Cymrodorion. 1899-1900.

Wales in the early Middle Ages. W. Davies. Leicester 1982.

'The Welsh Alliances of Earl Aelfgar'. K. L. Maund. A.N.S. 11 1989.

'Where did all the Charters Go? Anglo-Saxon Charters and the new Politics of the Eleventh Century.' C. Insley. A.N.S. 24. 2001.

William the Conqueror. D. Bates. Tempus 2004.

William the Conqueror. D. C. Douglas. London 1964.

The Witanagemot in the reign of Edward the Confessor. T.J. Oleson. Oxford
1955.

1066; the Year of the Three Battles. Frank McLynn. Pimlico 1066.

Notes

Chapter 1

1   G.N.D. 5.4 to 5.7.

2   Van Houts Collegium Medievale 12 1999 Countess Gunnor of Normandy.

3   De Boüard 43.

4   Historia Anglorum 752b.

5   G.N.D. 5.7.

6   Matthew. 32-34.

7   Aetheling from 'aethel' – noble and 'inge' – offspring. Dumville. A.S.E. The Aetheling. Prince of the Royal House.

8   Harmer Writs. No.104.

9   S.1148 Writ of King Edward granting Islip where he was born to Westminster.

10 S 911 & S 910

11 Barlow 28-32 discusses the question.

12 Vita Edwardi 7-8.

13 Matthew 39.

14 Inventio et Miracula S.Vulfranni 251, circa 1053-54.from St Wandrille.

15 Barlow. 7-8.

16 O'Brien 86.

17 See Bishop Brihtwald's vision;Vita Edwardi 8-9

18 See Vita Edwardi 60.

19 Encomium 18-19.

20 Barlow 32-33

21 Liber Eliensis II 91, page 191 in translation of Janet Fairweather.

22 John. Orbis Britanniae 159-60.Vita S. Oswaldi HCY i.449.

23 Encomium 22-28.

24 S 1115 Writs 68

25 Barlow 13.

26 Saga of Olaf Tryggvason; the Longer Saga. Cap.285.

27 Olaf's Saga Tryggvasonnar cap.286.

28 Olaf's Saga Helge caps 12-15

29 G.R.i.191.

30 Olaf's Saga Helge cap.16 & 20

31 Williams Aethelred. 135.

32 Flateyarbok; the Saga of Olaf cap.10.

33 Olaf's Drapa (1) Stanza 1.

34 Wright C.E. p.203

35 Charters and Documents of the Abbey of St. Peter no. 69

36 S 1002 with copies in the Ghent archives.

37 Vita p.8

38 S 949 Rammesleah between Winchelsea and Rye.

39 Worcester D 1043.

40 Encomium 32-3.

41 Harmer Writs no. 93 of doubtful authenticity.

Chapter 2

1 G.R. II 188.3.

2 Vita 75.

3 Vita 61-62

4 Onslow 120-21.

5 Stenton. 425-6.

6 Cap. 37.

7 Bates 24.

8 Jumièges V 7 81-2 Poitiers I p.2

9 Polycraticus I iv & v)

10 Vita Edwardi 40.

11 Barlow E.H.R.C. 109 1965

12 Poitiers II 174.

13 See McLynn . 13-14.

14 For the background to this see Barlow; William Rufus
    16-23. on the upbringing of Rufus.

15 Douglas William the Conqueror 162.

16 Onslow. 124. Saxo Gram. 1.193. Adam of Bremen ii 52. Glaber iv 6
    & 20.

17 Lawson 20.

18 G.N.D. vi 10.

19 Lawson Cnut. 110.

20 GND. II. I.7.

21 Barlow; The Norman Conquest and Beyond 1983. 101.

22 Bates 45.

23 Freeman Norman Conquest Vol. I 520.

24 Douglas. 44-45. and 162-3.

25 R.A.D.N. no. 70

26 R.A.D.N. no. 69

27 R.A.D.N. no. 111 S 1061

28 Lawson; Cnut 110.

29 R.A.D.N. no. 85.

30 Douglas 162. Keynes A.N.S. no. XIII.

31 Lawson op. cit. 110.

32 Abingdon Chronicle C 1036.

33 L.E. II. 90. Version F.

34 Twelfth century Calendar.

35 Vita Edwardi 20-21.

36   L.E. II. 90 versions E and F.

37   L.E.II 79.

38   G.G. i. cap.2.

39   Worcester D 1018.

40   Barlow E.H.R. 80 1965

41   Jumièges G.N.D. 120-21. Poitiers G.G. 4-6.

42   McLynn 4.

43   Encomium 41-47.

44   O'Brien 172.

45   See discussion in O'Brien 173-4.

46   Kemble C.D. 14 173 and 181. Rejected by Sawyer.

47   Hill. 73, Stenton 421. Florence. i. 195.

48   Theodric the Monk; History of Norway 46,
      Anonymous of Roskild; Danish Chronicle i.377,
      Saxo Grammaticus, Gesta Danorum 360,
      Snorre Sturlason, Heimskringla caps 6,37-8.

Chapter 3

1   Abingdon C and Worcester D. Peterborough E Notes only his
      return.

2   Encomium 52-3

3   Poitiers G.G. 12 and 28-31.

4   Barlow 49.

5   B. Mus. Add. MS 33241

6   Abingdon C & Worcester D 1041 and Florence of Worcester.

7   Stenton 423.

8   Oleson Witanagemot. 84-6.

9   Nelson Politics and Ritual.

10   S 994 & S 997.

11   Stafford Queen Emma and Queen Edith p.247.

12   S 993.

13   Stafford Queens, Concubines and Dowagers. 4.

14   Poitiers G.G. 30.Vita Edwardi 17.

15   Eccles. Hist.VI 168-9.

16   A.N.S. 17 The French in England before the Norman Conquest.

17   Discussed in E.H.R. 119 2004 by J.R. Maddicott.
     Edward the Confessor's return to England in 1041.

18   Aelfwine had been Cnut's priest, a bishop since 1032 and a
     prominent member of the Witan under Harthacnut.

19   Abingdon C and Worcester D 1041.

20   G.R.ii.196.

21   S.1001 1044; S1007 & 1008 1045; S 1013 1046; S 1152 &1151.

22   Williams in A.N.S. I.

23   See Chronicle, 'as was his natural right'; Encomium 52 'legitimate heir'.

24   William of Poitiers G.G. 14.

25   Loyn H.R. Footnote p.19.

26   L.E. II 97.

27   S 1103 Writs 51.

28   S 1104 Writs 54 and S 1151 Writs 109.

29   S 998 & S 1005 for Ordgar and S999 for Aelfstan.

30   S1004.

31   S1086 Writs 31.

32   S1001, S 1007 and S1008. DB I.155 & 41v.

33   S1009.

34   Vita 13-14 & Florence 1.195 1041.

35   Encomium 84-5 Malmesbury G.P. cap.21.

36   Miracula S. Mildredae in E.H.R. lxxiii 1958 Barlow.
     Theodoric the Monk Historia 39-48 Chron. Roskildensis 376-7.

37   Adam of Bremen II lxxvii, lxxviii.

38   See Charters S 1001 & 1006.

Chapter 4

1   Abingdon Chron. C 1043 and Peterborough E.

2   H.C.Y. I 438ff.

3   3 Kings I. 39

4   3 Kings i. 39.

5   Vita pp. 11–12.

6   Robertson; Charters cxx & xcv

7   Abingdon Chron. C end of annal for 1044.

8   Peterborough E

9   Osbert of Clare Vita Edwardi c. iv. possibly using the lost section of the *Vita Edwardi Regis*.

10   Osbert c.i vi and G.R. II 197.

11   Lawson Cnut. P. 265.

12   Leofric Missal pp.8b–9a.

13   Typical of this view is Robin Fleming in Kings & Lords in Conquest England.

14   Jerrold. Genealogical table C. p.568.

15   Stafford. (1) p.37.

16   Oleson Witanagemot p.42.

17   Fleming p. 9.

18   Vita 7, 15.

19   Stafford (1) p.99 citing Hincmar of Rheims' On the Governance of the Palace'.

20   Vita Edwardi. P.17.

21   Idem. p. 23.

Chapter 5

1   Orderic II 272–8

2   Osbert c.iv no doubt derived from the lost pages of the *Vita*.

3   Barlow (1) p.73.

4   S 1037 to the priest Scepio.

5   Stenton A.S.E. p.581.

6   Stenton p.427.

7   Peterborough E 1046 (correctly 1049).Abingdon C 1049.

8 Campbell J. The Anglo-Saxons p.208.

9 Op.Cit. p.212.

10 Vita 17 & footnotes.

11 Vita 76

12 Barlow (1) 94. Stenton ASE p.562.

13 Gest. Pont. I 94 and Florence 1046.

14 Barlow (91) 86-87.

15 See A.N. S. 19.

16 L.E. II 95.

17 S 998

18 Peterborough E 1043 (for 1044) Abingdon C 1044.

19 S 1123

20 Barlow (1) 84.

21 Articles in Blackwell.

22 S 1021.

23 According to witness lists on 3 forged charters. S 1030,1036 &1043.

24 S 1002.

25 Vita Wulfstani.p.18.

26 S. 1021 and Harmer, Writs No. 44.

Chapter 6

1 S 1009, S 1022.

2 Walker p.54.

3 Davies R.H. unpublished thesis Cardiff 1967. Williams A.N.S. 2 1979
Land & Power.

4 Figures derived from Domesday by the author.

5 Fleming Tables 3.1 and 3.3.

6 Grassi J.L. E.H.R. 117 2002. Lands and Revenue of Edward the
Confessor.

7 Campbell J.T.R.H.S. 5th series no.25.

8 See E.H.R. 93. 1978.

9   S 1026.

10 See discussion in Barlow (1) p.181ff. & English Romanesque Art
    1066–1200 Hayward Gallery 1984

Chapter 7

1   Abels p.103.

2   Loyn. Governance. P.121.

3   Barlow. P.156.

4   Williams. Aethelred pp151ff.

5   Abingdon C 1050.

6   D.B. fol.30.

7   Idem fol.100.

8   Idem. fol.336v.

9   Williams. Kingship and Government p.144-45.

10 D.B. II fols. 372;118;119v.

Chapter 8

1   Abels. P.80.

2   S. 986 Cnut to Archbishop Aethelnoth. S. 1091
    Edward to St Augustine's Canterbury.

3   D.B.II fol.310v.

4   Harmer Writs Appendix no.17.

5   II Edward the Elder cap.1. III Edmund cap.1.

6   VI Aethelstan Cap. 10.

7   II Aethelstan cap.22.

8   Laws of King Edward, a 12th century lawbook.

9   S.1090.

10 Campbell. The Anglo-Saxon Achievement; a maximum view. P. 34.

11 Eccles. Hist. IV 126-7.

12   Campbell J. The Anglo-Saxons pp 200–201.

13   S 986.

14   S. 1109

15   S. 1046 & D.B.II fol.372.

16   D.B. fol.32 Surrey.

17   D.B. Clamores Lincolnshire fol. 376.

Chapter 9

1   N.C.M.H. IV. I p.87.

2   Vita Edwardi p.7.

3   See relevant entries in the Chronicle 1047-51.

4   Stenton. P.574.

5   Higham. P.231.

6   Gospatric's Charter.

7   Worcester Chron. D 1046. Abingdon C. 1049.

8   Abingdon Chron. C 1056

9   Florence of Worcester 1049.

10   See Maps in Walker. Pp.210-211.

11   S 1036.

12   Worcester D 1046 and Waltham Chronicle. 1-27, 62-2.

13   Clarke P.A. The English Nobility.

14   Vita. P. 17.

15   D.B. fol. 56v Wallingford.

16   D.B. fol.. 252.

17   See discussion in A.N.S. 7. Hooper C. The Housecarl.

18   Worcester D 1051. Peterborough E 1070.

19   D.B. fols.56v. 75. 100.

20   L. E. II.97.

21   II Cnut 71.

Chapter 10

1 Peterborough E sub anno.

2 Abingdon C sub anno.

3 Worcester D 1051.

4 Florence 1047.

5 Worcester D 1047.

6 Florence 1048.

7 Peterborough E 1046 for 1048.

8 For all this see relevant entries in the Chronicles and Florence.

9 Stenton pp.431-2.

10 See S 1021.

11 G.R. II 197.

12 G.R. II 198.

13 Vita. P.18 – 20.

14 G.P. ch.21.

15 Robertson Charters No.CII.

16 Vita p.21

17 In this account the version in Peterborough E is mainly adopted, since for this period it is based on an original text written at St Augustine's, Canterbury.

18 Aethelred IV 4.. II Cnut 62.1.& 64.

19 Abingdon C 1041.

20 Florence sub anno & post-conquest bi-lingual Latin and English epitome of the Chronicle.

21 Florence sub anno.

22 Worcester D 1051.

23 In Peterborough E 1052.

24 G.R. Ch.22.

25 N.C.M.H. IV. II.p.58-9.

26 Vita p.30.

27 Poitiers G.G. and Jumièges G.N.D. pages 224 and 215 in E.H.D. II..

28 See John E. Reassessing. P.180.

Chapter 11

1 G.R. 197.6.
2 G.R. 199.9.
3 Vita p. 9 & 26.
4 H.H. Lamb. The Changing Climate 1966. p. 144.
5 Vita p.30.
6 Kapelle. P.11.
7 Quoted Oman p.612.
8 G.P. Malmes. Ch.23.
9 Vita p. 32.
10 Vita p.8-9.
11 Vita p.60-61.
12 G.R. II 221 Osbert of Clare Vita. C. ii fol.141.
13 G.R. II 197.3.
14 Vita p. 46-49.
15 A.N.S. 8 and 14. NCMH IV. II. Table 4.
16 A.N.S.18.
17 Vita p.33.
18 Grierson P. E.H.R. 51, 1936.
19 Vita p.33.
20 Peterborough E and Poem in Worcester D 1057.
21 G.R. 228. 1.

Chapter 12

1 Annales Cambriae 23-4. Hemming 1.278.
2 Conquest, Co-existence and Change; Wales 1063-1415 Davies R.R.
   p. 24.
3 Abingdon C 1046.
4 Peterborough E 1048.
5 Worcester D 1050.
6 Worcester D 1052.

7   Abingdon C 1052, Worcester D and Florence 1053.

8   Abingdon C 1053.

9   De Nugis Curialium 99–103.

10 Brut y Twysogion 42–3.

11 Gerald of Wales Description. Bk.2 Ch.3.

12 De Nugis p.100.

13 Abingdon C and Worcester D 1065.

14 Annals of Tigernach .399. Annales Cambriae p.25. Brut y Twysogion p.45.

15 Vita Wulfstani 16–18.

16 S 1237 and D.B. fol.222b.

17 Writ S 1140

18 Vita p.57.

19 Worcester D 1063.

20 John of Salisbury, Polycraticus iv 18.

21 Worcester D 1065.

22 Higham. Northumberland. P.330

23 Stenton. P.419.

24 S 1243 a Writ issued by Gospatric of Allerdale before 1064.

25 Higham. op.cit.p.231.

26 McLynn p.139.

27 Vita p.43.

28 Symeon H.R. ii 174–5.

29 Lines 5087–98

30 Kapelle p.91.

31 Eccles. Hist. iv. 270.

32 Vita p.43.

33 Vita p.54–5. Vita Wulstani. 16–17.

34 Vita p.34. G.P. Ch.115.

35 Liber Vitae Dunelm. Fol.12v.

36 Florence sub anno 1065. reports death of Gospatric and puts The other deaths in the 'previous year'.

37 Flor. 1065.

38   Kapelle. Note 36 p. 261.& p.98.

39   Vita p. 51.Abingdon C 1065.

40   H.D. I. p.94-97.

41   Hist. Trans. S.Cuthberti ii.1808.
      Symeon Opera i. 244-45.

42   Florence 1065.

43   Kapelle p. 260-61 note 35.

44   Op cit. page 260 note 33.

45   Kapelle.p. 96-7.

46   Walker. P.108. D.B.Yorkshire.

47   Florence 1065.

48   Abingdon C and Worcester d 1065.

49   Vita p.53.

50   Florence 1065, & Abingdon C.

51   Vita p.54.

52   Vita p. 73 from Osbert's text c.xix.

53   Vita p.75-80.

54   Vita p.80.Vigil of the Epiphany Abingdon C and Worcester D
      and Peterborough E.

55   Abingdon C,Worcester D, 1065.

56   Peterborough E.

57   Plate xxxii.

58   G.G. II. Caps 11 and 25.

59   Vita p.79.

Chapter 13

1   G.R. 180.10.

2   Malmesbury G.R. 196.4.

3   G.R. 188.4.

4   G.N.D. 7. p. 132-6.

5   G.R. 228.3.

6   D.C. Douglas, Edward the Confessor, Duke William
     Of Normandy and the English Succession E.H.R. 68. 1953.

7   G.G. sec. 16.

8   Poitiers G.G. p.178–213.

9   Mason. P. 78.

10 G.G.p.95.

11 G.R. 228.2.

12 Stubbs Select Charters p.62. cap.12 of Council.

13 E. Albu. The Normans in their Histories. Propaganda, Myth and
     Subversion. 2001.

14 Eccles. Hist. 7.3.

15 Idem 7.3.

16 Even William of Malmesbury, G.R. 228.3. says he was given
     'the hand of the duke's daughter', which means a betrothal.

17 Chronicle. M.G.H. ss vii p.361.

18 Chron. S. Andreas II c. 32 (circa 1133) and Waltham Chron. Sec.20.

19 Eccles. Hist. II 272–8.

20 Book I. p.431. This is not the Anglo-Saxon Chronicle.

21 Williams A.N.S. 1. Problems connected with the English
     royal succession 860–1066.

22 McLynn P.108. Farskinna p.202. Flatyarbok iii.285.

23 Adam of Bremen p.108. Saxo Grammaticus p.47.

24 Eccles. Hist. I. 178.

25 See E. John E.H.R. 94 1979. Jolliffe J.E.A.
     Constitutional History p.139. Sayles G.O. Med. Foundations p. 161.

26 Stafford p. Queens, Dowagers and Concubines.p.5.

27 John E. Reassessing. p. 184.

28 Hunter Blair. p.111.

29 Plates II and XV.

30 Stenton. P.547.

31 Encomium iii.1.

Chapter 14

1 Plates I, XXX –XXXII.
2 Vita p.3 & 11-13.
3 Vita p.13 & 27.
4 Vita p.27.
5 Encomium 52b.
6 Vita S. Edithae. 37-38.
7 G. R. II cap. 196.
8 L.E. II. 96-97.
9 History of Peterborough ed. Mellows. P.67 & 70.
10 Miracula S. Edmundi.
11 Dudo. Cols. 749-52.
12 Vita.p.23.
13 Vita.p.26.
14 Latham Revised Medieval Wordlist.
15 Vita pp. 3, 4, 23, 79.
16 Vita p.60-61. Osbert p.92-3.
17 Osbert c.iv.Vita p.28.
18 G.R.197.
19 Denzinger p.173 Alexander III and p.176 Innocent III.
20 B.M. Harl.526.
21 See Barlow's Edition Introduction lxxx.
22 Idem. xxxix.
23 See Stafford. Queen Emma & Queen Edith. p.42.
24 G.R. 218. 197.3.
25 G.R. 197.3.
26 G.N.D.VII.9.
27 There are late twelfth century tales accusing both Emma and Edith of adultery, usually with bishops!

Chapter 15

1 Vita p.75.
2 Vita. P.61-2. G.R. 223. G.P.pp.95,207,219,297.
3 Barlow;Vita p.69 footnotes.
4 G.R. 2221-227.
5 John E.Analecta Bollendiana 97 1979.
6 Eadmer p.143.
7 Osbert. Cap. XXX.
8 Osbert. P.125.
9 Letters of Osbert No. 14.
10 Denzinger H. Enchiridion Symbolorum..p.159.
11 Idem.No.19.
12 Idem. No.38.
13 Richard of Cirencester Speculum Historiale. Ii. 319ff.
14 Idem. ii.320.
15 Vatican Library Ms. Latin 6024;fol.150v-151v.
16 Richard of Cirencester ii.321-2.
17 Idem. ii. 324-5. Flete History of Westminster p.71-2.
18 Lanfranc was said to have attempted to depose Wulfstan
   who refused to surrender his crozier to the archbishop
   and returned it to King Edward by sticking the spiked
   end into Edward's gravestone, from which it could not
   be removed until he was re-instated as bishop.
   Osbert added the tale to his Vita.
19 A.L. Poole Domesday Book to Magna Carta p.5.
20 Hindley p.352.
21 Canonization and Authority in the Western Church. E.W. Kemp.
   1948. p.2.
22 P.L. ccxiv col.483.

Appendix One

1   Plates xxx &xxxi.
2   Vita p.45-46.
3   R. Gem. English Romanesque Architecture in
    English Romanesque Art 1066-1200, Hayward gallery London 1984.
    p.27ff.
4   Writs no.87. S.1131.
5   Idem. p.34.
6   Vita. P.45 notes 2, 3, 4 and 5.
7   Flete's History of Westminster. Ed. J. Armitage Robinson, 1909.
8   See Gem R. Proceedings of the Battle Conference
    Of Anglo-Norman Studies iii. 1981.
9   Wischermann H. Romanesque Architecture in Great Britain in
    Romansesque; Architecture .Sculpture .Painting. Ed. R. Toman.
    Königswinter. 2004. p217.

Appendix Two

1   British Library Cott. Tib. Bi ff 115v-164.
2   B.L. Cott. Tib. B iv ff 3-86.
3   Oxford, Bodleian Library MS Laud 636.
4   B.L. Cott. Dom. A viii ff 30-70.

List of Illustrations

Index

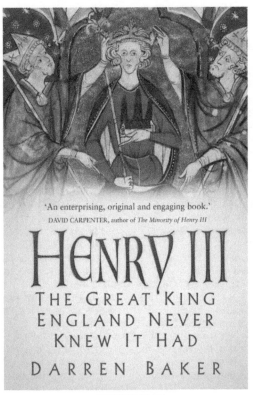

'An enterprising, original and engaging book.'
DAVID CARPENTER, author of *The Minority of Henry III*

HENRY III
THE GREAT KING
ENGLAND NEVER
KNEW IT HAD

DARREN BAKER

97807509932435

The History Press

The destination for history
www.thehistorypress.co.uk